NEW PERSPECTIVES ON
Microsoft® Access® 2010

BRIEF

Joseph J. Adamski
Grand Valley State University

Kathleen T. Finnegan

COURSE TECHNOLOGY
CENGAGE Learning™

Australia • Brazil • Japan • Korea • Mexico • Singapore • Spain • United Kingdom • United States

COURSE TECHNOLOGY
CENGAGE Learning™

New Perspectives on Microsoft Access 2010, Brief

Vice President, Publisher: Nicole Jones Pinard

Executive Editor: Marie L. Lee

Associate Acquisitions Editor: Brandi Shailer

Senior Product Manager: Kathy Finnegan

Product Manager: Leigh Hefferon

Product Manager: Katherine C. Russillo

Associate Product Manager: Julia Leroux-Lindsey

Editorial Assistant: Jacqueline Lacaire

Director of Marketing: Cheryl Costantini

Senior Marketing Manager: Ryan DeGrote

Marketing Coordinator: Kristen Panciocco

Developmental Editor: Jessica Evans

Content Project Manager: Jennifer Feltri

Composition: GEX Publishing Services

Art Director: Marissa Falco

Text Designer: Althea Chen

Cover Designer: Roycroft Design

Cover Art: © Veer Incorporated

Copyeditor: Camille Kiolbasa

Proofreader: Kathy Orrino

Indexer: Alexandra Nickerson

For product information and technology assistance, contact us at
Cengage Learning Customer & Sales Support, 1-800-354-9706

For permission to use material from this text or product, submit all requests online at **www.cengage.com/permissions**
Further permissions questions can be emailed to
permissionrequest@cengage.com

Some of the product names and company names used in this book have been used for identification purposes only and may be trademarks or registered trademarks of their respective manufacturers and sellers.

Microsoft and the Office logo are either registered trademarks or trademarks of Microsoft Corporation in the United States and/or other countries. Course Technology, Cengage Learning is an independent entity from the Microsoft Corporation, and not affiliated with Microsoft in any manner.

Disclaimer: Any fictional data related to persons or companies or URLs used throughout this book is intended for instructional purposes only. At the time this book was printed, any such data was fictional and not belonging to any real persons or companies.

Library of Congress Control Number: 2010929379

ISBN-13: 978-0-538-79849-5

ISBN-10: 0-538-79849-1

Course Technology
20 Channel Center Street
Boston, MA 02210
USA

Cengage Learning is a leading provider of customized learning solutions with office locations around the globe, including Singapore, the United Kingdom, Australia, Mexico, Brazil, and Japan. Locate your local office at:
international.cengage.com/global

Cengage Learning products are represented in Canada by Nelson Education, Ltd.

To learn more about Course Technology, visit **www.cengage.com/course technology**

To learn more about Cengage Learning, visit **www.cengage.com**

Purchase any of our products at your local college store or at our preferred online store **www.cengagebrain.com**

Printed in the United States of America
1 2 3 4 5 6 7 8 9 14 13 12 11 10

Preface

The New Perspectives Series' critical-thinking, problem-solving approach is the ideal way to prepare students to transcend point-and-click skills and take advantage of all that Microsoft Office 2010 has to offer.

In developing the New Perspectives Series, our goal was to create books that give students the software concepts and practical skills they need to succeed beyond the classroom. We've updated our proven case-based pedagogy with more practical content to make learning skills more meaningful to students.

With the New Perspectives Series, students understand *why* they are learning *what* they are learning, and are fully prepared to apply their skills to real-life situations.

About This Book

"This text provides students with excellent examples and screenshots of fundamental database concepts and skills. The key features of this book are the detailed explanations and the variety of exercises in which students can apply what they have learned."
—Matthew Alimagham
Spartanburg Community College

This book provides essential coverage of Microsoft Access 2010, and includes the following:

- Detailed, hands-on instruction of Microsoft Access 2010 basics, including creating and maintaining a database, querying a database, and creating forms and reports
- Coverage of important database concepts, including guidelines for designing databases, setting field properties, and defining table relationships
- Exploration of the exciting new features of Access 2010, including working in Backstage view, using the Data Type gallery to add new fields, and applying themes to database objects

New for this edition!

- Each session begins with a Visual Overview, a new two-page spread that includes colorful, enlarged screenshots with numerous callouts and key term definitions, giving students a comprehensive preview of the topics covered in the session, as well as a handy study guide.
- New ProSkills boxes provide guidance for how to use the software in real-world, professional situations, and related ProSkills exercises integrate the technology skills students learn with one or more of the following soft skills: decision making, problem solving, teamwork, verbal communication, and written communication.
- Important steps are now highlighted in yellow with attached margin notes to help students pay close attention to completing the steps correctly and avoid time-consuming rework.

System Requirements

This book assumes a typical installation of Microsoft Access 2010 and Microsoft Windows 7 Ultimate using an Aero theme. (You can also complete the material in this text using another version of Windows 7, such as Home Premium, or earlier versions of the Windows operating system. You will see only minor differences in how some windows look.) The browser used for any steps that require a browser is Internet Explorer 8.

www.cengage.com/ct/newperspectives

The New Perspectives Approach

"The clear step-by-step instructions, real-world data files, and helpful figures make New Perspectives texts excellent for courses taught in the classroom, the hybrid/blended format, or entirely online."
—Sylvia Amito'elau
Coastline Community College

Context
Each tutorial begins with a problem presented in a "real-world" case that is meaningful to students. The case sets the scene to help students understand what they will do in the tutorial.

Hands-on Approach
Each tutorial is divided into manageable sessions that combine reading and hands-on, step-by-step work. Colorful screenshots help guide students through the steps. **Trouble?** tips anticipate common mistakes or problems to help students stay on track and continue with the tutorial.

VISUAL OVERVIEW

Visual Overviews
New for this edition! Each session begins with a Visual Overview, a new two-page spread that includes colorful, enlarged screenshots with numerous callouts and key term definitions, giving students a comprehensive preview of the topics covered in the session, as well as a handy study guide.

PROSKILLS

ProSkills Boxes and Exercises
New for this edition! ProSkills boxes provide guidance for how to use the software in real-world, professional situations, and related ProSkills exercises integrate the technology skills students learn with one or more of the following soft skills: decision making, problem solving, teamwork, verbal communication, and written communication.

KEY STEP

Key Steps
New for this edition! Important steps are highlighted in yellow with attached margin notes to help students pay close attention to completing the steps correctly and avoid time-consuming rework.

INSIGHT

InSight Boxes
InSight boxes offer expert advice and best practices to help students achieve a deeper understanding of the concepts behind the software features and skills.

 TIP

Margin Tips
Margin Tips provide helpful hints and shortcuts for more efficient use of the software. The Tips appear in the margin at key points throughout each tutorial, giving students extra information when and where they need it.

REVIEW
APPLY

Assessment
Retention is a key component to learning. At the end of each session, a series of Quick Check questions helps students test their understanding of the material before moving on. Engaging end-of-tutorial Review Assignments and Case Problems have always been a hallmark feature of the New Perspectives Series. Colorful bars and brief descriptions accompany the exercises, making it easy to understand both the goal and level of challenge a particular assignment holds.

REFERENCE
TASK REFERENCE
GLOSSARY/INDEX

Reference
Within each tutorial, Reference boxes appear before a set of steps to provide a succinct summary and preview of how to perform a task. In addition, a complete Task Reference at the back of the book provides quick access to information on how to carry out common tasks. Finally, each book includes a combination Glossary/Index to promote easy reference of material.

www.cengage.com/ct/newperspectives

Our Complete System of Instruction

BRIEF

INTRODUCTORY

COMPREHENSIVE

Coverage To Meet Your Needs

Whether you're looking for just a small amount of coverage or enough to fill a semester-long class, we can provide you with a textbook that meets your needs.

- Brief books typically cover the essential skills in just 2 to 4 tutorials.
- Introductory books build and expand on those skills and contain an average of 5 to 8 tutorials.
- Comprehensive books are great for a full-semester class, and contain 9 to 12+ tutorials.

So if the book you're holding does not provide the right amount of coverage for you, there's probably another offering available. Go to our Web site or contact your Course Technology sales representative to find out what else we offer.

COURSECASTS

CourseCasts – Learning on the Go. Always available…always relevant.

Want to keep up with the latest technology trends relevant to you? Visit our site to find a library of podcasts, CourseCasts, featuring a "CourseCast of the Week," and download them to your mp3 player at http://coursecasts.course.com.

Our fast-paced world is driven by technology. You know because you're an active participant—always on the go, always keeping up with technological trends, and always learning new ways to embrace technology to power your life.

Ken Baldauf, host of CourseCasts, is a faculty member of the Florida State University Computer Science Department where he is responsible for teaching technology classes to thousands of FSU students each year. Ken is an expert in the latest technology trends; he gathers and sorts through the most pertinent news and information for CourseCasts so your students can spend their time enjoying technology, rather than trying to figure it out. Open or close your lecture with a discussion based on the latest CourseCast.

Visit us at http://coursecasts.course.com to learn on the go!

Instructor Resources

We offer more than just a book. We have all the tools you need to enhance your lectures, check students' work, and generate exams in a new, easier-to-use and completely revised package. This book's Instructor's Manual, ExamView testbank, PowerPoint presentations, data files, solution files, figure files, and a sample syllabus are all available on a single CD-ROM or for downloading at http://www.cengage.com/coursetechnology.

WebTUTOR

Content for Online Learning

Course Technology has partnered with the leading distance learning solution providers and class-management platforms today. To access this material, visit www.cengage.com/webtutor and search for your title. Instructor resources include the following: additional case projects, sample syllabi, PowerPoint presentations, and more. For students to access this material, they must have purchased a WebTutor PIN-code specific to this title and your campus platform. The resources for students might include (based on instructor preferences): topic reviews, review questions, practice tests, and more. For additional information, please contact your sales representative.

www.cengage.com/ct/newperspectives

SAM: Skills Assessment Manager

SAM is designed to help bring students from the classroom to the real world. It allows students to train and test on important computer skills in an active, hands-on environment.

SAM's easy-to-use system includes powerful interactive exams, training, and projects on the most commonly used Microsoft Office applications. SAM simulates the Office application environment, allowing students to demonstrate their knowledge and think through the skills by performing real-world tasks, such as bolding text or setting up slide transitions. Add in live-in-the-application projects, and students are on their way to truly learning and applying skills to business-centric documents.

Designed to be used with the New Perspectives Series, SAM includes handy page references, so students can print helpful study guides that match the New Perspectives textbooks used in class. For instructors, SAM also includes robust scheduling and reporting features.

Acknowledgments

Our sincere thanks to the following reviewers for their helpful feedback and valuable insights: Matthew Alimagham, Spartanburg Community College; Steve Ganz, Western Washington University; Kristen Hockman, University of Missouri–Columbia; Ahmed Kamel, Concordia College; Jean Luoma, Davenport University; Kelly Swain, Humber College; Karen Toreson, Shoreline Community College; Raymond Yu, Douglas College; and Violet Zhang, George Brown College. Many thanks to everyone at Course Technology, especially Marie Lee for her leadership and inspiration; Brandi Shailer and Leigh Hefferon for their contributions and friendship; Kate Russillo for her guidance in this text's development; Julia Leroux-Lindsey for ensuring the quality and timely delivery of supplements; Jacqueline Lacaire for her support; and Jennifer Feltri for her outstanding management of the production process. Thanks as well to the following Manuscript Quality Assurance staff members for their diligent efforts in ensuring the quality and accuracy of this text: Christian Kunciw, MQA Supervisor; and Serge Palladino, Danielle Shaw, and Teresa Storch, MQA Testers. To Jessica Evans, Developmental Editor extraordinaire— very special thanks for her commitment to excellence, incredible attention to detail, and many contributions to this book. I am grateful to have the continued support and encouragement of my parents, Ed and Mary Curran, and my two wonderful sons, Connor and Devon.
–Kathleen T. Finnegan

Thank you to all the people who guided and influenced me over the years during my educational, professional, and academic lives; specifically thanking those at Saint Francis School, Naugatuck High School, Tufts University, University of Massachusetts Amherst, United Technologies Research Laboratories, Rensselaer Polytechnic Institute, Associates Corporation of North America, and Grand Valley State University.
–Joseph J. Adamski

TABLE OF CONTENTS

OBJECTIVES

- Explore the programs in Microsoft Office
- Start programs and switch between them
- Explore common window elements
- Minimize, maximize, and restore windows
- Use the Ribbon, tabs, and buttons
- Use the contextual tabs, the Mini toolbar, and shortcut menus
- Save, close, and open a file
- Learn how to share files using SkyDrive
- Use the Help system
- Preview and print a file
- Exit programs

Getting Started with Microsoft Office 2010

Preparing a Meeting Agenda

Case | *Recycled Palette*

Recycled Palette, a company in Oregon founded by Ean Nogella in 2006, sells 100 percent recycled latex paint to both individuals and businesses in the area. The high-quality recycled paint is filtered to industry standards and tested for performance and environmental safety. The paint is available in both 1 gallon cans and 5 gallon pails, and comes in colors ranging from white to shades of brown, blue, green, and red. The demand for affordable recycled paint has been growing each year. Ean and all his employees use Microsoft Office 2010, which provides everyone in the company with the power and flexibility to store a variety of information, create consistent files, and share data. In this tutorial, you'll review how the company's employees use Microsoft Office 2010.

STARTING DATA FILES

Office → Tutorial Review

(none) Finances.xlsx
Letter.docx

VISUAL OVERVIEW

The File tab opens **Backstage view**, which provides access to file-level options and program settings.

The **Ribbon** is the main set of commands you click to execute tasks. It is organized into tabs and groups.

The **Quick Access Toolbar** provides one-click access to commonly used commands, such as Save, Undo, and Repeat.

A **button**, or icon, provides one-click access to a command. This button underlines text.

The **workspace** is the area that displays the file you are working on (a Word document, an Excel workbook, and so on).

The **status bar** provides information about the program, open file, or current task or selection. It also contains buttons and other controls for working with the file and its content.

The Ribbon is organized into tabs. Each **tab** has commands related to particular activities or tasks.

Buttons for related commands are organized on a tab in **groups**. The buttons in this group can be used to change the appearance of paragraphs.

The **insertion point** shows where characters will appear when you start to type.

You can click a program button on the taskbar to switch between open files and programs.

COMMON WINDOW ELEMENTS

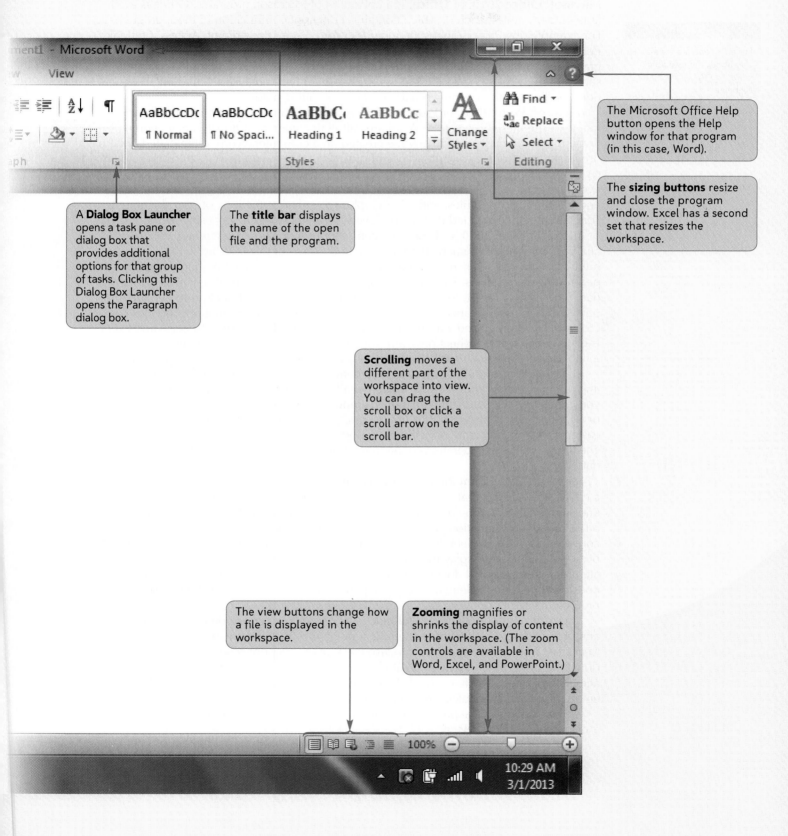

A **Dialog Box Launcher** opens a task pane or dialog box that provides additional options for that group of tasks. Clicking this Dialog Box Launcher opens the Paragraph dialog box.

The **title bar** displays the name of the open file and the program.

The Microsoft Office Help button opens the Help window for that program (in this case, Word).

The **sizing buttons** resize and close the program window. Excel has a second set that resizes the workspace.

Scrolling moves a different part of the workspace into view. You can drag the scroll box or click a scroll arrow on the scroll bar.

The view buttons change how a file is displayed in the workspace.

Zooming magnifies or shrinks the display of content in the workspace. (The zoom controls are available in Word, Excel, and PowerPoint.)

Exploring Microsoft Office 2010

Microsoft Office 2010, or **Office**, is a collection of Microsoft programs. Office is available in many suites, each of which contains a different combination of these programs. For example, the Professional suite includes Word, Excel, PowerPoint, Access, Outlook, Publisher, and OneNote. Other suites are available and can include more or fewer programs. Each Office program contains valuable tools to help you accomplish many tasks, such as composing reports, analyzing data, preparing presentations, compiling information, sending email, planning schedules, and compiling notes.

TIP

For additional information about the available suites, go to the Microsoft Web site.

Microsoft Word 2010, or **Word**, is a computer program you use to enter, edit, and format text. The files you create in Word are called **documents**, although many people use the term *document* to refer to any file created on a computer. Word, often called a word-processing program, offers many special features that help you compose and update all types of documents, ranging from letters and newsletters to reports, brochures, faxes, and even books, in attractive and readable formats. You can also use Word to create, insert, and position figures, tables, and other graphics to enhance the look of your documents. For example, the Recycled Palette employees create business letters using Word.

Microsoft Excel 2010, or **Excel**, is a computer program you use to enter, calculate, analyze, and present numerical data. You can do some of this in Word with tables, but Excel provides many more tools for recording and formatting numbers as well as performing calculations. The graphics capabilities in Excel also enable you to display data visually. You might, for example, generate a pie chart or a bar chart to help people quickly see the significance of and the connections between information. The files you create in Excel are called **workbooks** (commonly referred to as spreadsheets), and Excel is often called a spreadsheet program. The Recycled Palette accounting department uses a line chart in an Excel workbook to visually track the company's financial performance.

Microsoft Access 2010, or **Access**, is a computer program used to enter, maintain, and retrieve related information (or data) in a format known as a database. The files you create in Access are called **databases**, and Access is often referred to as a database or relational database program. With Access, you can create forms to make data entry easier, and you can create professional reports to improve the readability of your data. The Recycled Palette operations department tracks the company's inventory in an Access database.

Microsoft PowerPoint 2010, or **PowerPoint**, is a computer program you use to create a collection of slides that can contain text, charts, pictures, sound, movies, multimedia, and so on. The files you create in PowerPoint are called **presentations**, and PowerPoint is often called a presentation graphics program. You can show these presentations on your computer monitor, project them onto a screen as a slide show, print them, share them over the Internet, or display them on the Web. You can also use PowerPoint to generate presentation-related documents such as audience handouts, outlines, and speakers' notes. The Recycled Palette marketing department uses a PowerPoint slide presentation to promote its paints.

Microsoft Outlook 2010, or **Outlook**, is a computer program you use to send, receive, and organize email; plan your schedule; arrange meetings; organize contacts; create a to-do list; and record notes. You can also use Outlook to print schedules, task lists, phone directories, and other documents. Outlook is often referred to as an information management program. The Recycled Palette staff members use Outlook to send and receive email, plan their schedules, and create to-do lists.

Although each Office program individually is a strong tool, their potential is even greater when used together.

Teamwork: Integrating Office Programs

One of the main advantages of Office is **integration**, the ability to share information between programs. Integration ensures consistency and accuracy, and it saves time because you don't have to reenter the same information in several Office programs. It also means that team members can effortlessly share Office files. Team members can create files based on their skills and information that can be used by others as needed. The staff at Recycled Palette uses the integration features of Office every day, as described in the following examples:

• The accounting department created an Excel bar chart on fourth-quarter results for the previous two years, and inserted it into the quarterly financial report created in Word. The Word report includes a hyperlink that employees can click to open the Excel workbook and view the original data.

• The operations department included an Excel pie chart of sales percentages by paint colors on a PowerPoint slide, which is part of a presentation to stockholders.

• The marketing department produced a mailing to promote its recycled paints to local contractors and designers by combining a form letter created in Word with an Access database that stores the names and addresses of these potential customers.

• A sales representative merged the upcoming promotion letter that the marketing department created in Word with an Outlook contact list containing the names and addresses of prospective customers.

  Even these few examples of how information from one Office program can be integrated with another illustrate how integration can save time and effort. Each team member can focus on creating files in the program best suited to convey the information he or she is responsible for. Yet, everyone can share the files, using them as needed for their specific purpose.

Starting Office Programs

You can start any Office program from the Start menu on the taskbar. As soon as the program starts, you can immediately begin to create new files or work with existing ones.

Starting an Office Program

• On the taskbar, click the Start button.
• On the Start menu, click All Programs, click Microsoft Office, and then click the name of the program to start.
or
• Click the name of the program to start in the left pane of the Start menu.

You'll start Word using the Start button.

To start Word and open a new, blank document:

▶ **1.** Make sure your computer is on and the Windows desktop appears on your screen.

Trouble? If your screen varies slightly from those shown in the figures, your computer might be set up differently. The figures in this book were created while running Windows 7 with the Aero feature turned on, but how your screen looks depends on the version of Windows you are using, the resolution of your screen, and other settings.

▶ **2.** On the taskbar, click the **Start** button 🪟, and then click **All Programs** to display the All Programs list.

▶ **3.** Click **Microsoft Office**, and then point to **Microsoft Word 2010**. Depending on how your computer is set up, your desktop and menu might contain different icons and commands. See Figure 1.

Figure 1	Start menu with All Programs list displayed

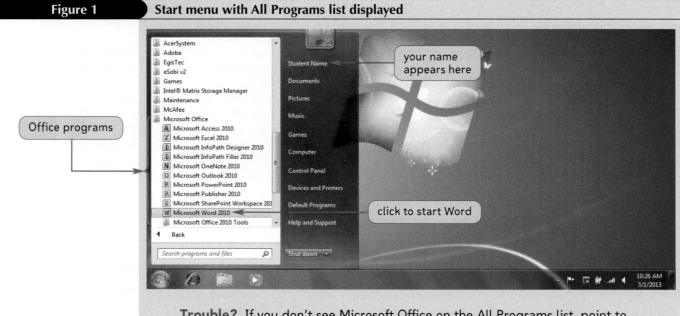

Trouble? If you don't see Microsoft Office on the All Programs list, point to Microsoft Word 2010 on the All Programs menu. If you still don't see Microsoft Word 2010, ask your instructor or technical support person for help.

▶ **4.** Click **Microsoft Word 2010**. Word starts and a new, blank document opens. Refer to the Visual Overview to review the common program window elements.

Trouble? If the Word window doesn't fill your entire screen as shown in the Visual Overview, the window is not maximized, or expanded to its full size. You'll maximize the window shortly.

You can have more than one Office program open at once. You'll use this same method to start Excel and open a new, blank workbook.

To start Excel and open a new, blank workbook:

1. On the taskbar, click the **Start** button, click **All Programs** to display the All Programs list, and then click **Microsoft Office**.

Trouble? If you don't see Microsoft Office on the All Programs list, point to Microsoft Excel 2010 on the All Programs list. If you still don't see Microsoft Excel 2010, ask your instructor or technical support person for help.

2. Click **Microsoft Excel 2010**. Excel starts and a new, blank workbook opens. See Figure 2.

Figure 2 New, blank Excel workbook

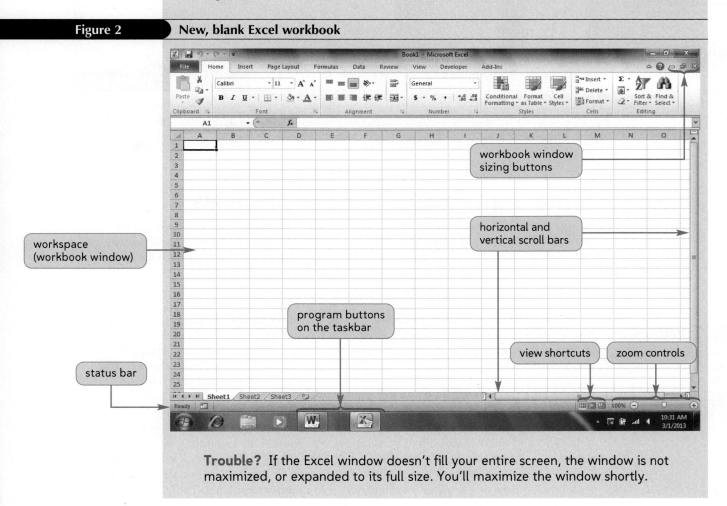

Trouble? If the Excel window doesn't fill your entire screen, the window is not maximized, or expanded to its full size. You'll maximize the window shortly.

Switching Between Open Programs and Files

Two programs are running at the same time—Word and Excel. The taskbar contains buttons for both programs. When you have two or more programs running or two files within the same program open, you can click the program buttons on the taskbar to switch from one program or file to another. When you point to a program button, a thumbnail (or small picture) of each open file in that program is displayed. You can then click the thumbnail of the file you want to make active. The employees at Recycled Palette often work in several programs and files at once.

To switch between the open Word and Excel files:

▶ **1.** On the taskbar, point to the **Microsoft Word** program button 🇼. A thumbnail of the open Word document appears. See Figure 3.

| Figure 3 | Thumbnail of the open Word document |

click the thumbnail that appears to make the file active

point to the Word program button

Excel program button

▶ **2.** Click the **Document1 - Microsoft Word** thumbnail. The active program switches from Excel to Word.

Exploring Common Window Elements

As you can see, many elements in both the Word and Excel program windows are the same. In fact, most Office programs have these same elements. Because these elements are the same in each program, after you've learned one program, it's easy to learn the others.

Resizing the Program Window and Workspace

There are three different sizing buttons that appear on the right side of a program window's title bar. The Minimize button [—], which is the left button, hides a window so that only its program button is visible on the taskbar. The middle button changes name and function depending on the status of the window—the Maximize button [□] expands the window to the full screen size or to the program window size, and the Restore Down button [❐] returns the window to a predefined size. The Close button [X], on the right, exits the program or closes the file.

The sizing buttons give you the flexibility to arrange the program and file windows to best fit your needs. Most often, you'll want to maximize the program window and workspace to take advantage of the full screen size you have available. If you have several files open, you might want to restore down their windows so that you can see more than one window at a time, or you might want to minimize programs or files you are not working on at the moment.

To resize the windows and workspaces:

▶ **1.** On the Word title bar, click the **Minimize** button [—]. The Word program window is reduced to a taskbar button. The Excel program window is visible again.

▶ **2.** On the Excel title bar, click the **Maximize** button [□] to expand the Excel program window to fill the screen, if necessary.

3. In the bottom set of Excel sizing buttons, click the **Restore Window** button. The workspace is resized smaller than the full program window. See Figure 4.

Figure 4 | Resized Excel window and workspace

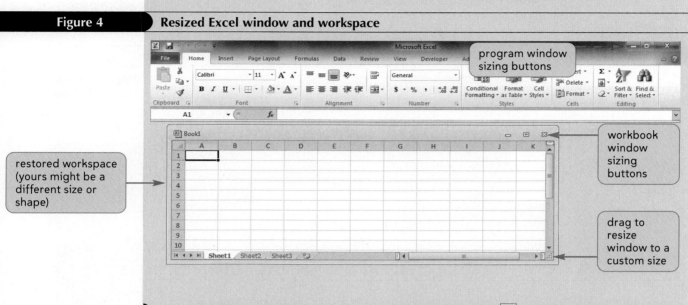

restored workspace (yours might be a different size or shape)

program window sizing buttons

workbook window sizing buttons

drag to resize window to a custom size

4. On the workbook window, click the **Maximize** button. The workspace expands to fill the program window.

5. On the taskbar, click the **Microsoft Word** program button. The Word program window returns to its previous size.

6. On the Word title bar, click the **Maximize** button if necessary to expand the Word program to fill the screen.

Switching Views

Each program has a variety of views, or ways to display the file in the workspace. For example, Word has five views: Print Layout, Full Screen Reading, Web Layout, Outline, and Draft. The content of the file doesn't change from view to view, although the presentation of the content does. In Word, for example, Print Layout view shows how the document would appear as a printed page, whereas Web Layout view shows how the document would appear as a Web page. You'll change views in later tutorials.

Zooming and Scrolling

You can zoom in to get a closer look at the content of an open document, worksheet, slide, or database report. Likewise, you can zoom out to see more of the content at a smaller size. You can select a specific percentage or size based on your file. The zoom percentage can range from 10 percent to 400 percent (Excel and PowerPoint) or 500 percent (Word). The figures shown in these tutorials show the workspace zoomed in to enhance readability. Zooming can shift part of the workspace out of view. To change which area of the workspace is visible in the program window, you can use the scroll bars. A scroll bar has arrow buttons that you can click to shift the workspace a small amount in the specified direction and a scroll box that you can drag to shift the workspace a larger amount in the direction you drag. Depending on the program and zoom level, you might see a vertical scroll bar, a horizontal scroll bar, or both.

To zoom and scroll in Word and Excel:

1. On the Word status bar, drag the **Zoom slider** ⬇ to the left until the percentage is **10%**. The document is reduced to its smallest size, which makes the entire page visible but unreadable. See Figure 5.

Figure 5   Word zoom level set to 10%

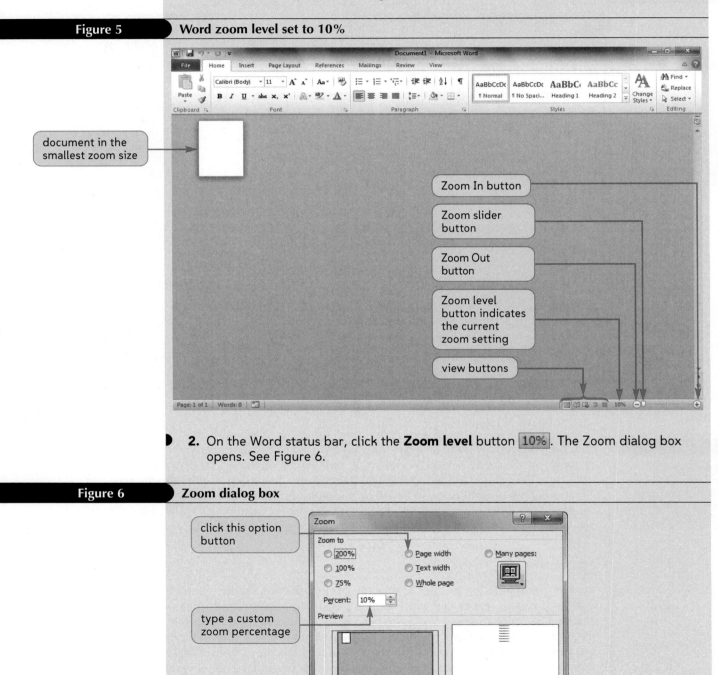

document in the smallest zoom size

Zoom In button

Zoom slider button

Zoom Out button

Zoom level button indicates the current zoom setting

view buttons

2. On the Word status bar, click the **Zoom level** button 10%. The Zoom dialog box opens. See Figure 6.

Figure 6   Zoom dialog box

click this option button

type a custom zoom percentage

click to accept the selected zoom setting

3. Click the **Page width** option button, and then click the **OK** button. The Word document is magnified to its page width, which matches how the Word figures appear in the tutorials.

4. On the taskbar, click the **Microsoft Excel** program button ⬚. The Excel program window is displayed.

5. On the status bar, click the **Zoom In** button ⊕ twice. The worksheet is magnified to 120%, which is the zoom level that matches the Excel figures shown in the tutorials.

6. On the horizontal scroll bar, click the **right arrow** button ▶ twice. The worksheet shifts two columns to the right. Columns A and B (labeled by letter at the top of the columns) shift out of view and two other columns shift into view.

7. On the horizontal scroll bar, drag the **scroll box** all the way to the left. The worksheet shifts left to display columns A and B again.

8. On the taskbar, click the **Microsoft Word** program button ⬚. The Word program window is displayed.

Using the Ribbon

TIP

To view more workspace, click the Minimize the Ribbon button, located below the sizing buttons, to reduce the Ribbon to a single line. Click the Expand the Ribbon button to redisplay the full Ribbon.

Although the tabs on the Ribbon differ from program to program, each program has two tabs in common. The first tab on the Ribbon, the File tab, opens Backstage view. Backstage view provides access to file-level features, such as creating new files, opening existing files, saving files, printing files, and closing files, as well as the most common program options. The second tab in each program—called the Home tab—contains the commands for the most frequently performed activities, including cutting and pasting, changing fonts, and using editing tools. In addition, the Insert, Review, and View tabs appear on the Ribbon in all Office programs except Access, although the commands they include might differ from program to program. Other tabs are program specific, such as the Design tab in PowerPoint and the Datasheet Tools tab in Access.

To use the Ribbon tabs:

1. In Word, point to the **Insert** tab on the Ribbon. The Insert tab is highlighted, though the Home tab with the options for using the Clipboard and formatting text remains visible.

2. Click the **Insert** tab. The Insert tab is displayed on the Ribbon. This tab provides access to all the options for adding objects such as shapes, pages, tables, illustrations, text, and symbols to a document. See Figure 7.

| Figure 7 | Insert tab on the Ribbon in Word |

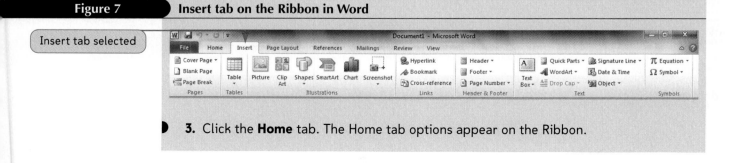

Insert tab selected

3. Click the **Home** tab. The Home tab options appear on the Ribbon.

Clicking Buttons

For the most part, when you click a button, something happens in the file. For example, the Clipboard group on the Home tab includes the Cut, Copy, Paste, and Format Painter buttons, which you can click to move or copy text, objects, and formatting.

Buttons can be **toggles**: one click turns the feature on and the next click turns the feature off. While the feature is on, the button remains colored or highlighted. For example, on the Home tab in Word, the Show/Hide ¶ button in the Paragraph group displays the nonprinting characters when toggled on and hides them when toggled off.

Some buttons have two parts: a button that accesses a command, and an arrow that opens a menu of all the commands or options available for that task. For example, the Paste button in the Clipboard group on the Home tab includes the Paste command and an arrow to access all the Paste commands and options. To select one of these commands or options, you click the button arrow and then click the command or option.

INSIGHT

How Buttons and Groups Appear on the Ribbon

The buttons and groups on the Ribbon change based on your monitor size, your screen resolution, and the size of the program window. With smaller monitors, lower screen resolutions, and reduced program windows, buttons can appear as icons without labels and a group can be condensed into a button that you click to display the group options. The figures in these tutorials were created using a screen resolution of 1024 × 768 and, unless otherwise specified, the program and workspace windows are maximized. If you are using a different screen resolution or window size, the buttons on the Ribbon might show more or fewer button names, and some groups might be reduced to a button.

You'll type text in the Word document, and then use the buttons on the Ribbon.

To use buttons on the Ribbon:

1. Type **Meeting Agenda** and then press the **Enter** key. The text appears in the first line of the document and the insertion point moves to the second line.

   Trouble? If you make a typing error, press the Backspace key to delete the incorrect letters, and then retype the text.

2. In the Paragraph group on the Home tab, click the **Show/Hide ¶** button ¶. The nonprinting characters appear in the document, and the Show/Hide ¶ button remains toggled on. See Figure 8.

Figure 8   **Button toggled on**

Home tab selected

Paragraph group

nonprinting paragraph mark and space symbols

Show/Hide ¶ button toggled on

Meeting·Agenda¶

Trouble? If the nonprinting characters disappear from your screen, the Show/Hide ¶ button was already on. Repeat Step 2 to show nonprinting characters.

▶ **3.** Position the insertion point to the left of the word "Meeting," press and hold the left mouse button, drag the pointer across the text of the first line but not the paragraph mark to highlight the text, and then release the mouse button. All the text in the first line of the document (but not the paragraph mark ¶) is selected.

▶ **4.** In the Clipboard group on the Home tab, click the **Copy** button 🖹. The selected text is copied to the Clipboard.

▶ **5.** Press the ↓ key. The text is deselected (no longer highlighted), and the insertion point moves to the second line in the document.

▶ **6.** In the Clipboard group on the Home tab, point to the top part of the **Paste** button 🖹. Both parts of the Paste button are outlined in yellow, but the icon at the top is highlighted to indicate that it will be selected if you click the mouse button.

▶ **7.** Point to the **Paste button arrow**. The button is outlined and the button arrow is highlighted.

▶ **8.** Click the **Paste button arrow**. The paste commands and options are displayed. See Figure 9.

Figure 9   Two-part Paste button

Paste button

click the button arrow to display more options and commands

Paste commands and options

▶ **9.** On the Paste Options menu, click the **Keep Text Only** button 🅰. The menu closes, and the text is duplicated in the second line of the document. The Paste Options button 🖹 (Ctrl) ▾ appears below the duplicated text, providing access to the same paste commands and options.

INSIGHT

Using Keyboard Shortcuts and Key Tips

Keyboard shortcuts can help you work faster and more efficiently. A **keyboard shortcut** is a key or combination of keys you press to access a feature or perform a command. You can use these shortcuts to access options on the Ribbon, on the Quick Access Toolbar, and in Backstage view without removing your hands from the keyboard. To access the options on the Ribbon, press the Alt key. A label, called a Key Tip, appears over each tab. To select a tab, press the corresponding key. The tab is displayed on the Ribbon and Key Tips appear over each available button or option on that tab. Press the appropriate key or keys to select a button.

You can also press combinations of keys to perform specific commands. For example, Ctrl+S is the keyboard shortcut for the Save command (you press and hold the Ctrl key while you press the S key). This type of keyboard shortcut appears in ScreenTips next to the command's name. Not all commands have this type of keyboard shortcut. Identical commands in each Office program use the same keyboard shortcut.

Using Galleries and Live Preview

Galleries and Live Preview let you quickly see how your file will be affected by a selection. A **gallery** is a menu or grid that shows a visual representation of the options available for a button. For example, the Bullet Library gallery in Word shows an icon of each bullet style you can select. Some galleries include a More button ⊡ that you click to expand the gallery to see all the options it contains. When you point to an option in a gallery, **Live Preview** shows the results that would occur in your file if you clicked that option. To continue the bullets example, when you point to a bullet style in the Bullet Library gallery, the selected text or the paragraph in which the insertion point is located appears with that bullet style. By moving the pointer from option to option, you can quickly see the text set with different bullet styles; you can then click the style you want.

To use the Bullet Library gallery and Live Preview:

1. In the Paragraph group on the Home tab, click the **Bullets button arrow** ⊞ ▾. The Bullet Library gallery opens.

2. Point to the **check mark bullet** style ✓. Live Preview shows the selected bullet style in your document. See Figure 10.

Figure 10	Live Preview of bullet icon

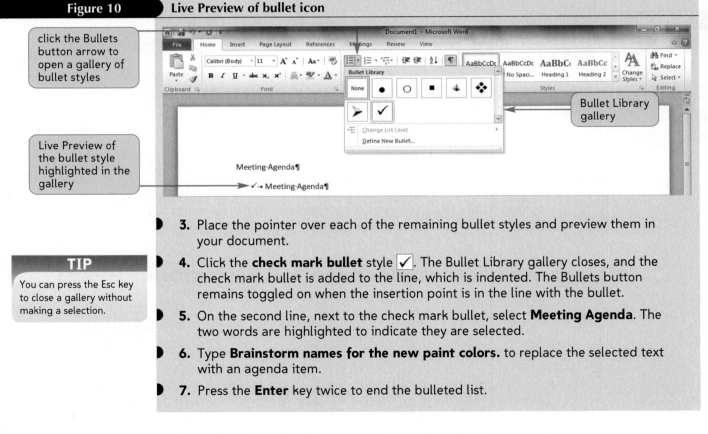

click the Bullets button arrow to open a gallery of bullet styles

Live Preview of the bullet style highlighted in the gallery

Bullet Library gallery

3. Place the pointer over each of the remaining bullet styles and preview them in your document.

4. Click the **check mark bullet** style ✓. The Bullet Library gallery closes, and the check mark bullet is added to the line, which is indented. The Bullets button remains toggled on when the insertion point is in the line with the bullet.

5. On the second line, next to the check mark bullet, select **Meeting Agenda**. The two words are highlighted to indicate they are selected.

6. Type **Brainstorm names for the new paint colors.** to replace the selected text with an agenda item.

7. Press the **Enter** key twice to end the bulleted list.

TIP

You can press the Esc key to close a gallery without making a selection.

Opening Dialog Boxes and Task Panes

The button to the right of some group names is the Dialog Box Launcher ⊡, which opens a task pane or dialog box related to that group of tasks. A **task pane** is a window that helps you navigate through a complex task or feature. For example, you can use the Clipboard task pane to paste some or all of the items that were cut or copied from any Office program during the current work session. A **dialog box** is a window from which you enter or choose settings for how you want to perform a task. For example, the Page Setup dialog box in Word contains options to change how the document looks. Some dialog boxes organize related information into tabs, and related options and settings are organized into groups, just as they are on the Ribbon. You select settings in a dialog box using option buttons, check boxes, text boxes, and lists to specify how you want to perform a task. In Excel, you'll use the Dialog Box Launcher to open the Page Setup dialog box.

To open the Page Setup dialog box using the Dialog Box Launcher:

1. On the taskbar, click the **Microsoft Excel** program button 🗙 to switch from Word to Excel.

2. On the Ribbon, click the **Page Layout** tab. The page layout options appear on the Ribbon.

3. In the Page Setup group, click the **Dialog Box Launcher**. The Page Setup dialog box opens with the Page tab displayed. See Figure 11.

| Figure 11 | Page tab in the Page Setup dialog box |

click this Dialog Box Launcher to open the Page Setup dialog box

click a tab to view a group of related options

click an option button to select that option

click in the box and type an entry

click to accept the changes and close the dialog box

click the up or down arrow to increase or decrease the number

click the arrow and then click an option in the list

click a button to open another dialog box or window

click to close the dialog box without making changes

4. Click the **Landscape** option button. The workbook's page orientation changes to a page wider than it is long.

5. Click the **Sheet** tab. The dialog box displays options related to the worksheet. You can click a check box to turn an option on (checked) or off (unchecked).

6. In the Print section of the dialog box, click the **Gridlines** check box and the **Row and column headings** check box. Check marks appear in both check boxes, indicating that these options are selected.

7. Click the **Cancel** button. The dialog box closes without making any changes to the page setup.

TIP

You can check more than one check box in a group, but you can select only one option button in a group.

Using Contextual Tools

Some tabs, toolbars, and menus come into view as you work. Because these tools become available only as you might need them, the workspace remains less cluttered. However, tools that appear and disappear as you work can take some getting used to.

Displaying Contextual Tabs

Any object that you can select in a file has a related contextual tab. An **object** is anything that appears on your screen that can be selected and manipulated, such as a table, a picture, a shape, a chart, or an equation. A **contextual tab** is a Ribbon tab that contains commands related to the selected object so you can manipulate, edit, and format that object. Contextual tabs appear to the right of the standard Ribbon tabs just below a title label. For example, Figure 12 shows the Table Tools contextual tabs that appear when you select a table in a Word document. Although contextual tabs appear only when you select an object, they function in the same way as standard tabs on the Ribbon. Contextual tabs disappear when you click elsewhere on the screen, deselecting the object. Contextual tabs can also appear as you switch views. You'll use contextual tabs in later tutorials.

Figure 12   Table Tools contextual tabs

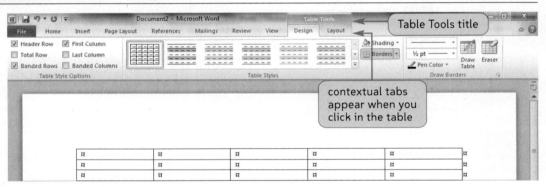

Accessing the Mini Toolbar

The **Mini toolbar**, which appears next to the pointer whenever you select text, contains buttons for the most commonly used formatting commands, such as font, font size, styles, color, alignment, and indents. The Mini toolbar buttons differ in each program. A transparent version of the Mini toolbar appears immediately after you select text. When you move the pointer over the Mini toolbar, it comes into full view so you can click the appropriate formatting button or buttons. The Mini toolbar disappears if you move the pointer away from the toolbar, press a key, or click in the workspace. The Mini toolbar can help you format your text faster, but initially you might find that the toolbar disappears unexpectedly. All the commands on the Mini toolbar are also available on the Ribbon. Note that Live Preview does not work with the Mini toolbar.

You'll use the Mini toolbar to format text you enter in the workbook.

To use the Mini toolbar to format text:

1. If necessary, click cell **A1** (the rectangle in the upper-left corner of the worksheet).

2. Type **Budget**. The text appears in the cell.

3. Press the **Enter** key. The text is entered in cell A1 and cell A2 is selected.

4. Type **2013** and then press the **Enter** key. The year is entered in cell A2 and cell A3 is selected.

5. Double-click cell **A1** to place the insertion point in the cell. Now you can select the text you typed.

6. Double-click **Budget** in cell A1. The selected text appears white with a black background, and the transparent Mini toolbar appears directly above the selected text. See Figure 13.

| Figure 13 | Transparent Mini toolbar |

Mini toolbar is transparent at first

select text to display the transparent Mini toolbar

Keep the pointer directly over the Mini toolbar; otherwise, it will disappear.

7. Move the pointer over the Mini toolbar. The Mini toolbar is now completely visible, and you can click buttons.

   Trouble? If the Mini toolbar disappears, you probably moved the pointer to another area of the worksheet. To redisplay the Mini toolbar, repeat Steps 6 and 7, being careful to move the pointer directly over the Mini toolbar in Step 7.

8. On the Mini toolbar, click the **Bold** button **B**. The text in cell A1 is bold. The Mini toolbar remains visible so you can continue formatting the selected text. See Figure 14.

| Figure 14 | Mini toolbar with the Bold button selected |

Mini toolbar remains open for additional formatting

Bold button toggled on

bold text in cell A1

9. Press the **Enter** key. The Mini toolbar disappears, and cell A2 is selected.

Opening Shortcut Menus

A **shortcut menu** is a list of commands related to a selection that opens when you click the right mouse button. Shortcut menus enable you to quickly access commands that you're most likely to need in the context of the task you're performing without using the tabs on the Ribbon. The shortcut menu includes commands that perform actions, commands that open dialog boxes, and galleries of options that provide Live Preview. The Mini toolbar also opens when you right-click. If you click a button on the Mini toolbar, the rest of the shortcut menu closes while the Mini toolbar remains open so you can continue formatting the selection. For example, you can right-click selected text to open a shortcut menu with a Mini toolbar; the menu will contain text-related commands such as Cut, Copy, and Paste, as well as other program-specific commands.

You'll use a shortcut menu to delete the content you entered in cell A1.

To use a shortcut menu to delete content:

1. Right-click cell **A1**. A shortcut menu opens, listing commands related to common tasks you'd perform in a cell, along with the Mini toolbar. See Figure 15.

Figure 15   Shortcut menu with Mini toolbar

Mini toolbar appears above the shortcut menu

click a command with ellipses to open a dialog box

click a command or button to perform an action

point to an arrow to open a submenu of additional options

2. On the shortcut menu, click **Clear Contents**. The shortcut menu closes, the Mini toolbar disappears, and the bold text is removed from cell A1.

3. Right-click cell **A2**, and then click **Clear Contents** on the shortcut menu. The year is removed from cell A2.

TIP

Press the Esc key to close an open menu, shortcut menu, list, or gallery without selecting an option.

Working with Files

The most common tasks you perform in any Office program are to create, open, save, and close files. All of these tasks can be done from Backstage view, and the processes for these tasks are basically the same in all Office programs. To begin working in a program, you need to create a new file or open an existing file. When you start Word, Excel, or PowerPoint, the program opens along with a blank file—ready for you to begin working on a new document, workbook, or presentation. When you start Access, the New tab in Backstage view opens, displaying options for creating a new database or opening an existing one.

Saving a File

As you create and modify an Office file, your work is stored only in the computer's temporary memory, not on a hard drive. If you were to exit the program without saving, turn off your computer, or experience a power failure, your work would be lost. To prevent losing work, save your file frequently—at least every 10 minutes. You can save files to the hard drive located inside your computer, an external hard drive, a network storage drive, or a portable storage drive such as a USB flash drive.

To save a file, you can click either the Save button on the Quick Access Toolbar or the Save command in Backstage view. If it is the first time you are saving a file, the Save As dialog box will open so that you can specify save options. You can also click the Save As command in Backstage view to open the Save As dialog box, in which you can name the file you are saving and specify a location to save it.

The first time you save a file, you need to name it. This **filename** includes a title you specify and a file extension assigned by Office to indicate the file type. You should specify a descriptive title that accurately reflects the content of the document, workbook, presentation, or database, such as "Shipping Options Letter" or "Fourth Quarter Financial Analysis." Your descriptive title can include uppercase and lowercase letters, numbers, hyphens, and spaces in any combination, but not the special characters ? " / \ < > * | and :. Each filename ends with a **file extension**, which is a period followed by several characters that Office adds to your descriptive title to identify the program in which that file was created. The default file extensions for Office 2010 are .docx for Word, .xlsx for Excel, .pptx for PowerPoint, and .accdb for Access. Filenames (the descriptive title and extension) can include a maximum of 255 characters. You might see file extensions depending on how Windows is set up on your computer. The figures in these tutorials do not show file extensions.

You also need to decide where to save the file—on which drive and in what folder. A **folder** is a container for your files. Just as you organize paper documents within folders stored in a filing cabinet, you can organize your files within folders stored on your computer's hard drive or on a removable drive such as a USB flash drive. Store each file in a logical location that you will remember whenever you want to use the file again. The default storage location for Office files is the Documents folder; you can create additional storage folders within that folder or navigate to a new location.

REFERENCE

Saving a File

To save a file the first time or with a new name or location:
- Click the File tab to open Backstage view, and then click the Save As command in the navigation bar (for an unnamed file, click the Save command or click the Save button on the Quick Access Toolbar).
- In the Save As dialog box, navigate to the location where you want to save the file.
- Type a descriptive title in the File name box, and then click the Save button.

To resave a named file to the same location with the same name:
- On the Quick Access Toolbar, click the Save button.

The text you typed in the Word window needs to be saved.

To save a file for the first time:

▶ **1.** On the taskbar, click the **Microsoft Word** program button W. Word becomes the active program.

▶ **2.** On the Ribbon, click the **File** tab. Backstage view opens with commands and tabs for creating new files, opening existing files, and saving, printing, and closing files. See Figure 16.

| Figure 16 | Backstage view |

click the File tab to open Backstage view

click a command in the navigation bar to perform an action

click a tab in the navigation bar to display related options

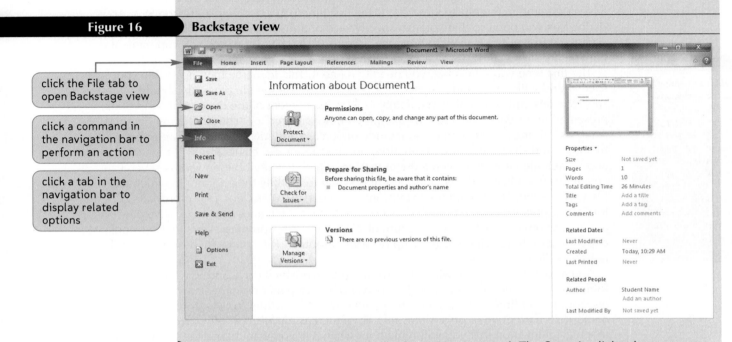

▶ **3.** In the navigation bar, click the **Save As** command. The Save As dialog box opens because you have not yet saved the file and need to specify a storage location and filename. The default location is set to the Documents folder, and the first few words of the first line appear in the File name box as a suggested title.

▶ **4.** In the Navigation pane along the left side of the dialog box, click the link for the location that contains your Data Files, if necessary.

Trouble? If you don't have the starting Data Files, you need to get them before you can proceed. Your instructor will either give you the Data Files or ask you to obtain them from a specified location (such as a network drive). In either case, make a backup copy of the Data Files before you start so that you will have the original files available in case you need to start over. If you have any questions about the Data Files, see your instructor or technical support person for assistance.

▶ **5.** In the file list, double-click the **Office** folder, and then double-click the **Tutorial** folder. This is the location where you want to save the document.

▶ **6.** Type **Agenda** in the File name box. This descriptive filename will help you more easily identify the file. See Figure 17 (your file path may differ).

| Figure 17 | Completed Save As dialog box |

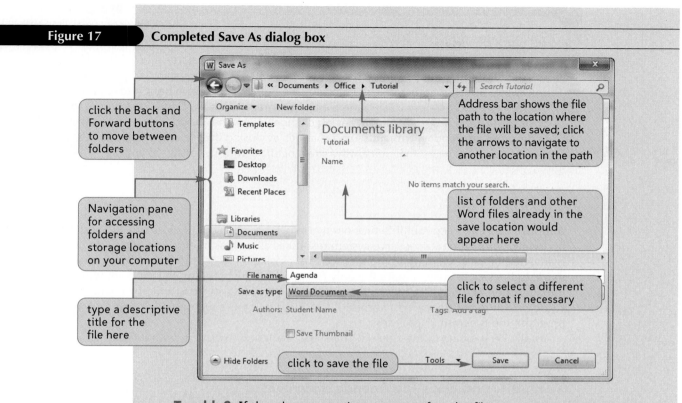

click the Back and Forward buttons to move between folders

Navigation pane for accessing folders and storage locations on your computer

type a descriptive title for the file here

Address bar shows the file path to the location where the file will be saved; click the arrows to navigate to another location in the path

list of folders and other Word files already in the save location would appear here

click to select a different file format if necessary

click to save the file

Trouble? If the .docx extension appears after the filename, your computer is configured to show file extensions. Continue with Step 7.

▶ **7.** Click the **Save** button. The Save As dialog box closes, and the name of your file appears in the Word window title bar.

The saved file includes everything in the document at the time you last saved it. Any new edits or additions you make to the document exist only in the computer's memory and are not saved in the file on the drive. As you work, remember to save frequently so that the file is updated to reflect the latest content.

Because you already named the document and selected a storage location, you don't need to use the Save As dialog box unless you want to save a copy of the file with a different filename or to a different location. If you do, the previous version of the file remains on your drive as well.

You need to add your name to the agenda. Then, you'll save your changes.

To modify and save the Agenda document:

▶ **1.** Type your name, and then press the **Enter** key. The text you typed appears on the next line.

▶ **2.** On the Quick Access Toolbar, click the **Save** button . The changes you made to the document are saved in the file stored on the drive.

INSIGHT

Saving Files Before Closing

As a standard practice, you should save files before closing them. However, Office has an added safeguard: if you attempt to close a file without saving your changes, a dialog box opens, asking whether you want to save the file. Click the Save button to save the changes to the file before closing the file and program. Click the Don't Save button to close the file and program without saving changes. Click the Cancel button to return to the program window without saving changes or closing the file and program. This feature helps to ensure that you always save the most current version of any file.

Closing a File

Although you can keep multiple files open at one time, you should close any file you are no longer working on to conserve system resources as well as to ensure that you don't inadvertently make changes to the file. You can close a file by clicking the Close command in Backstage view. If that's the only file open for the program, the program window remains open and no file appears in the window. You can also close a file by clicking the Close button in the upper-right corner of the title bar. If that's the only file open for the program, the program also closes.

You'll add the date to the agenda. Then, you'll attempt to close it without saving.

To modify and close the Agenda document:

1. Type today's date, and then press the **Enter** key. The text you typed appears below your name in the document.

2. On the Ribbon, click the **File** tab to open Backstage view, and then click the **Close** command in the navigation bar. A dialog box opens, asking whether you want to save the changes you made to the document.

3. Click the **Save** button. The current version of the document is saved to the file, and then the document closes. Word is still open, so you can create additional new files in the open program or you can open previously created and saved files.

Opening a File

When you want to open a blank document, workbook, presentation, or database, you create a new file. When you want to work on a previously created file, you must first open it. Opening a file transfers a copy of the file from the storage location (either a hard drive or a portable drive) to the computer's memory and displays it on your screen. The file is then in your computer's memory and on the drive.

Opening an Existing File

- Click the File tab to open Backstage view, and then click the Open command in the navigation bar.
- In the Open dialog box, navigate to the storage location of the file you want to open.
- Click the filename of the file you want to open.
- Click the Open button.
- If necessary, click the Enable Editing button in the Information Bar.

or

- Click the File tab, and then click the Recent tab in the navigation bar.
- Click a filename in the Recent list.

Any file you open that was downloaded from the Internet, accessed from a shared network, or received as an email attachment might open in a read-only format, called **Protected View**. In Protected View, you can see the file contents, but you cannot edit, save, or print them until you enable editing. To do so, click the Enable Editing button on the Information Bar, as shown in Figure 18.

| Figure 18 | **Protected View warning** |

You need to print the meeting agenda you typed for Ean. To do that, you'll reopen the Agenda document.

To open the Agenda document:

1. On the Ribbon, click the **File** tab to display Backstage view.

2. In the navigation bar, click the **Open** command. The Open dialog box, which works similarly to the Save As dialog box, opens.

3. In the Open dialog box, use the Navigation pane or the Address bar to navigate to the **Office\Tutorial** folder included with your Data Files. This is the location where you saved the Agenda document.

4. In the file list, click **Agenda**. See Figure 19.

| Figure 19 | Open dialog box |

file to open and print

folders and other
Word files stored in
this folder appear here

click to open the
selected file

5. Click the **Open** button. The Agenda file opens in the Word program window.

Sharing Files Using Windows Live SkyDrive

Often the purpose of creating a file is to share it with other people—sending it attached
to an email message for someone else to read or use, collaborating with others on the
same document, or posting it as a blog for others to review. You can do all of these things
in Backstage view from the Save & Send tab.

When you send a file using email, you can attach a copy of the file, send a link to
the file, or attach a copy of the file in a PDF or another file format. You can also save to
online workspaces where you can make the file available to others for review and collaboration. The Save to Web option on the Save & Send tab in Backstage view gives you
access to **Windows Live SkyDrive**, which is an online workspace provided by Microsoft;
your personal workspace comes with a Public folder for saving files to share as well as a
My Documents folder for saving files you want to keep private. (SkyDrive is not available for Access.) Figure 20 shows the Save to Web options on the Save & Send tab in
Backstage view of Word. SharePoint is an online workspace set up by an organization,
such as a school, business, or nonprofit group.

Files saved to an online workspace can be worked on by more than one person at the
same time. The changes are recorded in the files with each author's name and the date of
the change. A Web browser is used to access and edit the files. You choose who can have
access to the files.

Figure 20   Save to Web options on the Save & Send tab

Saving a File to SkyDrive

- Click the File tab to open Backstage view, and then click the Save & Send tab in the navigation bar.
- In the center pane, click Save to Web.
- In the right pane, click the Sign In button, and then use your Windows Live ID to log on to your Windows Live SkyDrive account.

REFERENCE

Getting Help

If you don't know how to perform a task or want more information about a feature, you can turn to Office itself for information on how to use it. This information is referred to simply as **Help**. You can get Help in ScreenTips and from the Help window.

Viewing ScreenTips

ScreenTips are a fast and simple method you can use to get information about objects you see on the screen. A **ScreenTip** is a box with descriptive text about an object or button. Just point to a button or object to display its ScreenTip. In addition to the button's name, a ScreenTip might include the button's keyboard shortcut if it has one, a description of the command's function, and, in some cases, a link to more information so that you can press the F1 key while the ScreenTip is displayed to open the Help window with the relevant topic displayed.

To view ScreenTips:

1. Point to the **Microsoft Office Word Help** button 📳. The ScreenTip shows the button's name, its keyboard shortcut, and a brief description. See Figure 21.

Figure 21   **ScreenTip for the Help button**

2. Point to other buttons on the Ribbon to display their ScreenTips.

Using the Help Window

For more detailed information, you can use the **Help window** to access all the Help topics, templates, and training installed on your computer with Office and available on Office.com. **Office.com** is a Web site maintained by Microsoft that provides access to the latest information and additional Help resources. For example, you can access current Help topics and training for Office. To connect to Office.com, you need to be able to access the Internet from your computer. Otherwise, you see only topics that are stored on your computer.

Each program has its own Help window from which you can find information about all of the Office commands and features as well as step-by-step instructions for using them. There are two ways to find Help topics—the search function and a topic list.

The Type words to search for box enables you to search the Help system for a task or a topic you need help with. You can click a link to open a Help topic with explanations and step-by-step instructions for a specific procedure. The Table of Contents pane displays the Help system content organized by subjects and topics, similar to a book's table of contents. You click main subject links to display related topic links. You click a topic link to display that Help topic in the Help window.

REFERENCE

Getting Help

- Click the Microsoft Office Help button (the button name depends on the Office program).
- Type a keyword or phrase in the Type words to search for box, click the Search button, and then click a Help topic in the search results list.
  or
  In the Table of Contents pane, click a "book," and then click a Help topic.
- Read the information in the Help window and then click other topics or links.
- On the Help window title bar, click the Close button.

You'll use Help to get information about printing a document in Word.

To search Help for information about printing:

1. Click the **Microsoft Office Word Help** button 🔘. The Word Help window opens.

▶ **2.** If the Table of Contents pane is not open on the left side of the Help window, click the **Show Table of Contents** button 🌣 on the toolbar to display the pane.

▶ **3.** Click the **Type words to search for** box, if necessary, and then type **print document**. You can specify where you want to search.

▶ **4.** Click the **Search button arrow**. The Search menu shows the online and local content available.

▶ **5.** If your computer is connected to the Internet, click **All Word** in the Content from Office.com list. If your computer is not connected to the Internet, click **Word Help** in the Content from this computer list.

▶ **6.** Click the **Search** button. The Help window displays a list of topics related to the keywords "print document" in the left pane. See Figure 22.

Figure 22   ▶ **Search results displaying Help topics**

Trouble? If your search results list differs from the one shown in Figure 22, your computer is not connected to the Internet or Microsoft has updated the list of available Help topics since this book was published. Continue with Step 7.

▶ **7.** Scroll through the list to review the Help topics.

▶ **8.** Click **Preview and print a file**. The topic content is displayed in the Help window so you can learn more about how to print a document. See Figure 23.

| Figure 23 | Preview and print a file Help topic |

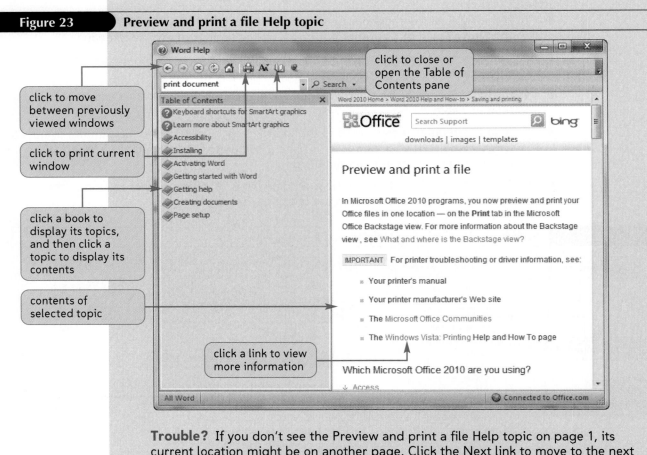

click to close or open the Table of Contents pane

click to move between previously viewed windows

click to print current window

click a book to display its topics, and then click a topic to display its contents

contents of selected topic

click a link to view more information

Trouble? If you don't see the Preview and print a file Help topic on page 1, its current location might be on another page. Click the Next link to move to the next page, and then scroll down to find the topic. Repeat as needed to search additional pages until you locate the topic.

9. Read the information, click the links within this topic, and then read the additional information.

10. On the Help window title bar, click the **Close** button [X] to close the window.

Printing a File

At times, you'll want a paper copy of Office files. Whenever you print, you should review and adjust the printing settings as needed. You can select the number of copies to print, the printer, the portion of the file to print, and so forth; the printing settings vary slightly from program to program. You should also check the file's print preview to ensure that the file will print as you intended. This simple review will help you to avoid reprinting, which requires additional paper, ink, and energy resources.

REFERENCE

Printing a File

- On the Ribbon, click the File tab to open Backstage view.
- In the navigation bar, click the Print tab.
- Verify the print settings and review the print preview.
- Click the Print button.

You will print the agenda for Ean.

To print the Agenda document:

1. Make sure your printer is turned on and contains paper.

2. On the Ribbon, click the **File** tab to open Backstage view.

3. In the navigation bar, click the **Print** tab. The print settings and preview appear. See Figure 24.

Figure 24   **Print tab in Backstage view**

verify the number of copies to print

click to print file

select a printer (yours may differ)

click to display the Print tab options

print and page layout settings to verify before printing

shows the number of pages in the file; use the arrows to move between pages

before printing, check the preview of how the page will appear when printed

use the Zoom slider to change the magnification of the preview

4. Verify that **1** appears in the Copies box.

5. Verify that the correct printer appears on the Printer button. If it doesn't, click the **Printer** button, and then click the correct printer from the list of available printers.

6. Click the **Print** button to print the document.

Trouble? If the document does not print, see your instructor or technical support person for help.

Exiting Programs

When you finish working with a program, you should exit it. As with many other aspects of Office, you can exit programs with a button or a command. You'll use both methods to exit Word and Excel. You can use the Exit command to exit a program and close an open file in one step. If you haven't saved the final version of the open file, a dialog box opens, asking whether you want to save your changes. Clicking the Save button in this dialog box saves the open file, closes the file, and then exits the program.

To exit the Word and Excel programs:

▶ **1.** On the Word title bar, click the **Close** button [x]. Both the Word document and the Word program close. The Excel window is visible again.

   Trouble? If a dialog box opens asking if you want to save the document, you might have inadvertently made a change to the document. Click the Don't Save button.

▶ **2.** On the Ribbon, click the **File** tab to open Backstage view, and then click the **Exit** command in the navigation bar. A dialog box opens asking whether you want to save the changes you made to the workbook. If you click the Save button, the Save As dialog box opens and Excel exits after you finish saving the workbook. This time, you don't want to save the workbook.

▶ **3.** Click the **Don't Save** button. The workbook closes without saving a copy, and the Excel program closes.

Exiting programs after you are done using them keeps your Windows desktop uncluttered for the next person using the computer, frees up your system's resources, and prevents data from being lost accidentally.

REVIEW

Quick Check

1. What Office program would be best to use to write a letter?
2. How do you start an Office program?
3. What is the purpose of Live Preview?
4. What is Backstage view?
5. Explain the difference between Save and Save As.
6. True or False. In Protected View, you can see file contents, but you cannot edit, save, or print them until you enable editing.
7. What happens if you open a file, make edits, and then attempt to close the file or exit the program without saving the current version of the file?
8. What are the two ways to get Help in Office?

Practice the skills you learned in the tutorial.

PRACTICE

Review Assignments

Data Files needed for the Review Assignments: Finances.xlsx, Letter.docx

You need to prepare for an upcoming meeting at Recycled Palette. You'll open and print documents for the meeting. Complete the following:

1. Start PowerPoint, and then start Excel.
2. Switch to the PowerPoint window, and then close the presentation but leave the PowerPoint program open. (*Hint*: Use the Close command in Backstage view.)
3. Open a blank PowerPoint presentation from the New tab in Backstage view. (*Hint*: Make sure Blank presentation is selected in the Available Templates and Themes section, and then click the Create button.)
4. Close the PowerPoint presentation and program using the Close button on the PowerPoint title bar; do not save changes if asked.
5. Open the **Finances** workbook located in the Office\Review folder. If the workbook opens in Protected View, click the Enable Editing button.
6. Use the Save As command to save the workbook as **Recycled Palette Finances** in the Office\Review folder.
7. In cell A1, type your name, press the Enter key to insert your name at the top of the worksheet, and then save the workbook.
8. Preview and print one copy of the worksheet using the Print tab in Backstage view.
9. Exit Excel using the Exit command in Backstage view.
10. Start Word, and then open the **Letter** document located in the Office\Review folder. If the document opens in Protected View, click the Enable Editing button.
11. Use the Save As command to save the document with the filename **Recycled Palette Letter** in the Office\Review folder.
12. Press and hold the Ctrl key, press the End key, and then release both keys to move the insertion point to the end of the letter, and then type your name.
13. Use the Save button to save the change to the Recycled Palette Letter document.
14. Preview and print one copy of the document using the Print tab in Backstage view.
15. Close the document, and then exit the Word program.
16. Submit the finished files to your instructor.

ASSESS

SAM: Skills Assessment Manager

For current SAM information, including versions and content details, visit SAM Central (http://samcentral.course.com). If you have a SAM user profile, you may have access to hands-on instruction, practice, and assessment of the skills covered in this tutorial. Since various versions of SAM are supported throughout the life of this text, check with your instructor for the correct instructions and URL/Web site for accessing assignments.

ENDING DATA FILES

Office → Tutorial   Review

Agenda.docx   Recycled Palette Finances.xlsx
Recycled Palette Letter.docx

Teamwork

Working on a Team

Teams consist of individuals who have skills, talents, and abilities that complement each other and, when joined, produce synergy—results greater than those a single individual could achieve. It is this sense of shared mission and responsibility for results that makes a team successful in its efforts to reach its goals. Teams are everywhere. In the workplace, a team might develop a presentation to introduce products. In the classroom, a team might complete a research project.

Teams meet face to face or virtually. A virtual team rarely, if ever, meets in person. Instead, technology makes it possible for members to work as if everyone was in the same room. Some common technologies used in virtual teamwork are corporate networks, email, tele-conferencing, and collaboration and integration tools, such as those found in Office 2010.

Even for teams in the same location, technology is a valuable tool. For example, teams commonly collaborate on a copy of a file posted to an online shared storage space, such as SkyDrive. In addition, team members can compile data in the program that best suits the information related to their part of the project. Later, that information can be integrated into a finished report, presentation, email message, and so on.

PROSKILLS

Collaborate with Others

At home, school, or work, you probably collaborate with others to complete many types of tasks—such as planning an event, creating a report, or developing a presentation. You can use Microsoft Office to streamline many of these tasks. Consider a project that you might need to work on with a team. Complete the following steps:

1. Start Word, and open a new document, if necessary.
2. In the document, type a list of all the tasks the team needs to accomplish. If you are working with a team, identify which team member would complete each task.
3. For each task, identify the type of Office file you would create to complete that task. For example, you would create a Word document to write a letter.
4. For each file, identify the Office program you would use to create that file, and explain why you would use that program.
5. Save the document with an appropriate filename in an appropriate folder location.
6. Use a Web browser to visit the Microsoft site at *www.microsoft.com* and research the different Office 2010 suites available. Determine which suite includes all the programs needed for the team to complete the tasks on the list.
7. In the document, type which Office suite you selected and a brief explanation of why.
8. Determine how the team can integrate the different programs in the Office suite you selected to create the files that complete the team's goal or task. Include this information at the end of the Word document. Save the document.
9. Develop an efficient way to organize the files that the team will create to complete the goal or task. Add this information at the end of the Word document.
10. If possible, sign in to SkyDrive, and then save a copy of the file in an appropriate subfolder within your Public folder. If you are working with a team, have your teammates access your file, review your notes, and add a paragraph with their comments and name.
11. Preview and print the finished document, and then submit it to your instructor.

ACCESS

Creating a Database

Creating a Database to Contain Customer, Contract, and Invoice Data

OBJECTIVES

Session 1.1
- Learn basic database concepts and terms
- Explore the Microsoft Access window and Backstage view
- Create a blank database
- Create and save a table in Datasheet view
- Enter field names and records in a table datasheet
- Open a table using the Navigation Pane

Session 1.2
- Open an Access database
- Copy and paste records from another Access database
- Navigate a table datasheet
- Create and navigate a simple query
- Create and navigate a simple form
- Create, preview, navigate, and print a simple report
- Learn how to compact, back up, and restore a database

Case | *Belmont Landscapes*

Soon after graduating with a degree in Landscape Architecture from nearby Michigan State University, Oren Belmont returned to his hometown of Holland, on the shores of Lake Michigan. There, Oren worked for a local firm that provided basic landscaping services to residential customers. After several years, Oren started his own landscape architecture firm, Belmont Landscapes, which specializes in landscape designs for residential and commercial customers and numerous public agencies.

Belmont Landscapes provides a wide range of services—from site analyses and feasibility studies, to drafting and administering construction documents—for projects of various scales. Oren and his staff depend on computers to help manage all aspects of the firm's operations, including financial and information management. Several months ago the company upgraded to Microsoft Windows and **Microsoft Access 2010** (or simply **Access**), a computer program used to enter, maintain, and retrieve related data in a format known as a database. Oren and his staff want to use Access to maintain such data as information about customers, contracts, and invoices. He asks for your help in creating the necessary Access database.

STARTING DATA FILES

Access1 →	Tutorial	Review	Case1	Case2	Case3	Case4
	Oren.accdb	Provider.accdb	School.accdb	Health.accdb	RRGroup.accdb	Travel.accdb

SESSION 1.1 VISUAL OVERVIEW

The Quick Access Toolbar provides one-click access to commonly used commands, such as Save.

The **Shutter Bar Open/Close Button** allows you to close and open the Navigation Pane; you might want to close the pane so that you have more room on the screen to view the object's contents.

Access assigns the default name "Table1" to the first new table you create. When you save the table, you give it a more meaningful name.

By default, Access creates the **ID column** as the primary key field for all new tables.

The **Click to Add column** provides another way for you to add new fields to a table.

The **Add & Delete group** contains options for adding different types of fields, including Text and Currency, to a table.

The **Fields tab** provides options for adding, removing, and formatting the fields in a table.

The **Navigation Pane** is the area that lists all the objects (tables, reports, and so on) in the database, and it is the main control center for opening and working with database objects.

Datasheet view shows the table's contents as a datasheet. The status bar indicates the current view, in this case, Datasheet view.

THE ACCESS WINDOW

...lmont : Database (Access 2007) - Microsoft Access

Data Type:

Format: Formatting

$ % , .0 .00 .00 .0

Required

Unique

Indexed

Validation

Formatting

Field Validation

The **Access window** is the program window that appears when you create a new database or open an existing database.

You use the window buttons to minimize, maximize, and close the Access window.

The Microsoft Access Help button opens the Help window, where you can find information about Access commands and features as well as instructions for using them.

The Ribbon provides the main Access commands organized by task into tabs and groups.

A **datasheet** displays the table's contents in rows and columns, similar to a table that you create in a Word document or an Excel spreadsheet. Each row will be a separate record in the table, and each column will contain the field values for one field in the table.

Modify
Expression

Memo
Settings

...odify
...nkups

...es

...ch

Introduction to Database Concepts

Before you begin using Access to create the database for Oren, you need to understand a few key terms and concepts associated with databases.

Organizing Data

Data is a valuable resource to any business. At Belmont Landscapes, for example, important data includes customers' names and addresses and contract amounts and dates. Organizing, storing, maintaining, retrieving, and sorting this type of data are critical activities that enable a business to find and use information effectively. Before storing data on a computer, however, you must organize the data.

Your first step in organizing data is to identify the individual fields. A **field** is a single characteristic or attribute of a person, place, object, event, or idea. For example, some of the many fields that Belmont Landscapes tracks are customer ID, first name, last name, company name, address, phone number, contract amount, contract signing date, and contract type.

Next, you group related fields together into tables. A **table** is a collection of fields that describes a person, place, object, event, or idea. Figure 1-1 shows an example of a Customer table that contains the following four fields: CustomerID, FirstName, LastName, and Phone.

Figure 1-1	Data organization for a table of customers

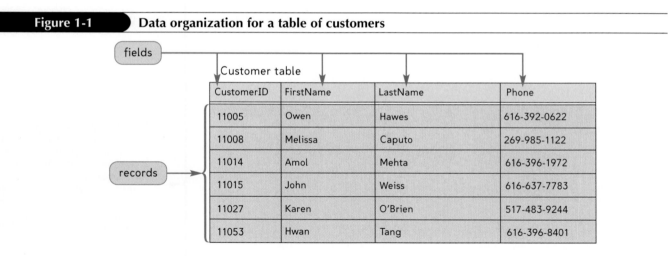

The specific value, or content, of a field is called the **field value**. In Figure 1-1, the first set of field values for CustomerID, FirstName, LastName, and Phone are, respectively: 11005; Owen; Hawes; and 616-392-0622. This set of field values is called a **record**. In the Customer table, the data for each customer is stored as a separate record. Figure 1-1 shows six records; each row of field values is a record.

Databases and Relationships

A collection of related tables is called a **database**, or a **relational database**. In this tutorial, you will create the database for Belmont Landscapes and a table named Contract to store data about contracts. In Tutorial 2, you will create two more tables, named Customer and Invoice, to store related information about customers and their invoices.

As Oren and his staff use the database that you will create, they will need to access information about customers and their contracts. To obtain this information, you must have a way to connect records in the Customer table to records in the Contract table. You connect the records in the separate tables through a **common field** that appears in both tables.

In the sample database shown in Figure 1-2, each record in the Customer table has a field named CustomerID, which is also a field in the Contract table. For example, Owen Hawes is the first customer in the Customer table and has a CustomerID field value of 11005. This same CustomerID field value, 11005, appears in three records in the Contract table. Therefore, Owen Hawes is the customer with these three contracts.

| Figure 1-2 | Database relationship between tables for customers and contracts |

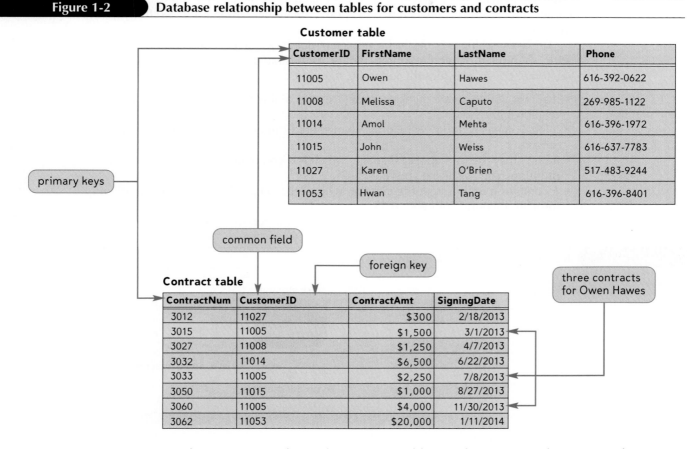

Customer table

CustomerID	FirstName	LastName	Phone
11005	Owen	Hawes	616-392-0622
11008	Melissa	Caputo	269-985-1122
11014	Amol	Mehta	616-396-1972
11015	John	Weiss	616-637-7783
11027	Karen	O'Brien	517-483-9244
11053	Hwan	Tang	616-396-8401

primary keys

common field

foreign key

three contracts for Owen Hawes

Contract table

ContractNum	CustomerID	ContractAmt	SigningDate
3012	11027	$300	2/18/2013
3015	11005	$1,500	3/1/2013
3027	11008	$1,250	4/7/2013
3032	11014	$6,500	6/22/2013
3033	11005	$2,250	7/8/2013
3050	11015	$1,000	8/27/2013
3060	11005	$4,000	11/30/2013
3062	11053	$20,000	1/11/2014

Each CustomerID value in the Customer table must be unique so that you can distinguish one customer from another. These unique CustomerID values also identify each customer's specific contracts in the Contract table. The CustomerID field is referred to as the primary key of the Customer table. A **primary key** is a field, or a collection of fields, whose values uniquely identify each record in a table. No two records can contain the same value for the primary key field. In the Contract table, the ContractNum field is the primary key because Belmont Landscapes assigns each contract a unique contract number.

When you include the primary key from one table as a field in a second table to form a relationship between the two tables, it is called a **foreign key** in the second table, as shown in Figure 1-2. For example, CustomerID is the primary key in the Customer table and a foreign key in the Contract table. Although the primary key CustomerID contains unique values in the Customer table, the same field as a foreign key in the Contract table does not necessarily contain unique values. The CustomerID value 11005, for example, appears three times in the Contract table because Owen Hawes has three contracts. Each foreign key value, however, must match one of the field values for the primary key in the other table. In the example shown in Figure 1-2, each CustomerID value in the Contract table must match a CustomerID value in the Customer table. The two tables are related, enabling users to connect the facts about customers with the facts about their contracts.

Relational Database Management Systems

To manage its databases, a company purchases a database management system. A **database management system (DBMS)** is a software program that lets you create databases and then manipulate data in them. Most of today's database management systems, including Access, are called relational database management systems. In a **relational database management system**, data is organized as a collection of tables. As stated earlier, a relationship between two tables in a relational DBMS is formed through a common field.

A relational DBMS controls the storage of databases on disk and facilitates the creation, manipulation, and reporting of data, as illustrated in Figure 1-3. Specifically, a relational DBMS provides the following functions:

- It allows you to create database structures containing fields, tables, and table relationships.
- It lets you easily add new records, change field values in existing records, and delete records.
- It contains a built-in query language, which lets you obtain immediate answers to the questions you ask about your data.
- It contains a built-in report generator, which lets you produce professional-looking, formatted reports from your data.
- It protects databases through security, control, and recovery facilities.

Figure 1-3	Relational database management system

A company such as Belmont Landscapes benefits from a relational DBMS because it allows users working in different groups to share the same data. More than one user can enter data into a database, and more than one user can retrieve and analyze data that other users entered. For example, the database for Belmont Landscapes will contain only one copy of the Contract table, and all employees will use it to meet their specific requests for contract information.

Finally, unlike other software programs, such as spreadsheet programs, a DBMS can handle massive amounts of data and can be used to create relationships among multiple tables. Each Access database, for example, can be up to two gigabytes in size, can contain up to 32,768 objects (tables, queries, forms, and so on), and can have up to 255 people using the database at the same time. For instructional purposes, the databases you will create and work with throughout this text contain a relatively small number of records compared to databases you would encounter outside the classroom, which likely contain tables with very large numbers of records.

Creating a Database

Now that you've learned some database terms and concepts, you're ready to start Access and create the Belmont database for Oren.

To start Access:

1. Click the **Start** button on the taskbar, click **All Programs**, click **Microsoft Office**, and then click **Microsoft Access 2010**. The Access program starts and opens in Backstage view. See Figure 1-4.

   Trouble? If you don't see the Microsoft Access 2010 option on the Microsoft Office menu, look for it on a different menu or as an option on the All Programs menu. If you still cannot find the Microsoft Access 2010 option, ask your instructor or technical support person for help.

Figure 1-4   **Backstage view in Access**

Trouble? If the Microsoft Access program window on your computer is not maximized, click the Maximize button on the program window title bar.

When you start Access, the first screen that appears is Backstage view, which is the starting place for your work in Access. Backstage view provides options for you to get information about the current database, create a new database, or open an existing database. To create a new database that does not contain any data or objects, you use the Blank database option. If the database you need to create contains objects that match those found in common databases, such as databases that store data about contacts or events, you can click Sample templates and use a template provided with Access. A **template** is a predesigned database that includes professionally designed tables, reports, and other database objects that can make it quick and easy for you to create a database. You can also search for a template and download it from Office.com.

In this case, the templates provided do not match Oren's needs for the Belmont Landscapes database, so you need to create a new, blank database from scratch.

To create the new Belmont database:

▶ **1.** Make sure you have created your copy of the Access starting Data Files, and that your computer can access them.

   Trouble? If you don't have the starting Data Files, you need to get them before you can proceed. Your instructor will either give you the Data Files or ask you to obtain them from a specified location (such as a network drive). In either case, make a backup copy of the Data Files before you start so that you will have the original files available in case you need to start over. If you have any questions about the Data Files, see your instructor or technical support person for assistance.

▶ **2.** Make sure the **New** tab is selected in the navigation bar, and that the **Blank database** option is selected (see Figure 1-4).

> Be sure to type **Belmont** or you'll create a database named Database1.

▶ **3.** In the File Name box on the right side of the screen, select the default name provided by Access, and then type **Belmont**. Next you need to specify the location for the file.

▶ **4.** Click the **Browse** button 📂 to the right of the File Name box. The File New Database dialog box opens.

▶ **5.** Navigate to the drive that contains your Data Files.

   Trouble? If you do not know where your Data Files are located, consult with your instructor about where to save your Data Files.

▶ **6.** Navigate to the **Access1\Tutorial** folder. This is the folder in which you will store the database file you create.

▶ **7.** Make sure the "Save as type" box displays "Microsoft Access 2007 Databases."

   Trouble? If your computer is set up to show filename extensions, you will see the Access filename extension ".accdb" in the Save as type box.

> **TIP**
>
> If you don't type the filename extension, Access adds it automatically.

▶ **8.** Click the **OK** button. You return to Backstage view, and the File Name box now shows the name Belmont.accdb. The filename extension ".accdb" identifies the file as an Access 2007 database.

▶ **9.** Click the **Create** button. Access creates the new database, saves it to the specified drive, and then opens an empty table named Table1.

INSIGHT

Understanding the Database File Type

Access 2010 uses the .accdb file extension, which is the same file extension used for databases created with Microsoft Access 2007. To ensure compatibility between databases created with Access 2007 and Access 2010, new databases created using Access 2010 have the same file extension and file format as Access 2007 databases. This is why the File New Database dialog box provides the Microsoft Access 2007 Databases option in the "Save as type" box. In addition, the notation "(Access 2007)" appears in the title bar next to the name of an open database in Access 2010.

Refer back to the Session 1.1 Visual Overview and spend some time becoming familiar with the components of the Access window.

Creating a Table in Datasheet View

Tables contain all the data in a database and are the fundamental objects for your work in Access. There are different ways to create a table in Access, including entering the fields and records for a table directly in Datasheet view.

REFERENCE

Creating a Table in Datasheet View

- Click the Create tab on the Ribbon.
- In the Tables group, click the Table button.
- Accept the default ID primary key field with the AutoNumber data type, or rename the field and change its data type, if necessary.
- In the Add & Delete group on the Fields tab, click the button for the type of field you want to add to the table (for example, click the Text button), and then type the field name. Repeat this step to add all the necessary fields to the table.
  or
  In the table datasheet, click the Click to Add column heading, click the type of field you want to add from the list that opens, type the field name, and then press the Tab or Enter key to move to the next column in the datasheet. Repeat this step to add all the necessary fields to the table.
- In the first row below the field names, enter the value for each field in the first record, pressing the Tab or Enter key to move to the next field.
- After entering the value for the last field in the first record, press the Tab or Enter key to move to the next row, and then enter the values for the next record. Continue this process until you have entered all the records for the table.
- Click the Save button on the Quick Access Toolbar, enter a name for the table, and then click the OK button.

For Belmont Landscapes, Oren needs to track information about the company's contracts with its customers. He asks you to create the Contract table according to the plan shown in Figure 1-5.

Figure 1-5   **Plan for the Contract table**

Field	Purpose
ContractNum	Unique number assigned to each contract; will serve as the table's primary key
CustomerID	Unique number assigned to each customer; common field that will be a foreign key to connect to the Customer table
ContractAmt	Dollar amount for the full contract
SigningDate	Date on which the customer signed the contract
ContractType	Brief description of the contract

As shown in Oren's plan, he wants to store data about contracts in five fields, including fields to contain the amount of each contract, when it was signed, and the contract type. These are the most important aspects of a contract and, therefore, must be tracked. Also, notice that the ContractNum field will be the primary key for the table; each contract at Belmont Landscapes has a unique contract number, so this field is the logical choice for the primary key. Finally, the CustomerID field is needed in the Contract table as a foreign key to connect the information about contracts to customers. The data about customers and their invoices will be stored in separate tables, which you will create in Tutorial 2.

Notice the name of each field in Figure 1-5. You need to name each field, table, and other object in an Access database.

PROSKILLS

Decision Making: Naming Database Fields and Objects in Access

One of the most important tasks in creating a table is deciding what names to specify for the table's fields. Keep the following guidelines in mind when you assign field names:
- A field name can consist of up to 64 characters, including letters, numbers, spaces, and special characters, except for a period (.), exclamation mark (!), accent grave (`), and square brackets ([ ]).
- A field name cannot begin with a space.
- Capitalize the first letter of each word in a field name that combines multiple words, for example SigningDate.
- Use concise field names that are easy to remember and reference, and that won't take up a lot of space in the table datasheet.
- Use standard abbreviations, such as Num for Number, Amt for Amount, and Qty for Quantity.
- Give fields descriptive names so that you can easily identify them when you view or edit records.
- Although Access supports the use of spaces in field names (and in other object names), experienced database developers avoid using spaces because they can cause errors when the objects are involved in programming tasks.

By spending time obtaining and analyzing information about the fields in the table, and understanding the rules for naming Access fields and objects, you can determine the most appropriate object names and create a well-designed database that will be easy for others to use.

Renaming the Default Primary Key Field

As noted earlier, Access provides the ID field as the default primary key for a new table you create in Datasheet view. Recall that a primary key is a field, or a collection of fields, whose values uniquely identify each record in a table. However, according to Oren's plan, the ContractNum field should be the primary key for the Contract table. You'll begin by renaming the default ID field to create the ContractNum field.

To rename the ID field to the ContractNum field:

‣ **1.** Right-click the **ID** column heading to open the shortcut menu, and then click **Rename Field**. The column heading ID is selected, so that whatever text you type next will replace it.

‣ **2.** Type **ContractNum** and then click the row below the heading. The column heading changes to ContractNum and the insertion point moves to the row below the heading. See Figure 1-6.

Figure 1-6	ID field renamed to ContractNum

ContractNum field name entered in the column heading

option for specifying the data type for a field

AutoNumber data type assigned to the default primary key field (ID)

Trouble? If you make a mistake while typing the field name, use the Backspace key to delete characters to the left of the insertion point or the Delete key to delete characters to the right of the insertion point. Then type the correct text. To correct a field name by replacing it entirely, press the Esc key, and then type the correct text.

Trouble? The entire field name "ContractNum" might not be visible in the column heading. You'll learn how to resize columns to display the full field names later in this tutorial.

You have renamed the default primary key field, ID, to ContractNum. However, the ContractNum field still retains the characteristics of the ID field, including its data type. Your next task is to change the data type of this field.

Changing the Data Type of the Default Primary Key Field

Notice the Formatting group on the Fields tab. One of the options available in this group is the Data Type option (see Figure 1-6). Each field in an Access table must be assigned a data type. The **data type** determines what field values you can enter for the field. In this case, the AutoNumber data type is displayed. Access assigns the AutoNumber data type to the default ID primary key field because the **AutoNumber** data type automatically inserts a unique number in this field for every record. Therefore, it can serve as the primary key for any table you create.

Contract numbers at Belmont Landscapes are specific, four-digit numbers, so the AutoNumber data type is not appropriate for the ContractNum field, which is the primary key field in the table you are creating. A better choice is the **Text** data type, which allows field values containing letters, digits, and other characters, and which is appropriate for identifying numbers, such as contract numbers, that are never used in calculations. So, Oren asks you to change the data type for the ContractNum field from AutoNumber to Text.

To change the data type for the ContractNum field:

1. Make sure that the ContractNum column is selected. A column is selected when you click a field value, in which case the background color of the column heading changes (the default color is orange) and the insertion point appears in the field value. You can also click the column heading to select a column, in which case the background color of both the column heading and the field value changes (the default colors are gray and blue, respectively).

2. In the Formatting group on the Fields tab, click the **Data Type arrow**, and then click **Text**. The ContractNum field is now a Text field. See Figure 1-7.

Figure 1-7	Text data type assigned to the ContractNum field

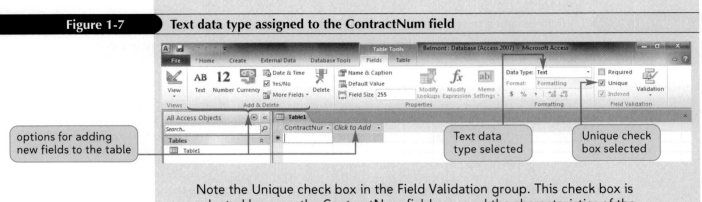

options for adding new fields to the table

Text data type selected

Unique check box selected

Note the Unique check box in the Field Validation group. This check box is selected because the ContractNum field assumed the characteristics of the default primary key field, ID, including the fact that each value in the field must be unique. No two records in the Contract table will be allowed to have the same value in the ContractNum field.

With the ContractNum field created and established as the primary key, you can now enter the rest of the fields in the Contract table.

Adding New Fields

When you create a table in Datasheet view, you can use the options in the Add & Delete group on the Fields tab to add fields to your table. You can also use the Click to Add column in the table datasheet to add new fields. (See Figure 1-7.) You'll use both methods to add the four remaining fields to the Contract table. The next field you need to add is the CustomerID field. Similar to the ContractNum field, the CustomerID field will also contain numbers that will not be used in calculations, so it should be a Text field.

To add the rest of the fields to the Contract table:

▶ **1.** In the Add & Delete group on the Fields tab, click the **Text** button. Access adds a new field named "Field1" to the right of the ContractNum field. See Figure 1-8.

Figure 1-8	New Text field added to the table

new field added as the second field in the table

default name highlighted in the new field

indicates the data type of the new field

The text "Field1" is selected, so you can simply type the new field name to replace it.

▶ **2.** Type **CustomerID**. The second field is added to the table. Next, you'll add the ContractAmt field. According to Oren's plan, this field will contain the dollar amount of each contract. The most appropriate data type for displaying dollar amounts is the Currency data type.

▶ **3.** In the Add & Delete group, click the **Currency** button. Access adds a third field to the table, this time with the Currency data type.

4. Type **ContractAmt** to replace the highlighted name "Field1." The fourth field in the Contract table is the SigningDate field. Because this field will contain date values, you'll add a field with the Date/Time data type next—this time using the Click to Add column.

5. Click the **Click to Add** column heading. Access displays a list of available data types from which you can choose the data type for the new field you're adding.

6. Click **Date & Time** in the list. Access adds a fourth field to the table.

7. Type **SigningDate** to replace the highlighted name "Field1," and then press the **Enter** key. The Click to Add column becomes active and displays the list of field data types. The fifth and final field in the Contract table is the ContractType field, which will contain brief descriptions of the contracts. The Text data type is suitable for this field.

TIP

You can also type the first letter of a data type to select it and close the Click to Add list.

8. Click **Text** in the list, and then type **ContractType** to replace the highlighted name "Field1." All five fields are now entered for the Contract table.

Some of the field names are not completely visible, so you need to resize the datasheet columns.

Trouble? If you pressed the Tab or Enter key after typing the ContractType field name, press the Esc key to close the Click to Add list.

9. Place the pointer on the vertical line between the ContractNum and CustomerID field names until the pointer changes to a ↔ shape.

10. Double-click the pointer. The ContractNum column is resized and now displays the full field name.

Trouble? If you click the arrow on the ContractNum column heading by mistake, a menu will open. Simply click the arrow again to close the menu, and then repeat Steps 9 and 10.

11. Double-click the ↔ pointer on the vertical line to the right of the CustomerID, ContractAmt, SigningDate, and ContractType column headings to resize the columns in the datasheet. When finished, click the first column for row 1. Your datasheet should now look like the one shown in Figure 1-9.

Figure 1-9	Table with all fields entered

The table contains three Text fields (ContractNum, CustomerID, and ContractType), one Currency field (ContractAmt), and one Date/Time field (SigningDate). You'll learn more about field data types in Tutorial 2.

As noted earlier, Datasheet view shows a table's contents in rows (records) and columns (fields). Each column is headed by a field name inside a field selector, and each row has a record selector to its left (see Figure 1-9). Clicking a **field selector** or a **record selector** selects that entire column or row (respectively), which you then can manipulate. A field selector is also called a **column selector**, and a record selector is also called a **row selector**.

Entering Records

With the fields in place for the table, you can now enter the field values for each record. Oren requests that you enter eight records in the Contract table, as shown in Figure 1-10.

Figure 1-10	Contract table records

ContractNum	CustomerID	ContractAmt	SigningDate	ContractType
3011	11001	$4,000.00	2/9/2013	Residential landscape plan
3026	11038	$165,000.00	3/11/2013	Landscape plans for large-scale housing development
3012	11027	$300.00	2/18/2013	Consultation for backyard, residential
3015	11005	$1,500.00	3/1/2013	Schematic plan for backyard, residential
3022	11043	$22,000.00	4/14/2013	Landscape design for two entrances
3017	11012	$2,250.00	3/1/2013	Peer plan review for town
3023	11070	$39,000.00	3/22/2013	Renovation of large multifamily housing open space
3021	11040	$28,000.00	5/3/2013	Landscape plans for multifamily housing site

To enter records in a table datasheet, you type the field values below the column headings for the fields. The first record you enter will go in the first row (see Figure 1-9).

To enter the first record for the Contract table:

Be sure to type the numbers "0" and "1" and not the letters "O" and "l" in the field value.

1. In the first row for the ContractNum field, type **3011** (the ContractNum field value for the first record), and then press the **Tab** key. Access adds the field value and moves the insertion point to the right, in the CustomerID column. See Figure 1-11.

Figure 1-11	First field value entered

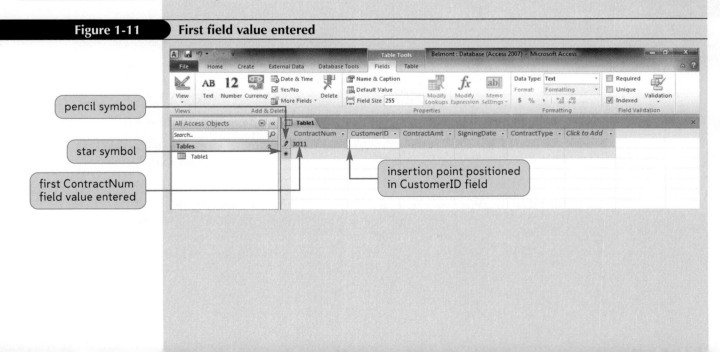

Trouble? If you make a mistake when typing a value, use the Backspace key to delete characters to the left of the insertion point or the Delete key to delete characters to the right of the insertion point. Then type the correct value. To correct a value by replacing it entirely, press the Esc key, and then type the correct value.

Notice the pencil symbol that appears in the row selector for the new record. The **pencil symbol** indicates that the record is being edited. Also notice the star symbol that appears in the row selector for the second row. The **star symbol** identifies the second row as the next row available for a new record.

▶ **2.** Type **11001** (the CustomerID field value for the first record), and then press the **Tab** key. Access enters the field value and moves the insertion point to the ContractAmt column.

▶ **3.** Type **4000** (the ContractAmt field value for the first record), and then press the **Tab** key. Notice that Access formats the field value with a dollar sign, a comma, and two decimal places—displaying it as $4,000.00—even though you did not enter the value this way. This is because the ContractAmt field has the Currency data type, which automatically formats field values in this way. You'll learn more about formatting field values later in this text.

▶ **4.** Type **2/9/13** (the SigningDate field value for the first record), and then press the **Tab** key. Access displays the year as "2013" even though you entered only the final two digits of the year. This is because the SigningDate field has the Date/Time data type, which automatically formats dates with four-digit years.

Trouble? Depending on your Windows date setting, your SigningDate field values might be displayed in a different format. This difference will not cause any problems.

▶ **5.** Type **Residential landscape plan** (the ContractType field value for the first record), and then press the **Tab** key. The first record is entered into the table, and the insertion point is positioned in the ContractNum field for the second record. The pencil symbol is removed from the first row because the record in that row is no longer being edited. The table is now ready for you to enter the second record. See Figure 1-12.

| Figure 1-12 | Datasheet with first record entered |

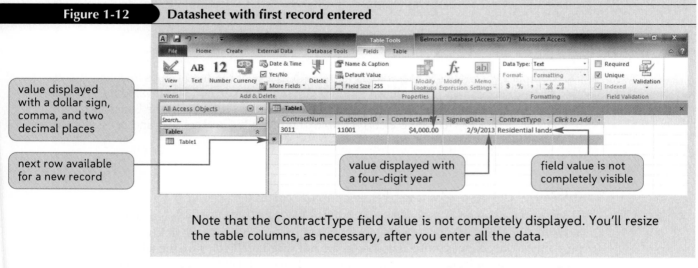

value displayed with a dollar sign, comma, and two decimal places

next row available for a new record

value displayed with a four-digit year

field value is not completely visible

Note that the ContractType field value is not completely displayed. You'll resize the table columns, as necessary, after you enter all the data.

Now you can enter the remaining seven records in the Contract table.

TIP

You can also press the Enter key instead of the Tab key to move from one field to another, and to the next row.

To enter the remaining records in the Contract table:

1. Referring to Figure 1-10, enter the values for records 2 through 8, pressing the **Tab** key to move from field to field and to the next row for a new record. Keep in mind that you do not have to type the dollar sign, comma, or decimal places in the ContractAmt values, because Access will add them automatically. Similarly, you do not have to type all four digits of the year in the SigningDate field values; you can enter only the final two digits and Access will display all four.

   Trouble? If you enter a value in the wrong field by mistake, such as entering a ContractType field value in the ContractAmt field, a menu might open with options for addressing the problem. If this happens, click the "Enter new value" option in the menu. You'll return to the field with the incorrect value highlighted, which you can then replace by typing the correct value.

   To see more of the table datasheet and the full field values, you'll close the Navigation Pane and resize the ContractType column.

2. Click the **Shutter Bar Open/Close Button** ⟨⟨ at the top of the Navigation Pane. The Navigation Pane closes, and you can see the complete table datasheet.

3. Place the pointer on the vertical line to the right of the ContractType field name until the pointer changes to a ↔ shape, and then double-click the pointer. All the ContractType field values are now fully displayed. See Figure 1-13.

Figure 1-13	Datasheet with eight records entered

Navigation Pane is closed

field values are completely visible

ContractNum	CustomerID	ContractAmt	SigningDate	ContractType
3011	11001	$4,000.00	2/9/2013	Residential landscape plan
3026	11038	$165,000.00	3/11/2013	Landscape plans for large-scale housing development
3012	11027	$300.00	2/18/2013	Consultation for backyard, residential
3015	11005	$1,500.00	3/1/2013	Schematic plan for backyard, residential
3022	11043	$22,000.00	4/14/2013	Landscape design for two entrances
3017	11012	$2,250.00	3/1/2013	Peer plan review for town
3023	11070	$39,000.00	3/22/2013	Renovation of large multifamily housing open space
3021	11040	$28,000.00	5/3/2013	Landscape plans for multifamily housing site

Carefully compare your ContractNum and CustomerID values with those in the figure and correct any errors before continuing.

4. Compare your table to the one in Figure 1-13. If any of the field values in your table do not match those shown in the figure, you can correct a field value by clicking to position the insertion point in the value, and then using the Backspace key or Delete key to delete incorrect text. Then type the correct text and press the Enter key.

Saving a Table

The records you enter are immediately stored in the database as soon as you enter them; however, the table's design—the field names and characteristics of the fields themselves, plus any layout changes to the datasheet—are not saved until you save the table. When you save a new table for the first time, you should give it a name that best identifies the information it contains. Like a field name, a table name can contain up to 64 characters, including spaces.

REFERENCE

Saving a Table

- Click the Save button on the Quick Access Toolbar. The Save As dialog box opens.
- In the Table Name box, type the name for the table.
- Click the OK button.

According to Oren's plan, you need to save the table with the name "Contract."

To save and name the Contract table:

TIP

You can also use the Save command in Backstage view to save and name a new table.

1. Click the **Save** button 🖫 on the Quick Access Toolbar. The Save As dialog box opens.

2. With the default name Table1 selected in the Table Name box, type **Contract**, and then click the **OK** button. The tab for the table now displays the name "Contract," and the Contract table design is saved in the Belmont database.

Notice that after you saved and named the Contract table, Access sorted and displayed the records in order by the values in the ContractNum field because it is the primary key. If you compare your screen to Figure 1-10, which shows the records in the order you entered them, you'll see that the current screen shows the records in order by the ContractNum field values.

Oren asks you to add two more records to the Contract table. When you add a record to an existing table, you must enter the new record in the next row available for a new record; you cannot insert a row between existing records for the new record. In a table with just a few records, such as the Contract table, the next available row is visible on the screen. However, in a table with hundreds of records, you would need to scroll the datasheet to see the next row available. The easiest way to add a new record to a table is to use the New button, which scrolls the datasheet to the next row available so you can enter the new record.

To enter additional records in the Contract table:

1. If necessary, click the first record's ContractNum field value (**3011**) to make it the current record.

2. Click the **Home** tab on the Ribbon.

3. In the Records group, click the **New** button. The insertion point is positioned in the next row available for a new record, which in this case is row 9. See Figure 1-14.

Figure 1-14 Entering a new record

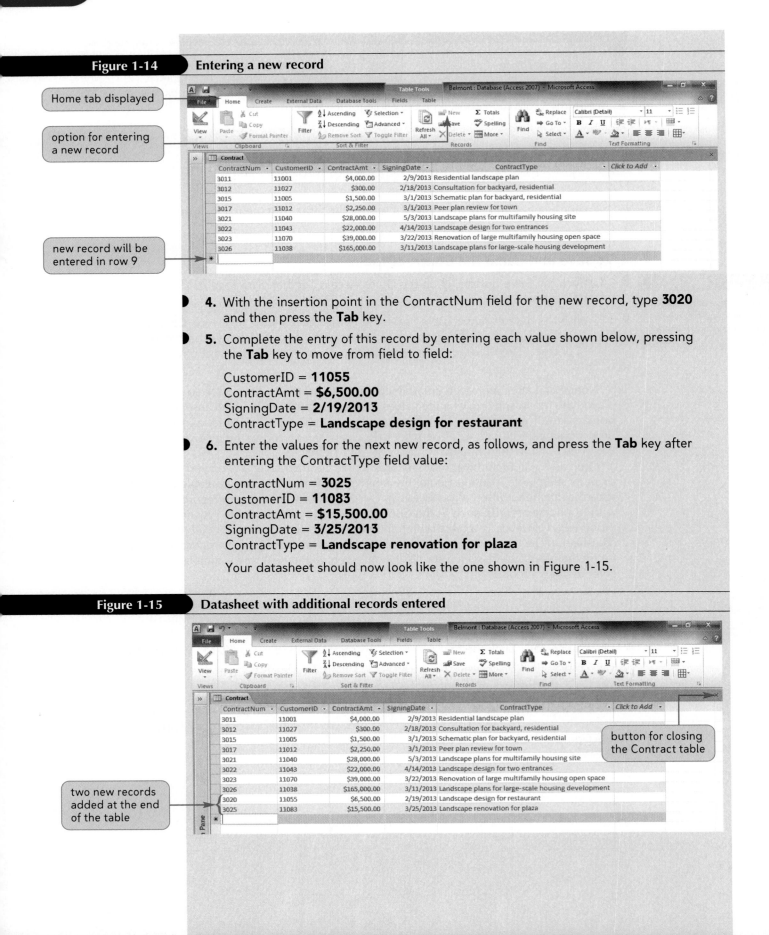

Home tab displayed

option for entering a new record

new record will be entered in row 9

4. With the insertion point in the ContractNum field for the new record, type **3020** and then press the **Tab** key.

5. Complete the entry of this record by entering each value shown below, pressing the **Tab** key to move from field to field:

   CustomerID = **11055**
   ContractAmt = **$6,500.00**
   SigningDate = **2/19/2013**
   ContractType = **Landscape design for restaurant**

6. Enter the values for the next new record, as follows, and press the **Tab** key after entering the ContractType field value:

   ContractNum = **3025**
   CustomerID = **11083**
   ContractAmt = **$15,500.00**
   SigningDate = **3/25/2013**
   ContractType = **Landscape renovation for plaza**

   Your datasheet should now look like the one shown in Figure 1-15.

Figure 1-15 Datasheet with additional records entered

two new records added at the end of the table

button for closing the Contract table

The new records you added appear at the end of the table, and are not sorted in order by the primary key field values. For example, ContractNum 3020 should be the fifth record in the table, placed between ContractNum 3017 and ContractNum 3021. When you add records to a table datasheet, they appear at the end of the table. The records are not displayed in primary key order until you close and reopen the table, or switch between views.

▶ **7.** Click the **Close 'Contract'** button ✕ on the object tab (see Figure 1-15 for the location of this button). The Contract table closes, and the main portion of the Access window is now blank because no database object is currently open.

Opening a Table

The tables in a database are listed in the Navigation Pane. You open a table, or any Access object (query, form, report), by double-clicking the object name in the Navigation Pane. Next, you'll open the Contract table so you can see the order of all the records you've entered.

To open the Contract table:

▶ **1.** On the Navigation Pane, click the **Shutter Bar Open/Close Button** ≫ to open the pane. Note that the Contract table is listed.

▶ **2.** Double-click **Contract** to open the table in Datasheet view. See Figure 1-16.

Figure 1-16 — **Table with 10 records entered and displayed in primary key order**

Contract table object in the Belmont database

two records added now appear in primary key order

records listed in order by the values in the primary key field

Current Record box indicates the table contains 10 records

The two records you added, with ContractNum field values of 3020 and 3025, now appear in the correct primary key order. The table now contains a total of 10 records, as indicated by the Current Record box at the bottom of the datasheet. The **Current Record box** displays the number of the current record as well as the total number of records in the table.

Each record contains a unique ContractNum value because this field is the primary key. Other fields, however, can contain the same value in multiple records; for example, note the two values of 3/1/2013 in the SigningDate field.

3. If you are not continuing on to Session 1.2, click the **Close** button [X] on the program window title bar. Access closes the Contract table and the Belmont database, and then the Access program closes.

INSIGHT

Saving a Database

Unlike the Save buttons in other Office programs, the Save button on the Quick Access Toolbar in Access does not save the active document (database) to your disk. Instead, you use the Save button to save the design of an Access object, such as a table (as you saw earlier), or to save datasheet format changes, such as resizing columns. Access does not have a button or option you can use to save the active database.

Access saves changes to the active database to your disk automatically when you change or add a record or close the database. If your database is stored on a removable medium, such as a USB drive, you should never remove the drive while the database file is open. If you do, Access will encounter problems when it tries to save the database, which might damage the database.

Now that you've become familiar with database concepts and Access, and created the Belmont database and the Contract table, Oren wants you to add more records to the table and work with the data stored in it to create database objects including a query, form, and report. You will complete these tasks in Session 1.2.

REVIEW

Session 1.1 Quick Check

1. A(n) _____ is a single characteristic of a person, place, object, event, or idea.

2. You connect the records in two separate tables through a(n) _____ that appears in both tables.

3. The _____, whose values uniquely identify each record in a table, is called a(n) _____ when it is placed in a second table to form a relationship between the two tables.

4. The _____ is the area of the Access window that lists all the objects in a database, and it is the main control center for opening and working with database objects.

5. Which field does Access create, by default, as the primary key field for a new table in Datasheet view?

6. Which group on the Fields tab contains the options you use to add new fields to a table?

7. What does a pencil symbol at the beginning of a record represent? A star symbol?

8. Explain how the saving process in Access is different from saving in other Office programs.

SESSION 1.2 VISUAL OVERVIEW

The Forms group contains options for creating a **form**, which is a database object you use to enter, edit, and view records in a database.

The **Query Wizard** button opens a dialog box with different types of wizards that guide you through the steps to create a query. One of these, the **Simple Query Wizard**, allows you to select records and fields quickly to display in the query results.

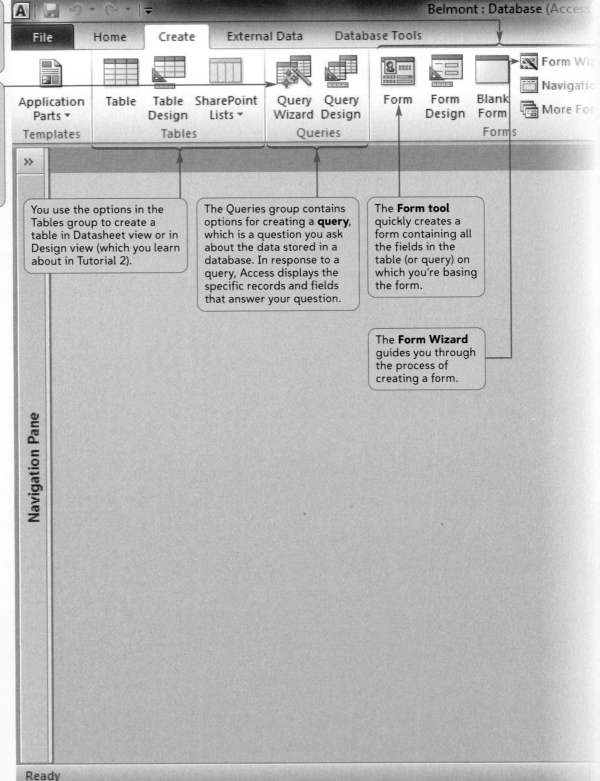

You use the options in the Tables group to create a table in Datasheet view or in Design view (which you learn about in Tutorial 2).

The Queries group contains options for creating a **query**, which is a question you ask about the data stored in a database. In response to a query, Access displays the specific records and fields that answer your question.

The **Form tool** quickly creates a form containing all the fields in the table (or query) on which you're basing the form.

The **Form Wizard** guides you through the process of creating a form.

THE CREATE TAB OPTIONS

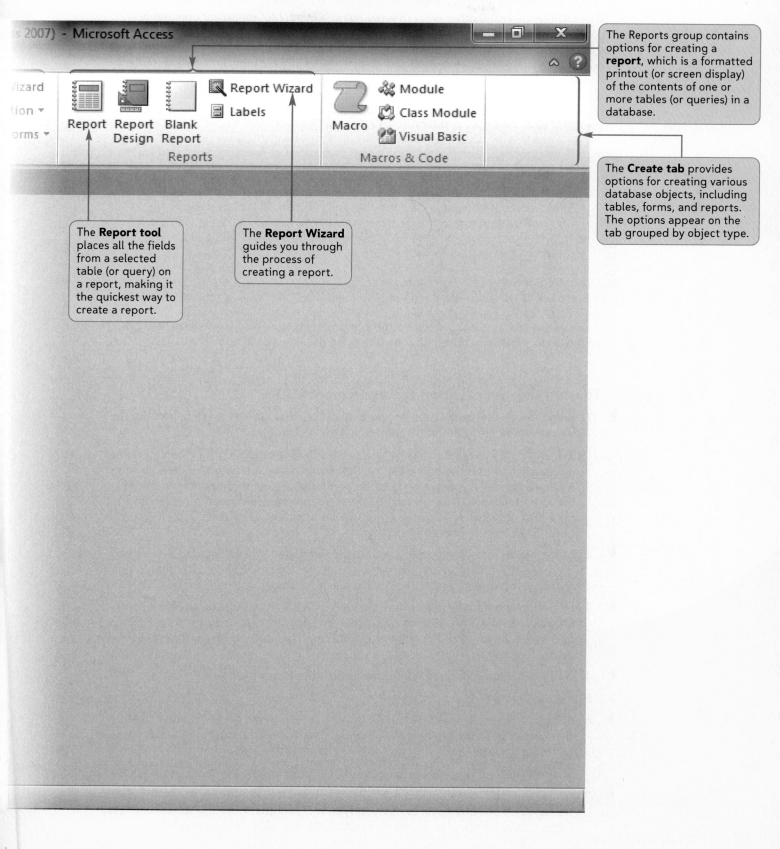

The Reports group contains options for creating a **report**, which is a formatted printout (or screen display) of the contents of one or more tables (or queries) in a database.

The **Create tab** provides options for creating various database objects, including tables, forms, and reports. The options appear on the tab grouped by object type.

The **Report tool** places all the fields from a selected table (or query) on a report, making it the quickest way to create a report.

The **Report Wizard** guides you through the process of creating a report.

Copying Records from Another Access Database

When you created the Contract table, you entered records directly into the table datasheet. There are many other ways to enter records in a table, including copying and pasting records from a table into the same database or into a different database. To use this method, however, the tables must have the same structure—that is, the tables must contain the same fields, with the same design and characteristics, in the same order.

Oren has already created a table named Agreement that contains additional records with contract data. The Agreement table is contained in a database named Oren located in the Access1\Tutorial folder included with your Data Files. The Agreement table has the same table structure as the Contract table you created.

REFERENCE

Opening a Database

- Start Access. If necessary, click the File tab to display Backstage view.
- Click the Open command in the navigation bar to display the Open dialog box.
- Navigate to the database file you want to open, and then click the file.
- Click the Open button.

Your next task is to copy the records from the Agreement table and paste them into your Contract table. To do so, you need to open the Oren database.

To copy the records from the Agreement table:

1. If you took a break after the previous session, make sure that the Belmont database is open, and the Contract table is open in Datasheet view.

   Trouble? If you need to open the Belmont database, a Security Warning might appear below the Ribbon indicating that some active content has been disabled. Access provides this warning because some databases might contain content that could harm your computer. Because the Belmont database does not contain objects that could be harmful, you can open it safely. Click the Enable Content button next to the Security Warning.

2. In the Navigation Pane, click the **Shutter Bar Open/Close Button** « to close the pane (if necessary) and display more of the table datasheet. To open a second database, you need to start another copy of Access.

3. Click the **Start** button ⊙ on the taskbar, click **All Programs**, click **Microsoft Office**, and then click **Microsoft Access 2010**. The Access program opens in Backstage view. To open an existing database, you use the Open command in the navigation bar.

4. In the navigation bar, click **Open** to display the Open dialog box.

5. Navigate to the drive that contains your Data Files.

6. Navigate to the **Access1\Tutorial** folder, click the database file named **Oren**, and then click the **Open** button. The Oren database opens in a second Access window. Note that the database contains only one object, the Agreement table.

   Trouble? If the Security Warning opens, click the Enable Content button to close it.

7. In the Navigation Pane, double-click **Agreement** to open the Agreement table in Datasheet view. The table contains 55 records and the same five fields, with the same characteristics, as the fields in the Contract table. See Figure 1-17.

Figure 1-17   **Agreement table in the Oren database**

same fields as in the Contract table

click the datasheet selector to select all the records in the table

table contains a total of 55 records

Oren wants you to copy all the records in the Agreement table. You can select all the records by clicking the **datasheet selector**, which is the box to the left of the first field name in the table datasheet (see Figure 1-17).

8. Click the **datasheet selector** to the left of the ContractNum field. Access selects all the records in the table.

9. In the Clipboard group on the Home tab, click the **Copy** button. All the records are copied to the Clipboard.

10. Click the **Close 'Agreement'** button ✖ on the object tab. A dialog box opens asking if you want to save the data you copied to the Clipboard. This dialog box opens only when you copy a large amount of data to the Clipboard.

11. Click the **Yes** button. The dialog box closes, and then the Agreement table closes.

12. Click the **Close** button ✖ on the Access window title bar to close the Oren database and the second Access program window. .

With the records copied to the Clipboard, you can now paste them into the Contract table.

To paste the records into the Contract table:

1. With the Belmont database's Contract table open in Datasheet view, position the pointer on the row selector for row 11 (the next row available for a new record) until the pointer changes to a ➡ shape, and then click to select the row.

Trouble? If you have difficulty displaying the correct pointer shape, click an empty area of the table datasheet to establish the window as the active window. Then repeat Step 1.

2. In the Clipboard group on the Home tab, click the **Paste** button. The pasted records are added to the table, and a dialog box opens asking you to confirm that you want to paste all the records (55 total).

   Trouble? If the Paste button isn't active, click the ➡ pointer on the row selector for row 11, making sure the entire row is selected, and then repeat Step 2.

3. Click the **Yes** button. The dialog box closes, and the pasted records are highlighted. See Figure 1-18. Notice that the table now contains a total of 65 records—10 records that you entered and 55 records that you copied and pasted.

Figure 1-18   **Contract table after copying and pasting records**

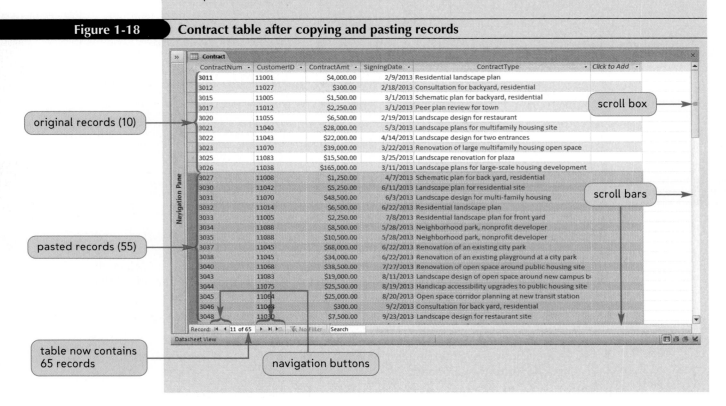

Navigating a Datasheet

The Contract table now contains 65 records, but only some of the records are visible on the screen. To view fields or records not currently visible on the screen, you can use the horizontal and vertical scroll bars shown in Figure 1-18 to navigate the data. The **navigation buttons**, shown in Figure 1-18 and also described in Figure 1-19, provide another way to move vertically through the records. The Current Record box appears between the two sets of navigation buttons and displays the number of the current record as well as the total number of records in the table. Figure 1-19 shows which record becomes the current record when you click each navigation button. Note the New (blank) record button, which works in the same way as the New button on the Home tab you used earlier to enter a new record in the table.

Figure 1-19	Navigation buttons

Navigation Button	Record Selected	Navigation Button	Record Selected
⏮	First record	⏭	Last record
◀	Previous record	▶✱	New (blank) record
▶	Next record		

Oren suggests that you use the various navigation techniques to move through the Contract table and become familiar with its contents.

TIP

You can make a field the current field by clicking anywhere within the column for that field.

To navigate the Contract datasheet:

▶ 1. Click the first record's ContractNum field value (**3011**). The Current Record box shows that record 1 is the current record.

▶ 2. Click the **Next record** navigation button ▶. The second record is now highlighted, which identifies it as the current record. Also, notice that the second record's value for the ContractNum field is selected, and the Current Record box displays "2 of 65" to indicate that the second record is the current record.

▶ 3. Click the **Last record** navigation button ⏭. The last record in the table, record 65, is now the current record.

▶ 4. Drag the scroll box in the vertical scroll bar (see Figure 1-18) up to the top of the bar. Notice that record 65 is still the current record, as indicated in the Current Record box. Dragging the scroll box changes the display of the table datasheet, but does not change the current record.

▶ 5. Drag the scroll box in the vertical scroll bar back down until you can see the end of the table and the current record (record 65).

▶ 6. Click the **Previous record** navigation button ◀. Record 64 is now the current record.

▶ 7. Click the **First record** navigation button ⏮. The first record is now the current record and is visible on the screen.

The Contract table now contains all the data about the customer contracts for Belmont Landscapes. To better understand how to work with this data, Oren asks you to create simple objects for the other main types of database objects—queries, forms, and reports.

Creating a Simple Query

As noted earlier, a query is a question you ask about the data stored in a database. When you create a query, you tell Access which fields you need and what criteria Access should use to select the records that will answer your question. Then Access displays only the information you want, so you don't have to navigate through the entire database for the information. In the Contract table, for example, Oren might create a query to display only those records for contracts that were signed in a specific month. Even though a query can display table information in a different way, the information still exists in the table as it was originally entered.

Oren wants to focus on the amount of each contract and the contract type. He doesn't want the list to include all the fields in the Contract table, such as CustomerID and

SigningDate. To produce this list for Oren, you'll use the Simple Query Wizard to create a query based on the Contract table.

To start the Simple Query Wizard:

▶ **1.** Click the **Create** tab on the Ribbon.

▶ **2.** In the Queries group on the Create tab, click the **Query Wizard** button. The New Query dialog box opens.

▶ **3.** Make sure **Simple Query Wizard** is selected, and then click the **OK** button. The first Simple Query Wizard dialog box opens. See Figure 1-20.

Figure 1-20 | **First Simple Query Wizard dialog box**

Because the Contract table is the only object in the Belmont database, it is listed in the Tables/Queries box by default. If the database contained more objects, you could click the Tables/Queries arrow and choose another table or a query as the basis for the new query you are creating. The Available Fields box lists all the fields in the Contract table.

You need to select fields from the Available Fields box to include them in the query. To select fields one at a time, click a field and then click the > button. The selected field moves from the Available Fields box on the left to the Selected Fields box on the right. To select all the fields, click the >> button. If you change your mind or make a mistake, you can remove a field by clicking it in the Selected Fields box and then clicking the < button. To remove all selected fields, click the << button.

Each Simple Query Wizard dialog box contains buttons on the bottom that allow you to move to the previous dialog box (Back button), move to the next dialog box (Next button), or cancel the creation process (Cancel button). You can also finish creating the object (Finish button) and accept the wizard's defaults for the remaining options.

Oren wants his list to include data from only the following fields: ContractNum, ContractAmt, and ContractType. You need to select these fields to include them in the query.

To create the query using the Simple Query Wizard:

▶ **1.** Click **ContractNum** in the Available Fields box to select the field (if necessary), and then click the ⟩ button. The ContractNum field moves to the Selected Fields box.

▶ **2.** Repeat Step 1 for the fields **ContractAmt** and **ContractType**, and then click the **Next** button. The second Simple Query Wizard dialog box opens and asks if you want a detail or summary query. This dialog box opens when the values in one of the fields selected for the query could be used in calculations—in this case, the ContractAmt field. Oren wants to see every field of every record and does not want to perform summary calculations on the ContractAmt field values, so you need to create a detail query.

▶ **3.** Make sure the **Detail** option button is selected, and then click the **Next** button. The third, and final, Simple Query Wizard dialog box opens and asks you to choose a name (title) for your query. Access suggests the name "Contract Query" because the query you are creating is based on the Contract table. You'll change the suggested name to "ContractList."

▶ **4.** Click at the end of the suggested name, use the **Backspace** key to delete the word "Query" and the space, and then type **List**. Now you can view the query results.

▶ **5.** Click the **Finish** button to complete the query. Access displays the query results in Datasheet view, on a new tab named "ContractList." A query datasheet is similar to a table datasheet, showing fields in columns and records in rows—but only for those fields and records you want to see, as determined by the query specifications you select.

▶ **6.** Place the pointer on the vertical line to the right of the ContractType field name until the pointer changes to a ↔ shape, and then double-click the pointer. All the ContractType field values are now fully displayed. See Figure 1-21.

Figure 1-21   Query results

only the three selected fields are displayed in the query datasheet

all 65 records are included in the results

The ContractList query datasheet displays the three selected fields for each record in the Contract table. The fields are shown in the order you selected them in the Simple Query Wizard, from left to right. The records are listed in order by the primary key field, ContractNum. Even though the query datasheet displays only the three fields you chose for the query, the Contract table still includes all the fields for all records.

Notice that the navigation buttons are located at the bottom of the window. You navigate a query datasheet in the same way that you navigate a table datasheet.

▶ **7.** Click the **Last record** navigation button ▶|. The last record in the query datasheet is now the current record.

▶ **8.** Click the **Previous record** navigation button ◀. Record 64 in the query datasheet is now the current record.

▶ **9.** Click the **First record** navigation button |◀. The first record is now the current record.

▶ **10.** Click the **Close 'ContractList'** button ✕ on the object tab. A dialog box opens asking if you want to save the changes to the layout of the query. This dialog box opens because you resized the ContractType column.

▶ **11.** Click the **Yes** button to save the query layout changes and close the query.

The query results are not stored in the database; however, the query design is stored as part of the database with the name you specified. You can re-create the query results at any time by opening the query again. You'll learn more about creating and working with queries in Tutorial 3.

Next, Oren asks you to create a form for the Contract table so that Belmont Landscapes employees can use the form to enter and work with data in the table easily.

Creating a Simple Form

As noted earlier, you use a form to enter, edit, and view records in a database. Although you can perform these same functions with tables and queries, forms can present data in many customized and useful ways.

Oren wants a form for the Contract table that shows all the fields for one record at a time, with fields listed one below another in a column. This type of form will make it easier for his staff to focus on all the data for a particular contract. You'll use the Form tool to create this form quickly and easily.

To create the form using the Form tool:

▶ **1.** Make sure the Contract table is still open in Datasheet view. The table or other database object you're using as the basis for the form must either be open or selected in the Navigation Pane when you use the Form tool.

   Trouble? If the Contract table is not open, click the Shutter Bar Open/Close Button ≫ to open the Navigation Pane. Then double-click Contract to open the Contract table in Datasheet view. Click the Shutter Bar Open/Close Button ≪ to close the pane.

▶ **2.** In the Forms group on the Create tab, click the **Form** button. The Form tool creates a simple form showing every field in the Contract table and places it on a tab named "Contract." Access assigns this name because the form is based on the Contract table. See Figure 1-22.

Figure 1-22 **Form created by the Form tool**

- new tab for the form
- field values for the first record displayed
- record 1 of 65 total records
- form displayed in Layout view
- depending on your computer's settings, your field value boxes might be a different width

The form displays one record at a time in the Contract table, providing another view of the data that is stored in the table and allowing you to focus on the values for one record. Access displays the field values for the first record in the table and selects the first field value (ContractNum) by placing a border around the value. Each field name appears on a separate line and on the same line as its field value, which appears in a box to the right. Depending on your computer's settings, the field value boxes in your form might be wider or narrower than those shown in the figure. As indicated in the status bar, the form is displayed in Layout view. In **Layout view**, you can make design changes to the form while it is displaying data, so that you can see the effects of the changes you make immediately.

To view and maintain data using a form, you must know how to move from field to field and from record to record. Notice that the form contains navigation buttons, similar to those available in Datasheet view, which you can use to display different records in the form. You'll use these now to navigate the form; then you'll save and close the form.

To navigate, save, and close the form:

1. Click the **Next record** navigation button ▶. The form now displays the values for the second record in the Contract table.

2. Click the **Last record** navigation button ▶I to move to the last record in the table. The form displays the information for contract number 3110.

3. Click the **Previous record** navigation button ◀ to move to record 64.

4. Click the **First record** navigation button I◀ to return to the first record in the Contract table.

Next, you'll save the form with the name "ContractData" in the Belmont database. Then the form will be available for later use.

▶ **5.** Click the **Save** button 🖫 on the Quick Access Toolbar. The Save As dialog box opens.

▶ **6.** In the Form Name box, click at the end of the highlighted word "Contract," type **Data**, and then press the **Enter** key. Access saves the form as ContractData in the Belmont database and closes the dialog box. The tab containing the form now displays the name ContractData.

▶ **7.** Click the **Close 'ContractData'** button ☒ on the object tab to close the form.

INSIGHT

Saving Database Objects

In general, it is best to save a database object—query, form, or report—only if you anticipate using the object frequently or if it is time consuming to create because all objects use storage space on your disk. For example, you most likely would not save a form you created with the Form tool because you can re-create it easily with one mouse click. (However, for the purposes of this text, you usually need to save the objects you create.)

After attending a staff meeting, Oren returns with another request. He would like to see the information in the Contract table presented in a more readable format. You'll help Oren by creating a report.

Creating a Simple Report

As noted earlier, a report is a formatted printout (or screen display) of the contents of one or more tables or queries. You'll use the Report tool to quickly produce a report based on the Contract table for Oren. The Report tool creates a report based on the selected table or query.

To create the report using the Report tool:

▶ **1.** With the Contract table open in Datasheet view, click the **Create** tab on the Ribbon.

▶ **2.** In the Reports group, click the **Report** button. The Report tool creates a simple report showing every field in the Contract table and places it on a tab named "Contract." Again, Access assigns this name because the object you created (the report) is based on the Contract table. See Figure 1-23.

Trouble? The records in your report might appear in a different order from the records shown in Figure 1-23. This difference will not cause any problems.

Figure 1-23   **Report created by the Report tool**

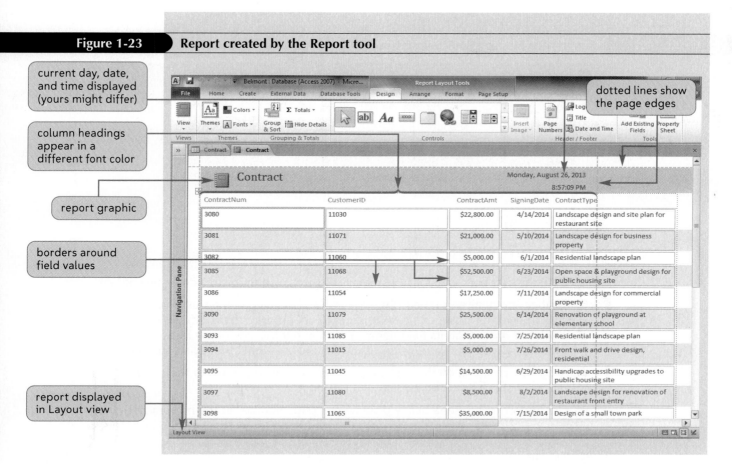

current day, date, and time displayed (yours might differ)

column headings appear in a different font color

report graphic

borders around field values

report displayed in Layout view

dotted lines show the page edges

The report shows each field in a column, with the field values for each record in a row, similar to a datasheet. However, the report offers a more visually appealing format for the data, with the column headings in a different color, borders around each field value, a graphic of a report at the top left, and the current day, date, and time at the top right. Also notice the dotted horizontal and vertical lines on the top and right, respectively; these lines mark the edges of the page and show where text will print on the page.

The report needs some design changes to better display the data. The columns are much wider than necessary for the ContractNum and CustomerID fields, and the ContractType field's values and borders are not completely displayed within the page area defined by the dotted lines, which means they would not appear on the printed report. You can resize the columns easily in Layout view.

To resize the ContractNum and CustomerID columns:

1. Position the pointer on the right border of any field value in the ContractNum column until the pointer changes to a ↔ shape.

2. Click and drag the mouse to the left; dark outlines surround the field name and each field value to show the column width as you change it. Drag to the left until the column is slightly wider than the ContractNum field name.

3. Release the mouse button. The ContractNum column is now narrower, and the other four columns shifted to the left. The ContractType field, values, and borders are almost completely within the page area. See Figure 1-24.

Figure 1-24   Report after resizing the ContractNum column

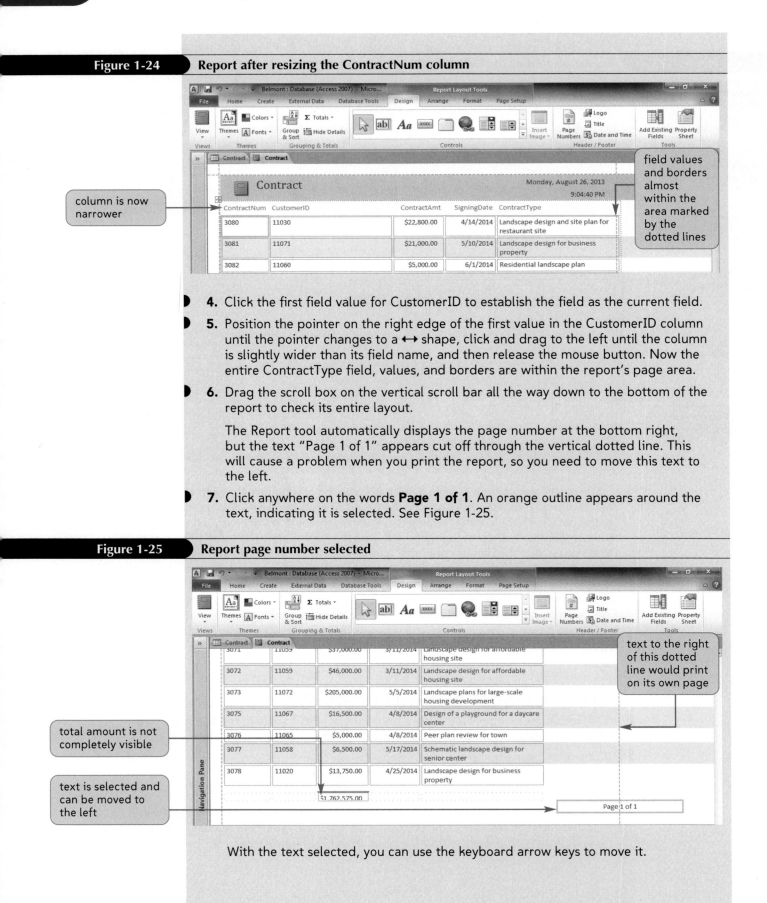

column is now narrower

field values and borders almost within the area marked by the dotted lines

4. Click the first field value for CustomerID to establish the field as the current field.

5. Position the pointer on the right edge of the first value in the CustomerID column until the pointer changes to a ↔ shape, click and drag to the left until the column is slightly wider than its field name, and then release the mouse button. Now the entire ContractType field, values, and borders are within the report's page area.

6. Drag the scroll box on the vertical scroll bar all the way down to the bottom of the report to check its entire layout.

The Report tool automatically displays the page number at the bottom right, but the text "Page 1 of 1" appears cut off through the vertical dotted line. This will cause a problem when you print the report, so you need to move this text to the left.

7. Click anywhere on the words **Page 1 of 1**. An orange outline appears around the text, indicating it is selected. See Figure 1-25.

Figure 1-25   Report page number selected

text to the right of this dotted line would print on its own page

total amount is not completely visible

text is selected and can be moved to the left

With the text selected, you can use the keyboard arrow keys to move it.

TIP

You can also use the mouse to drag the selected page number.

8. Press the ← key repeatedly until the selected page number is to the left of the vertical dotted line (roughly 35 times). The page number text is now completely within the page area and will print on the same page as the rest of the report.

Notice the total amount shown at the end of the report for the ContractAmt field. The Report tool calculated this amount and displayed it on the report. Often, you want to include information such as summaries and totals in a report; in this case, the Report tool generated it for you automatically. However, the amount looks partially cut off at the left and bottom and might not print correctly. To be sure the entire value is displayed in the report, you'll resize the box containing it.

9. Click to select the total contract amount, **$1,762,575.00**. An orange outline surrounds the value, indicating it is selected.

10. Place the pointer on the right side of the box until the pointer changes to a ↔ shape, and then click and drag to the right just a little until the dollar sign is completely visible; then place the pointer on the bottom of the box until the pointer changes to ↕, and then click and drag down a little until the full field value is displayed. The report scrolls up after you release the mouse button. See Figure 1-26.

| Figure 1-26 | Report after moving the page number and resizing the total |

11. Drag the scroll box back up to redisplay the top of the report.

The report is displayed in Layout view, which doesn't show how many pages there are in the report. To see this, you need to switch to Print Preview.

To view the report in Print Preview:

1. In the Views group on the Design tab, click the **View button arrow**, and then click **Print Preview**. The first page of the report is displayed in Print Preview. See Figure 1-27.

Figure 1-27 First page of the report in Print Preview

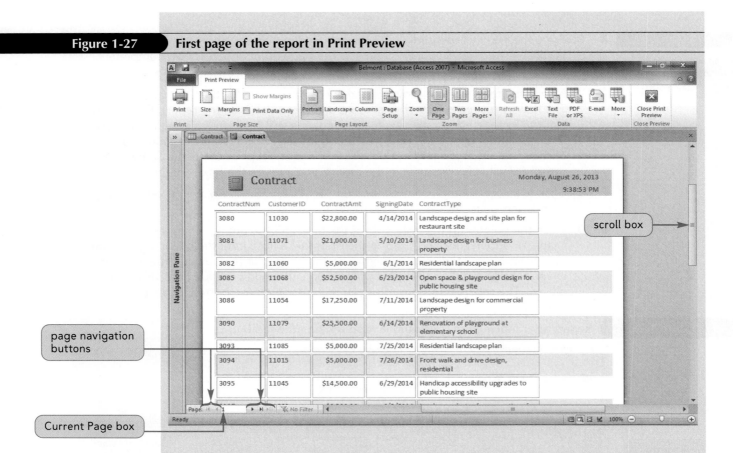

page navigation buttons

Current Page box

Print Preview shows exactly how the report will look when printed. Notice that Print Preview provides page navigation buttons at the bottom of the window, similar to the navigation buttons you've used to move through records in a table, query, and form.

2. Click the **Next Page** navigation button ▶. The second page of the report is displayed in Print Preview.

3. Click the **Last Page** navigation button ▶| to move to the last page of the report.

4. Drag the scroll box in the vertical scroll bar (see Figure 1-27) down until the bottom of the report page is displayed. The notation "Page 3 of 3" appears at the bottom of the page, indicating that you are on page 3 out of a total of 3 pages in the report. Also note the total displayed for the ContractAmt field.

   Trouble? Depending on the printer you are using, your report might have more or fewer pages, and some of the pages might be blank. If so, don't worry. Different printers format reports in different ways, sometimes affecting the total number of pages and the number of records printed per page.

5. Click the **First Page** navigation button |◀ to return to the first page of the report, and then drag the scroll box in the vertical scroll bar back up so that the top of the report is displayed.

   Next you'll save the report as ContractDetails, and then print it.

6. Click the **Save** button 🖫 on the Quick Access Toolbar. The Save As dialog box opens.

▶ **7.** In the Report Name box, click at the end of the highlighted word "Contract," and then type **Details** and press the **Enter** key. Access saves the report as ContractDetails in the Belmont database and closes the dialog box. The tab containing the report now displays the name "ContractDetails."

Printing a Report

After creating a report, you typically print it to distribute it to others who need to view the report's contents. You can print a report without changing any print settings, or display the Print dialog box and select options for printing.

REFERENCE

Printing a Report

- Open the report in any view, or select the report in the Navigation Pane.
- To print the report with the default print settings, click the File tab to display Backstage view, click the Print tab, and then click Quick Print.
  or
  To display the Print dialog box and select the options you want for printing the report, click the File tab, click the Print tab, and then click Print (or, if the report is displayed in Print Preview, click the Print button in the Print group on the Print Preview tab).

Oren asks you to print the entire report with the default settings, so you'll use the Quick Print option in Backstage view.

Note: To complete the following steps, your computer must be connected to a printer.

To print the report and then close it:

▶ **1.** Click the **File** tab on the Ribbon to display Backstage view.

▶ **2.** Click the **Print** tab in the navigation bar, and then click **Quick Print**. The report prints with the default print settings.

   Trouble? If your report did not print, make sure that your computer is connected to a printer, and that the printer is turned on and ready to print. Then repeat Steps 1 and 2.

▶ **3.** Click the **Close 'ContractDetails'** button ⊠ on the object tab to close the report.

▶ **4.** Click the **Close 'Contract'** button ⊠ on the object tab to close the Contract table.

You can also use the Print dialog box to print other database objects, such as table and query datasheets. Most often, these objects are used for viewing and entering data, and reports are used for printing the data in a database.

Viewing Objects in the Navigation Pane

The Belmont database now contains four objects—the Contract table, the ContractList query, the ContractData form, and the ContractDetails report. You can view and work with these objects in the Navigation Pane.

To view the objects in the Belmont database:

▶ 1. Click the **Shutter Bar Open/Close Button** ⨠ on the Navigation Pane to open the pane. See Figure 1-28.

Figure 1-28   **Belmont database objects displayed in the Navigation Pane**

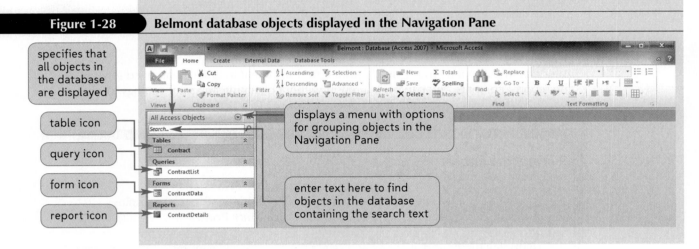

The Navigation Pane currently displays the default category, **All Access Objects**, which lists all the database objects in the pane. Each object type (Tables, Queries, Forms, and Reports) appears in its own group. Each database object (the Contract table, the ContractList query, the ContractData form, and the ContractDetails report) has a unique icon to its left to indicate the type of object. This makes it easy for you to identify the objects and choose which one you want to open and work with.

The arrow on the All Access Objects bar displays a menu with options for various ways to group and display objects in the Navigation Pane. The Search box enables you to enter text for Access to find; for example, you could search for all objects that contain the word "Contract" in their names. Note that Access searches for objects only in the categories and groups currently displayed in the Navigation Pane.

As you continue to build the Belmont database and add more objects to it in later tutorials, you'll learn how to use the options in the Navigation Pane.

Managing a Database

One of the main tasks involved in working with database software is managing your databases and the data they contain. By managing your databases, you can ensure that they operate in the most efficient way, that the data they contain is secure, and that you can work with the data effectively. Some of the activities involved in database management include compacting and repairing a database and backing up and restoring a database.

Compacting and Repairing a Database

Whenever you open an Access database and work in it, the size of the database increases. Further, when you delete records or when you delete or replace database objects—such as queries, forms, and reports—the space that had been occupied on the disk by the deleted or replaced records or objects does not automatically become available for other records or objects. To make the space available, you must compact the database. **Compacting** a database rearranges the data and objects in a database to decrease its file size, thereby making more space available on your disk and letting you open and close the database more quickly. Figure 1-29 illustrates the compacting process.

Figure 1-29 **Compacting a database**

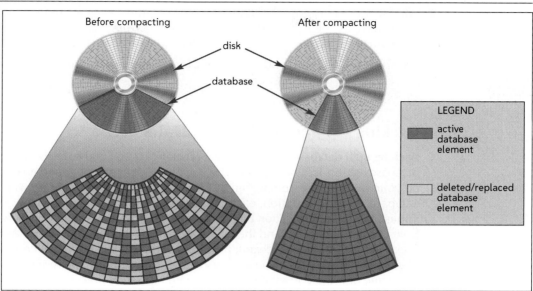

When you compact a database, Access repairs the database at the same time. In many cases, Access detects that a database is damaged when you try to open it and gives you the option to compact and repair it at that time. For example, the data in your database might become damaged, or corrupted, if you exit the Access program suddenly by turning off your computer. If you think your database might be damaged because it is behaving unpredictably, you can use the Compact & Repair Database option to fix it.

REFERENCE

Compacting and Repairing a Database

- Make sure the database file you want to compact and repair is open.
- Click the File tab to display Backstage view.
- Make sure the Info tab is selected in the navigation bar.
- Click the Compact & Repair Database button.

Access also allows you to set an option to compact and repair a database file automatically every time you close it. The Compact on Close option is available in the Current Database section of the Access Options dialog box, which you open from Backstage view by clicking the Options command in the navigation bar. By default, the Compact on Close option is turned off.

Next, you'll compact the Belmont database manually using the Compact & Repair Database option. This will make the database smaller and cause it to use disk space more efficiently. After compacting the database, you'll close it.

To compact and repair the Belmont database:

1. Click the **File** tab on the Ribbon to display Backstage view. The Info tab in the navigation bar is selected.

   Trouble? Check with your instructor before selecting the option to compact and repair the database. If your instructor tells you not to select this option, click the Exit command in the navigation bar and skip the next two steps.

▶ **2.** Click the **Compact & Repair Database** button. Access closes Backstage view and returns to the Home tab. Although nothing visible happens on the screen, Access compacts the Belmont database, making it smaller, and repairs it at the same time.

▶ **3.** Click the **File** tab, and then click **Close Database** in the navigation bar. Access closes the Belmont database.

Backing Up and Restoring a Database

Backing up a database is the process of making a copy of the database file to protect your database against loss or damage. The Back Up Database command enables you to back up your database file from within the Access program, while you are working on your database. To use this option, click the File tab to display Backstage view, click the Save & Publish tab in the navigation bar, click Back Up Database in the Advanced section of the Save Database As pane, and then click the Save As button. In the Save As dialog box that opens, Access provides a default filename for the backup copy that consists of the same filename as the database you are backing up (for example, "Belmont"), and an underscore character, plus the current date. This filenaming system makes it easy for you to keep track of your database backups and when they were created. To restore a backup database file, you simply copy the backup from the drive on which it is stored to your hard drive, or whatever device you use to work in Access, and start working with the restored database file. (You will not actually back up the Belmont database in this tutorial.)

PROSKILLS

Problem Solving: Planning and Performing Database Backups

Experienced database users make it a habit to back up a database before they work with it for the first time, keeping the original data intact, and to make frequent backups while continuing to work with a database. Most users back up their databases on tapes, USB drives, recordable CDs or DVDs, external hard drives, or network hard drives. Also, it is recommended to store the backup copy in a different location from the original. For example, if the original database is stored on a USB drive, you should not store the backup copy on the same USB drive. If you lose the drive or the drive is damaged, you would lose both the original database and its backup copy.

If the original database file and the backup copy have the same name, restoring the backup copy might replace the original. If you want to save the original file, rename it before you restore the backup copy. To ensure that the restored database has the most current data, you should update the restored database with any changes made to the original between the time it became damaged or lost and the time you created the backup copy.

By properly planning for and performing backups, you can avoid losing data and prevent the time-consuming effort required to rebuild a lost or damaged database.

With the Contract table in place, you can continue to build the Belmont database so that Oren and his staff members can use it to store, manipulate, and retrieve important data for Belmont Landscapes. In the following tutorials, you'll help Oren complete and maintain the database, and you'll use it to meet the specific information needs of the firm's employees.

REVIEW

Session 1.2 Quick Check

1. True or False: You can copy records from any Access database table and paste them in another table.
2. A(n) _____ is a question you ask about the data stored in a database.
3. The quickest way to create a form is to use the _____.
4. To see the total number of pages in a report and navigate through the report pages, you need to display the report in _____.
5. In the Navigation Pane, each database object has a unique _____ to its left that identifies the object's type.
6. _____ a database rearranges the data and objects in a database to decrease its file size.
7. _____ a database is the process of making a copy of the database file to protect the database against loss or damage.

Review Assignments

Data File needed for the Review Assignments: Provider.accdb

In the Review Assignments, you'll create a new database to contain information about the suppliers that Belmont Landscapes works with on its landscape design projects. Complete the following steps:

1. Create a new, blank database named **Supplier**, and save it in the Access1\Review folder provided with your Data Files.

2. In Datasheet view for the Table1 table, rename the default ID primary key field to **CompanyID**. Change the data type of the CompanyID field to Text.

3. Add the following 10 fields to the new table in the order shown; all of them are Text fields *except* InitialContact, which is a Date/Time field: **Company**, **Product**, **Address**, **City**, **State**, **Zip**, **Phone**, **ContactFirst**, **ContactLast**, and **InitialContact**. Resize the columns as necessary so that the complete field names are displayed. Save the table as **Company**.

4. Enter the records shown in Figure 1-30 in the Company table. For the first record, be sure to enter your first name in the ContactFirst field and your last name in the ContactLast field.

Figure 1-30	Company table records

CompanyID	Company	Product	Address	City	State	Zip	Phone	ContactFirst	ContactLast	InitialContact
AND225	Anderson OnSite	Site furnishings	200 Lincoln Dr	Kalamazoo	MI	49007	269-337-9266	Student First	Student Last	6/3/2012
HOL292	Holland Nursery	Plants	380 W 20th St	Holland	MI	49424	616-396-9330	Brenda	Ehlert	9/2/2013
BES327	Best Paving	Pavers	780 N. Main St	Rockford	MI	49341	616-866-6364	Shirley	Hauser	2/14/2013
MID312	Midwest Lighting	Outdoor lighting	435 Central Dr	Battle Creek	MI	49014	269-979-3970	Weston	Caldwell	5/15/2012
BAC200	Backyard Structures	Play equipment	105 E 8th St	Holland	MI	49423	616-396-3989	Alan	Bastian	4/15/2012

5. Oren created a database named Provider that contains a Business table with supplier data. The Company table you created has the same design as the Business table. Copy all the records from the **Business** table in the **Provider** database (located in the Access1\Review folder provided with your Data Files) and paste them at the end of the Company table in the Supplier database.

6. Resize columns in the datasheet, as necessary, so that all the field values are completely displayed, and then save the Company table.

7. Close the Company table, and then use the Navigation Pane to reopen it. Note that the records are displayed in primary key order.

8. Use the Simple Query Wizard to create a query that includes the Company, Product, ContactFirst, ContactLast, and Phone fields (in that order) from the Company table. Name the query **CompanyList**, and then close the query.

9. Use the Form tool to create a form for the Company table. Save the form as **CompanyInfo**, and then close it.

10. Use the Report tool to create a report based on the Company table. In Layout view, resize the CompanyID, City, State, Zip, Phone, ContactFirst, ContactLast, and InitialContact fields so they are slightly wider than the longest entry (either the field name itself or an entry in the field). Also, resize the box containing the total amount that appears below the CompanyID column so that the amount is completely displayed. Display the report in Print Preview and verify that all the fields fit across two pages in the report. Save the report as **CompanyDetails**, and then close it.

11. Close the Company table, and then compact and repair the Supplier database.

12. Close the Supplier database.

Case Problem 1

If you have a SAM 2010 user profile, your instructor may have assigned an autogradable version of this assignment. If so, log into the SAM 2010 Web site at www.cengage.com/sam2010 to download the instructions and start files.

Data File needed for this Case Problem: School.accdb

Pine Hill Music School   After giving private piano lessons from her home for several years, Yuka Koyama founded the Pine Hill Music School in Portland, Oregon. Because of her popularity as a music teacher, Yuka attracted top-notch students, and her school quickly established a reputation for excellence. During the past two years, other qualified teachers have joined Yuka to offer instruction in voice, violin, cello, guitar, percussion, and other instruments. As her school continues to grow, Yuka wants to use Access to keep track of information about students, teachers, and contracts. You'll help Yuka create and maintain an Access database to store data about her school. Complete the following:

1. Create a new, blank database named **Pinehill**, and save it in the Access1\Case1 folder provided with your Data Files.

2. In Datasheet view for the Table1 table, rename the default primary key ID field to **TeacherID**. Change the data type of the TeacherID field to Text.

3. Add the following five fields to the new table in the order shown; all of them are Text fields *except* HireDate, which is a Date/Time field: **FirstName**, **LastName**, **Degree**, **School**, and **HireDate**. Save the table as **Teacher**.

4. Enter the records shown in Figure 1-31 in the Teacher table. For the first record, be sure to enter your first name in the FirstName field and your last name in the LastName field.

Figure 1-31   **Teacher table records**

TeacherID	FirstName	LastName	Degree	School	HireDate
55-5310	Student First	Student Last	BA	Lewis & Clark College	4/21/2012
13-1100	Yuka	Koyama	MM	Pacific University	1/13/2012
17-1798	Richard	Jacobson	PhD	Pacific University	1/15/2012
22-0102	Andre	Dvorak	BM	University of Portland	3/3/2012
34-4506	Marilyn	Schwartz	BM	University of Portland	5/1/2012

5. Yuka created a database named School that contains a Faculty table with teacher data. The Teacher table you created has the same design as the Faculty table. Copy all the records from the **Faculty** table in the **School** database (located in the Access1\Case1 folder provided with your Data Files) and paste them at the end of the Teacher table in the Pinehill database.

6. Resize columns in the datasheet, as necessary, so that all the field values are completely displayed, and then save the Teacher table.

7. Close the Teacher table, and then use the Navigation Pane to reopen it. Note that the records are displayed in primary key order.

8. Use the Simple Query Wizard to create a query that includes the FirstName, LastName, and HireDate fields (in that order) from the Teacher table. Name the query **StartDate**, and then close the query.

9. Use the Form tool to create a form for the Teacher table. Save the form as **TeacherInfo**, and then close it.

10. Use the Report tool to create a report based on the Teacher table. In Layout view, resize each field so it is slightly wider than the longest entry (either the field name itself or an entry in the field). All six fields should fit within the page area after resizing. Move the

text "Page 1 of 1" to the left so it is within the page area. Also, resize the box containing the total amount that appears below the TeacherID column so that the amount is completely displayed. Display the report in Print Preview and verify that the fields and page number appear within the page area. Save the report as **TeacherList**, print the report (only if asked by your instructor to do so), and then close it.

11. Close the Teacher table, and then compact and repair the Pinehill database.

12. Close the Pinehill database.

Apply what you learned to create a database for a business in the fitness industry.

APPLY

Case Problem 2

Data File needed for this Case Problem: Health.accdb

Parkhurst Health & Fitness Center   After many years working in various corporate settings, Martha Parkhurst decided to turn her lifelong interest in health and fitness into a new business venture and opened the Parkhurst Health & Fitness Center in Richmond, Virginia. In addition to providing the usual fitness classes and weight training facilities, the center also offers specialized programs designed to meet the needs of athletes—both young and old—who participate in certain sports or physical activities. Martha's goal in establishing such programs is twofold: to help athletes gain a competitive edge through customized training, and to ensure the health and safety of all participants through proper exercises and physical preparation. Martha wants to use Access to maintain information about the members who have joined the center and the types of programs offered. She needs your help in creating this database. Complete the following steps:

1. Create a new, blank database named **Fitness**, and save it in the Access1\Case2 folder provided with your Data Files.

2. In Datasheet view for the Table1 table, rename the default primary key ID field to **ProgramID**. Change the data type of the ProgramID field to Text.

3. Add the following three fields to the new table in the order shown; all of them are Text fields *except* MonthlyFee, which is a Currency field: **ProgramType**, **MonthlyFee**, and **PhysicalRequired**. Resize the columns as necessary so that the complete field names are displayed. Save the table as **Program**.

4. Enter the records shown in Figure 1-32 in the Program table.

Figure 1-32   Program table records

ProgramID	ProgramType	MonthlyFee	PhysicalRequired
201	Junior Full (ages 13-17)	$40.00	Yes
202	Junior Limited (ages 13-17)	$30.00	Yes
203	Young Adult Full (ages 18-25)	$50.00	No
204	Young Adult Limited (ages 18-25)	$35.00	No

5. Martha created a database named Health that contains a Class table with program data. The Program table you created has the same design as the Class table. Copy all the records from the **Class** table in the **Health** database (located in the Access1\Case2 folder provided with your Data Files) and paste them at the end of the Program table in the Fitness database.

6. Resize columns in the datasheet, as necessary, so that all the field values are completely displayed, and then save the Program table.

7. Use the Simple Query Wizard to create a query that includes all the fields from the Program table. In the second Simple Query Wizard dialog box, select the Detail option. Save the query as **ProgramData**. Resize the columns in the query datasheet so that all the field values are completely displayed, if necessary, and then close the query.

8. Use the Form tool to create a form for the Program table. Save the form as **ProgramInfo**, and then close it.

9. Use the Report tool to create a report based on the Program table. In Layout view, resize the ProgramID and PhysicalRequired fields so they are slightly wider than the longest entry (either the field name itself or an entry in the field). All four fields should fit within the page area after resizing. Move the text "Page 1 of 1" to the left so it is within the page area. Also, resize the box containing the total amount that appears below the MonthlyFee column so that the amount is completely displayed. Display the report in Print Preview and verify that the fields and page number fit within the page area. Save the report as **ProgramList**, print the report (only if asked by your instructor to do so), and then close it.

10. Close the Program table, and then compact and repair the Fitness database.

11. Close the Fitness database.

Expand your skills to create a database for an agency that recycles household goods.

CHALLENGE

Case Problem 3

Data File needed for this Case Problem: RRGroup.accdb

Rossi Recycling Group   The Rossi Recycling Group is a not-for-profit agency in Salina, Kansas that provides recycled household goods to needy people and families at no charge. Residents of Salina and surrounding communities donate cash and goods, such as appliances, furniture, and tools, to the Rossi Recycling Group. The group's volunteers then coordinate with local human services agencies to distribute the goods to those in need. The Rossi Recycling Group was established by Mary and Tom Rossi, who live on the outskirts of Salina on a small farm. Mary and Tom organize the volunteers to collect the goods and store the collected items in their barn for distribution. Tom wants to create an Access database to manage information about donors, their donations, and the human services agencies. Complete the following steps:

1. Create a new, blank database named **Rossi**, and then save it in the Access1\Case3 folder provided with your Data Files.

2. In Datasheet view for the Table1 table, rename the default primary key ID field to **DonorID**. Change the data type of the DonorID field to Text.

3. Add the following four Text fields to the new table in the order shown: **Title**, **FirstName**, **LastName**, and **Phone**. Resize the columns, if necessary, so that the complete field names are displayed. Save the table as **Donor**.

4. Enter the records shown in Figure 1-33 in the Donor table. For the first record, be sure to enter your title in the Title field, your first name in the FirstName field, and your last name in the LastName field.

Figure 1-33	Donor table records

DonorID	Title	FirstName	LastName	Phone
36012	Student Title	Student First	Student Last	785-823-9275
36016	Mr.	Doug	Showers	620-793-8477
36001	Mrs.	Janis	Fendrick	785-452-8736
36020	Mrs.	JoAnn	Randolph	785-309-6540
36019	Ms.	Connie	Springen	785-452-1178

5. Tom created a database named RRGroup that contains a Contributors table with data about donors. The Donor table you created has the same design as the Contributors table. Copy all the records from the **Contributors** table in the **RRGroup** database (located in the Access1\Case3 folder provided with your Data Files) and paste them at the end of the Donor table in the Rossi database.

6. If necessary, resize the columns in the datasheet so that all the field values are completely displayed, and then save the Donor table.

7. Close the Donor table, and then use the Navigation Pane to reopen it. Note that the records are displayed in primary key order.

✦ **EXPLORE**   8. Use the Simple Query Wizard to create a query that includes all the fields in the Donor table *except* the Title field. (*Hint*: Use the ⟩⟩ and ⟨ buttons to select the necessary fields.) Save the query using the name **DonorPhoneList**.

✦ **EXPLORE**   9. The query results are displayed in order by the DonorID field values. You can specify a different order by sorting the query. Display the Home tab. Then, click the insertion point anywhere in the LastName column to make it the current field. In the Sort & Filter group on the Home tab, click the Ascending button. The records are now listed in order by the values in the LastName field. Save and close the query.

✦ **EXPLORE**   10. Use the Form tool to create a form for the Donor table. In the new form, navigate to record 8, and then print the form *for the current record only*. (*Hint*: You must use the Print dialog box in order to print only the current record. Go to Backstage view, click the Print command, and then click Print to open the Print dialog box. Click the Selected Record(s) option button and then click the OK button to print the current record.) Save the form as **DonorInfo**, and then close it.

11. Use the Report tool to create a report based on the Donor table. In Layout view, resize each field so it is slightly wider than the longest entry (either the field name itself or an entry in the field). All five fields should fit within the page area after resizing. Move the text "Page 1 of 1" to the left so it is within the page area. Also, resize the box containing the total amount that appears below the DonorID column so that the amount is completely displayed. Display the report in Print Preview and verify that the fields and page number fit within the page area. Save the report as **DonorList**. Print the report (only if asked by your instructor to do so), and then close it.

12. Close the Donor table, and then compact and repair the Rossi database.

13. Close the Rossi database.

Explore some new skills to create a database for a luxury rental company.

CHALLENGE

Case Problem 4

Data File needed for this Case Problem: Travel.accdb

GEM Ultimate Vacations   As guests of a friend, Griffin and Emma MacElroy spent two weeks at a magnificent villa in the south of France. This unforgettable experience stayed with them upon returning to their home in a suburb of Chicago, Illinois. As a result, they decided to open their own agency, GEM Ultimate Vacations, which specializes in locating and booking luxury rental properties, primarily in Europe. Recently, Griffin and Emma expanded their business to include properties in Africa as well. From the beginning, Griffin and Emma used computers to help them manage all aspects of their business. They recently installed Access and now would like you to create a database to store information about guests, properties, and reservations. Complete the following:

1. Create a new, blank database named **GEM**, and then save it in the Access1\Case4 folder provided with your Data Files.

2. In Datasheet view for the Table1 table, rename the default primary key ID field to **GuestID**. Change the data type of the GuestID field to Text.

3. Add the following eight Text fields to the new table in the order shown: **GuestFirst**, **GuestLast**, **Address**, **City**, **State/Prov**, **PostalCode**, **Country**, and **Phone**. Resize the columns, if necessary, so that the complete field names are displayed. Save the table as **Guest**.

4. Enter the records shown in Figure 1-34 in the Guest table. For the first record, be sure to enter your first name in the GuestFirst field and your last name in the GuestLast field.

Figure 1-34   **Guest table records**

GuestID	GuestFirst	GuestLast	Address	City	State/Prov	PostalCode	Country	Phone
201	Student First	Student Last	153 Summer Ave	Evanston	IL	60201	USA	847-623-0975
203	Tom	Davis	5003 Wilson Blvd	Chicago	IL	60603	USA	312-897-4515
206	Li	Zhu	6509 Great Rd	Gary	IN	46401	USA	219-655-8109
202	Ingrid	Gorman	207 Riverside Dr West	Windsor	ON	N9A 5K4	Canada	519-977-8577
205	Richard	Nelson	34 Settlers Dr	Tinley Park	IL	60477	USA	708-292-4441

5. Emma created a database named Travel that contains a Client table with data about guests. The Guest table you created has the same design as the Client table. Copy all the records from the **Client** table in the **Travel** database (located in the Access1\Case4 folder provided with your Data Files) and paste them at the end of the Guest table in the GEM database.

6. Resize columns in the datasheet, as necessary, so that all the field values are completely displayed, and then save the Guest table.

7. Close the Guest table, and then use the Navigation Pane to reopen it. Note that the records are displayed in primary key order.

8. Use the Simple Query Wizard to create a query that includes the following fields from the Guest table, in the order shown: GuestID, GuestLast, GuestFirst, City, and Phone. Name the query **GuestData**.

⊕ **EXPLORE**   9. The query results are displayed in order by the GuestID field values. You can specify a different order by sorting the query. Display the Home tab. Then, click the insertion point anywhere in the GuestLast column to make it the current field. In the Sort & Filter group on the Home tab, click the Ascending button. The records are now listed in order by the values in the GuestLast field. Save and close the query.

⊕ **EXPLORE**   10. Use the Form tool to create a form for the Guest table. In the new form, navigate to record 12, and then print the form *for the current record only*. (*Hint*: You must use the Print dialog box in order to print only the current record. Go to Backstage view, click the Print command, and then click Print to open the Print dialog box. Click the Selected Record(s) option button and then click the OK button to print the current record.) Save the form as **GuestInfo**, and then close it.

11. Use the Report tool to create a report based on the Guest table. In Layout view, resize each field so it is slightly wider than the longest entry (either the field name itself or an entry in the field). Move the text "Page 1 of 1" to the left so it is within the page area on the report's first page. Also, resize the box containing the total amount that appears below the GuestID column so that the amount is completely displayed. Display the report in Print Preview and notice that the columns of the report are spread across two pages. Save the report as **GuestList**.

⊕ **EXPLORE**   12. In the Close Preview group, click the Close Print Preview button to return to the report in Layout view. To make more room on the first page, you'll delete the Address, PostalCode, and Country columns from the report. Click anywhere in the Address column to make it active. Click the Report Layout Tools Arrange tab, and then click the Select Column button in the Rows & Columns group. Click the Home tab, and then click the Delete button in the Records group to delete the selected column. Repeat this process to delete the PostalCode and Country columns. The remaining six fields should now all fit on the report's first page.

13. Save the report, print it (only if asked by your instructor to do so), and then close it.

14. Close the Guest table, and then compact and repair the GEM database.

15. Close the GEM database.

SAM: Skills Assessment Manager

ASSESS

For current SAM information, including versions and content details, visit SAM Central (http://samcentral.course.com). If you have a SAM user profile, you may have access to hands-on instruction, practice, and assessment of the skills covered in this tutorial. Since various versions of SAM are supported throughout the life of this text, check with your instructor for the correct instructions and URL/Web site for accessing assignments.

ENDING DATA FILES

Access1 →	**Tutorial** Belmont.accdb	**Review** Supplier.accdb	**Case1** Pinehill.accdb

Case2 Fitness.accdb	**Case3** Rossi.accdb	**Case4** GEM.accdb

ACCESS

Building a Database and Defining Table Relationships

Creating the Invoice and Customer Tables

OBJECTIVES

Session 2.1
- Learn the guidelines for designing databases and setting field properties
- Modify the format of a field in Datasheet view
- Create a table in Design view
- Define fields and specify a table's primary key
- Modify the structure of a table

Session 2.2
- Import data from an Excel worksheet
- Create a table by importing an existing table structure
- Add fields to a table with the Data Type gallery
- Delete, rename, and move fields
- Add data to a table by importing a text file
- Define a relationship between two tables

Case | *Belmont Landscapes*

The Belmont database currently contains one table, the Contract table. Oren also wants to track information about the firm's customers, both residential and commercial, and the invoices sent to customers for services provided by Belmont Landscapes. This information includes such items as each customer's name and address and the invoice amount and invoice date.

In this tutorial, you'll create two new tables in the Belmont database—named Invoice and Customer—to contain the additional data Oren wants to track. You will use two different methods for creating the tables, and learn how to modify the fields. After adding records to the tables, you will define the necessary relationships between the tables in the Belmont database to relate the tables, enabling Oren and his staff to work with the data more efficiently.

STARTING DATA FILES

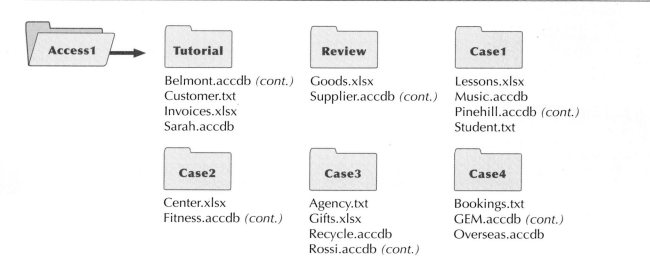

Access1 →

Tutorial

Belmont.accdb *(cont.)*
Customer.txt
Invoices.xlsx
Sarah.accdb

Review

Goods.xlsx
Supplier.accdb *(cont.)*

Case1

Lessons.xlsx
Music.accdb
Pinehill.accdb *(cont.)*
Student.txt

Case2

Center.xlsx
Fitness.accdb *(cont.)*

Case3

Agency.txt
Gifts.xlsx
Recycle.accdb
Rossi.accdb *(cont.)*

Case4

Bookings.txt
GEM.accdb *(cont.)*
Overseas.accdb

SESSION 2.1 VISUAL OVERVIEW

The default name for a new table you create in Design view is Table1. This name appears on the tab for the new table.

| Table Tools | Belmont : Data... |

File   Home   Create   External Data   Database Tools   Design

View
Views

Primary Key   Builder   Test Validation Rules

Insert Rows
Delete Rows
Modify Lookups
Tools

Property Sheet   Indexes
Show/Hide

Create Data Macros ▾   Rename/D... Macro
Field, Record & Table E...

Table1

Navigation Pane

Field Name   Data Type

The top portion of the Table window in Design view is called the **Table Design grid**. Here, you enter values for the Field Name, Data Type, and Description field properties.

In the Field Name column, you enter the name for each new field in the table. When you first open a new Table window in Design view, Field Name is the current property.

In the Data Type column, you select the appropriate data type for each new field in the table. The data type determines what field values you can enter for a field and what other properties the field will have. The default data type for a new field is Text.

Field Properti...

General Lookup

After you assign a data type to a field, the General tab displays additional field properties for that data type. Initially, most field properties are assigned default values.

When defining the fields in a table, you can move from the Table Design grid to the Field Properties pane by pressing the **F6** key.

Design view. F6 = Switch panes. F1 = Help.

TABLE WINDOW IN DESIGN VIEW

Belmont : Database (Access 2007) - Microsoft Access

Create Data Macros ▾

Rename/Delete Macro

Field, Record & Table Events

Relationships

Object Dependencies

Relationships

Description

Field Properties

A field name can be up to 64 characters long, including spaces. Press F1 for help on field names.

Design view allows you to define or modify a table structure or the properties of the fields in a table.

You can use the **Description property** to enter an optional description for a field to explain its purpose or usage. A field's Description property can be up to 255 characters long, and its value appears on the status bar when you view the table datasheet.

The bottom portion of the Table window in Design view is called the **Field Properties pane**. Here, you select values for all other field properties, most of which are optional.

The purpose or characteristics of the current property (Field Name, in this case) appear in this section of the Field Properties pane.

You can display more complete Help information about the current property by pressing the F1 key.

Guidelines for Designing Databases

A database management system can be a useful tool, but only if you first carefully design the database so that it meets the needs of its users. In database design, you determine the fields, tables, and relationships needed to satisfy the data and processing requirements. When you design a database, you should follow these guidelines:

- **Identify all the fields needed to produce the required information.** For example, Oren needs information about contracts, invoices, and customers. Figure 2-1 shows the fields that satisfy these information requirements.

Figure 2-1	Oren's data requirements

ContractNum   ContractAmt
CustomerID   SigningDate
Company   InvoiceDate
FirstName   ContractType
LastName   Phone
Address   InvoicePaid
City   InvoiceNum
State   InvoiceAmt
Zip

- **Organize each piece of data into its smallest useful part.** For example, Oren could store each customer's complete name in one field called CustomerName instead of using two fields called FirstName and LastName, as shown in Figure 2-1. However, doing so would make it more difficult to work with the data. If Oren wanted to view the records in alphabetical order by last name, he wouldn't be able to do so with field values such as "Tom Cotter" and "Ray Yost" stored in a CustomerName field. He could do so with field values such as "Cotter" and "Yost" stored separately in a LastName field.
- **Group related fields into tables.** For example, Oren grouped the fields related to contracts into the Contract table, which you created in Tutorial 1. The fields related to invoices are grouped into the Invoice table, and the fields related to customers are grouped into the Customer table. Figure 2-2 shows the fields grouped into all three tables for the Belmont database.

Figure 2-2	Oren's fields grouped into tables

Contract table	Invoice table	Customer table
ContractNum	InvoiceNum	CustomerID
CustomerID	ContractNum	Company
ContractAmt	InvoiceAmt	FirstName
SigningDate	InvoiceDate	LastName
ContractType	InvoicePaid	Phone
		Address
		City
		State
		Zip

- **Determine each table's primary key.** Recall that a primary key uniquely identifies each record in a table. For some tables, one of the fields, such as a credit card number, naturally serves the function of a primary key. For other tables, two or more fields might be needed to function as the primary key. In these cases, the primary key is called a

composite key. For example, a school grade table would use a combination of student number and course code to serve as the primary key. For a third category of tables, no single field or combination of fields can uniquely identify a record in a table. In these cases, you need to add a field whose sole purpose is to serve as the table's primary key. For Oren's tables, ContractNum is the primary key for the Contract table, InvoiceNum is the primary key for the Invoice table, and CustomerID is the primary key for the Customer table.

- **Include a common field in related tables.** You use the common field to connect one table logically with another table. For example, Oren's Contract and Customer tables include the CustomerID field as a common field. Recall that when you include the primary key from one table as a field in a second table to form a relationship, the field is called a foreign key in the second table; therefore, the CustomerID field is a foreign key in the Contract table. With this common field, Oren can find all contracts for a particular customer; he can use the CustomerID value for a customer and search the Contract table for all records with that CustomerID value. Likewise, he can determine which customer has a particular contract by searching the Customer table to find the one record with the same CustomerID value as the corresponding value in the Contract table. Similarly, the ContractNum field is a common field, serving as the primary key in the Contract table and a foreign key in the Invoice table.
- **Avoid data redundancy.** When you store the same data in more than one place, **data redundancy** occurs. With the exception of common fields to connect tables, you should avoid data redundancy because it wastes storage space and can cause inconsistencies. An inconsistency would exist, for example, if you type a field value one way in one table and a different way in the same table or in a second table. Figure 2-3, which contains portions of potential data stored in the Customer and Contract tables, shows an example of incorrect database design that has data redundancy in the Contract table. In Figure 2-3, the Company field in the Contract table is redundant, and one value for this field was entered incorrectly, in three different ways.

Figure 2-3	Incorrect database design with data redundancy

Customer table

CustomerID	Company	FirstName	LastName
11067	Blossom Day Care Center	Christina	Garrett
11068	Grand Rapids Housing Authority	Jessica	Ropiak
11070	Legacy Companies, LTD.	Michael	Faraci
11071	Blue Star Mini Golf	Vanetta	Walker
11072	Sierra Investment Company	Rodrigo	Valencia

data redundancy

Contract table

ContractNum	CustomerID	Company	ContractAmt	SigningDate
3023	11070	Legacy Company	$39,000.00	3/22/2013
3040	11068	Grand Rapids Housing Authority	$38,500.00	7/27/2013
3042	11070	Legacies Co. Limited	$48,500.00	6/3/2013
3073	11072	Sierra Investment Company	$205,000.00	5/5/2014
3081	11071	Blue Star Mini Golf	$21,000.00	5/10/2014
3085	11070	Legacy Corp. Ltd	$30,800.00	12/28/2013
3099	11067	Blossom Day Care Center	$6,500.00	7/25/2014

inconsistent data

- **Determine the properties of each field.** You need to identify the **properties**, or characteristics, of each field so that the DBMS knows how to store, display, and process the field values. These properties include the field's name, maximum number of characters or digits, description, valid values, and other field characteristics. You will learn more about field properties later in this tutorial.

The Invoice and Customer tables you need to create will contain the fields shown in Figure 2-2. Before creating these new tables in the Belmont database, you first need to learn some guidelines for setting field properties.

Guidelines for Setting Field Properties

As just noted, the last step of database design is to determine which values to assign to the properties, such as the name and data type, of each field. When you select or enter a value for a property, you **set** the property. Access has rules for naming fields and objects, assigning data types, and setting other field properties.

Naming Fields and Objects

You must name each field, table, and other object in an Access database. Access then stores these items in the database, using the names you supply. It's best to choose a field or object name that describes the purpose or contents of the field or object so that later you can easily remember what the name represents. For example, the three tables in the Belmont database will be named Contract, Invoice, and Customer because these names suggest their contents. Note that a table or query name must be unique within a database. A field name must be unique within a table, but it can be used again in another table. Refer to the ProSkills box, "Decision Making: Naming Database Fields and Objects in Access," in Tutorial 1 for a reminder of the guidelines to follow when naming fields and database objects.

Assigning Field Data Types

Each field must have a data type, which is either assigned automatically by Access or specifically by the table designer. The data type determines what field values you can enter for the field and what other properties the field will have. For example, the Invoice table will include an InvoiceDate field, which will store date values, so you will assign the Date/Time data type to this field. Then Access will allow you to enter and manipulate only dates or times as values in the InvoiceDate field.

Figure 2-4 lists the most commonly used data types in Access, describes the field values allowed for each data type, explains when you should use each data type, and indicates the field size of each data type. You can find more complete information about all available data types in Access Help.

Figure 2-4	Common data types

Data Type	Description	Field Size
Text	Allows field values containing letters, digits, spaces, and special characters. Use for names, addresses, descriptions, and fields containing digits that are not used in calculations.	0 to 255 characters; default is 255
Memo	Allows field values containing letters, digits, spaces, and special characters. Use for long comments and explanations.	1 to 65,535 characters; exact size is determined by entry
Number	Allows positive and negative numbers as field values. Numbers can contain digits, a decimal point, commas, a plus sign, and a minus sign. Use for fields that will be used in calculations, except those involving money.	1 to 15 digits
Date/Time	Allows field values containing valid dates and times from January 1, 100 to December 31, 9999. Dates can be entered in month/day/year format, several other date formats, or a variety of time formats, such as 10:35 PM. You can perform calculations on dates and times, and you can sort them. For example, you can determine the number of days between two dates.	8 bytes
Currency	Allows field values similar to those for the Number data type, but is used for storing monetary values. Unlike calculations with Number data type decimal values, calculations performed with the Currency data type are not subject to round-off error.	Accurate to 15 digits on the left side of the decimal point and to 4 digits on the right side
AutoNumber	Consists of integer values created automatically by Access each time you create a new record. You can specify sequential numbering or random numbering, which guarantees a unique field value, so that such a field can serve as a table's primary key.	9 digits
Yes/No	Limits field values to yes and no, on and off, or true and false. Use for fields that indicate the presence or absence of a condition, such as whether an order has been filled or whether an invoice has been paid.	1 character
Hyperlink	Consists of text used as a hyperlink address, which can have up to four parts: the text that appears in a field or control; the path to a file or page; a location within the file or page; and text displayed as a ScreenTip.	Up to 65,535 characters total for the four parts of the Hyperlink data type

Setting Field Sizes

The **Field Size property** defines a field value's maximum storage size for Text, Number, and AutoNumber fields only. The other data types have no Field Size property because their storage size is either a fixed, predetermined amount or is determined automatically by the field value itself, as shown in Figure 2-4. A Text field has a default field size of 255 characters; you can also set its field size by entering a number from 0 to 255. For example, the FirstName and LastName fields in the Customer table will be Text fields with a size of 20 characters and 25 characters, respectively. These field sizes will accommodate the values that will be entered in each of these fields.

PROSKILLS

Decision Making: Specifying the Field Size Property for Number Fields

When you use the Number data type to define a field, you need to decide what the most appropriate Field Size setting should be for the field. You should set the Field Size property based on the largest value that you expect to store in that field. Access processes smaller data sizes faster, using less memory, so you can optimize your database's performance and its storage space by selecting the correct field size for each field. Field Size property settings for Number fields are as follows:

- **Byte:** Stores whole numbers (numbers with no fractions) from 0 to 255 in one byte
- **Integer:** Stores whole numbers from –32,768 to 32,767 in two bytes
- **Long Integer** (default): Stores whole numbers from –2,147,483,648 to 2,147,483,647 in four bytes
- **Single:** Stores positive and negative numbers to precisely seven decimal places and uses four bytes
- **Double:** Stores positive and negative numbers to precisely 15 decimal places and uses eight bytes
- **Replication ID:** Establishes a unique identifier for replication of tables, records, and other objects in databases created using Access 2003 and earlier versions and uses 16 bytes
- **Decimal:** Stores positive and negative numbers to precisely 28 decimal places and uses 12 bytes

Choosing an appropriate field size is important to optimize efficiency. For example, it would be wasteful to use the Long Integer field size for a Number field that will store only whole numbers ranging from 0 to 255 because the Long Integer field size uses four bytes of storage space. A better choice would be the Byte field size, which uses one byte of storage space to store the same values. By first gathering and analyzing information about the number values that will be stored in a Number field, you can make the best decision for the field's Field Size property and ensure the most efficient user experience for the database.

Setting the Caption Property for Fields

The **Caption property** for a field specifies how the field name is displayed in database objects, including table and query datasheets, forms, and reports. If you don't set the Caption property, Access displays the field name as the column heading or label for a field. For example, field names such as ContractAmt and SigningDate in the Contract table can be difficult to read. Setting the Caption property for these fields to "Contract Amt" and "Signing Date" would make it easier for users to read the field names and work with the database.

INSIGHT

Setting the Caption Property vs. Naming Fields

Although Access allows you to include spaces in field names, this practice is not recommended because the spaces cause problems when you try to perform more complex tasks with the data in your database. Setting the Caption property allows you to follow best field naming practices, such as not including spaces in field names, while still providing users with more readable field names in datasheets, forms, and reports.

In Tutorial 1, you created the Belmont database and the Contract table. Before you create the new tables for the database, Oren suggests that you view the formatting of the fields in the Contract table to determine if any changes are needed to improve how the data is displayed.

Changing the Format of a Field in Datasheet View

The Formatting group on the Fields tab in Datasheet view allows you to modify some formatting for certain field types. When you format a field, you change the way data is displayed, but not the actual values stored in the table. Next, you'll open the Contract table in the Belmont database to view the formatting of the fields in the table.

To view the formatting of the Contract table's fields:

▶ **1.** Start Access, open the **Belmont** database you created in Tutorial 1, and make sure the Navigation Pane is open. This database file should be located in the Access1\Tutorial folder provided with your Data Files.

   Trouble? If the Security Warning is displayed below the Ribbon, click the Enable Content button.

▶ **2.** In the Navigation Pane, double-click the **Contract** table to open it in Datasheet view.

▶ **3.** On the Navigation Pane, click the **Shutter Bar Open/Close Button** « to close the pane and view more of the table datasheet. See Figure 2-5.

| Figure 2-5 | Contract table datasheet |

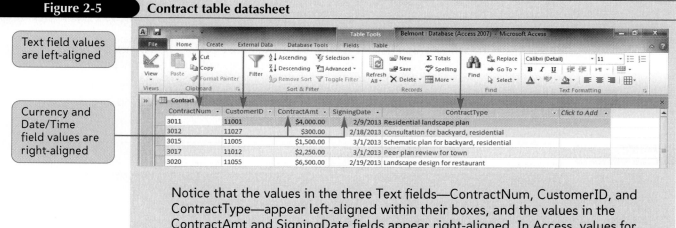

Text field values are left-aligned

Currency and Date/Time field values are right-aligned

Notice that the values in the three Text fields—ContractNum, CustomerID, and ContractType—appear left-aligned within their boxes, and the values in the ContractAmt and SigningDate fields appear right-aligned. In Access, values for Text fields are left-aligned, and values for Number, Date/Time, and Currency fields are right-aligned.

The ContractAmt field contains dollar values representing the total amount of each Belmont Landscapes contract. Oren knows that these dollar amounts will never contain cents because the contracts are drawn up in whole amounts only; therefore, the two decimal places currently shown for the values are unnecessary. Further, Oren feels that the dollar signs clutter the datasheet and are also unnecessary. He asks you to modify the format of the ContractAmt field to remove the dollar signs and decimal places. You can make these changes in Datasheet view using options on the Fields tab. You'll also check the format of the SigningDate field and modify it, if necessary.

To modify the format of the ContractAmt and SigningDate fields:

▶ **1.** Click the **Fields** tab on the Ribbon.

2. Click the first field value in the ContractAmt column. The options in the Formatting group indicate that this field has the Currency data type and the Currency format. See Figure 2-6.

Figure 2-6	Format of the ContractAmt field

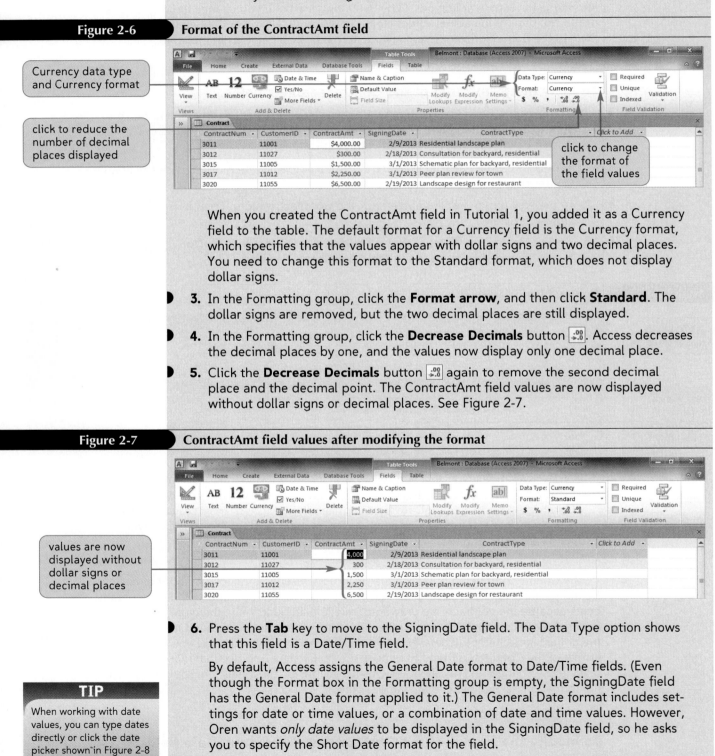

Currency data type and Currency format

click to reduce the number of decimal places displayed

click to change the format of the field values

When you created the ContractAmt field in Tutorial 1, you added it as a Currency field to the table. The default format for a Currency field is the Currency format, which specifies that the values appear with dollar signs and two decimal places. You need to change this format to the Standard format, which does not display dollar signs.

3. In the Formatting group, click the **Format arrow**, and then click **Standard**. The dollar signs are removed, but the two decimal places are still displayed.

4. In the Formatting group, click the **Decrease Decimals** button. Access decreases the decimal places by one, and the values now display only one decimal place.

5. Click the **Decrease Decimals** button again to remove the second decimal place and the decimal point. The ContractAmt field values are now displayed without dollar signs or decimal places. See Figure 2-7.

Figure 2-7	ContractAmt field values after modifying the format

values are now displayed without dollar signs or decimal places

6. Press the **Tab** key to move to the SigningDate field. The Data Type option shows that this field is a Date/Time field.

By default, Access assigns the General Date format to Date/Time fields. (Even though the Format box in the Formatting group is empty, the SigningDate field has the General Date format applied to it.) The General Date format includes settings for date or time values, or a combination of date and time values. However, Oren wants *only date values* to be displayed in the SigningDate field, so he asks you to specify the Short Date format for the field.

7. In the Formatting group, click the **Format arrow**, and then click **Short Date**. See Figure 2-8.

TIP

When working with date values, you can type dates directly or click the date picker shown in Figure 2-8 to select a date from an interactive calendar.

Figure 2-8 ▶ **SigningDate field after modifying the format**

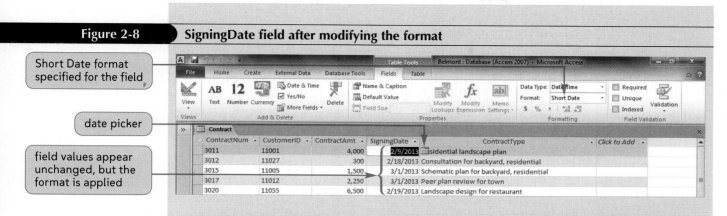

Short Date format specified for the field

date picker

field values appear unchanged, but the format is applied

Although no change is apparent in the worksheet—the SigningDate field values already appear with the Short Date setting (for example, 2/9/2013), as part of the default General Date format—the field now has the Short Date format applied to it. This ensures that only date field values, and not time or date/time values, are allowed in the field.

▶ **8.** Click the **Close 'Contract'** button ☒ on the object tab to close the table.

According to his plan for the Belmont database, Oren wants to track information about the invoices the firm sends to its customers. Next, you'll create the Invoice table for Oren—this time, working in Design view.

Creating a Table in Design View

Creating a table in Design view involves entering the field names and defining the properties for the fields, specifying a primary key for the table, and then saving the table structure. Oren documented the design for the new Invoice table by listing each field's name, data type, size (if applicable), and description, as shown in Figure 2-9.

Figure 2-9 ▶ **Design for the Invoice table**

Field Name	Data Type	Field Size	Description	Other
InvoiceNum	Text	4	Primary key	Caption = Invoice Num
ContractNum	Text	4	Foreign key	Caption = Contract Num
InvoiceAmt	Currency			Format = Currency
				Decimal Places = 2
				Caption = Invoice Amt
InvoiceDate	Date/Time			Format = mm/dd/yyyy
				Caption = Invoice Date
InvoicePaid	Yes/No			Caption = Invoice Paid
				Format = Yes/No

You will use Oren's design as a guide for creating the Invoice table in the Belmont database.

To begin creating the Invoice table:

▸ 1. Click the **Create** tab on the Ribbon.

▸ 2. In the Tables group on the Create tab, click the **Table Design** button. A new table named Table1 opens in Design view. Refer to the Session 2.1 Visual Overview for a complete description of the Table window in Design view.

Defining Fields

When you first create a table in Design view, the insertion point is located in the first row's Field Name box, ready for you to begin defining the first field in the table. You enter values for the Field Name, Data Type, and Description (optional) field properties and then select values for all other field properties in the Field Properties pane. These other properties will appear when you move to the first row's Data Type box.

REFERENCE

Defining a Field in Design View

- In the Field Name box, type the name for the field, and then press the Tab key.
- Accept the default Text data type, or click the arrow and select a different data type for the field. Press the Tab key.
- Enter an optional description for the field, if necessary.
- Use the Field Properties pane to type or select other field properties, as appropriate.

The first field you need to define is the InvoiceNum field. This field will be the primary key for the Invoice table.

TIP

You can also press the Enter key to move from one property to the next in the Table Design grid.

To define the InvoiceNum field:

▸ 1. Type **InvoiceNum** in the first row's Field Name box, and then press the **Tab** key to advance to the Data Type box. The default data type, Text, appears highlighted in the Data Type box, which now also contains an arrow, and the field properties for a Text field appear in the Field Properties pane. See Figure 2-10.

Notice that the right side of the Field Properties pane now provides an explanation for the current property, Data Type.

Trouble? If you make a typing error, you can correct it by clicking to position the insertion point, and then using either the Backspace key to delete characters to the left of the insertion point or the Delete key to delete characters to the right of the insertion point. Then type the correct text.

| Figure 2-10 | Table window after entering the first field name |

field name entered

default data type

click to display a
list of data types

properties for a
Text field

pressing the F1 key
displays Help information

default property
values for a Text field

The data type determines the kind of values
that users can store in the field. Press F1 for
help on data types.

Because the InvoiceNum field values will not be used in calculations, you will
accept the default Text data type for the field.

▶ **2.** Press the **Tab** key to accept Text as the data type and to advance to the
Description box.

Next you'll enter the Description property value as "Primary key." The value you
enter for the Description property will appear on the status bar when you view the
table datasheet. Note that specifying "Primary key" for the Description property
does *not* establish the current field as the primary key; you use a button on the
Ribbon to specify the primary key in Design view, which you will do later in this
session.

▶ **3.** Type **Primary key** in the Description box.

Notice the Field Size property for the field. The default setting of 255 for Text
fields is displayed. You need to change this number to 4 because all invoice numbers at Belmont Landscapes contain only four digits.

▶ **4.** Double-click the number **255** in the Field Size property box to select it, and then
type **4**.

Finally, you need to set the Caption property for the field so that its name appears
with a space, as "Invoice Num."

> **5.** Click the **Caption** property box, and then type **Invoice Num**. The definition of the first field is complete. See Figure 2-11.

| Figure 2-11 | InvoiceNum field defined |

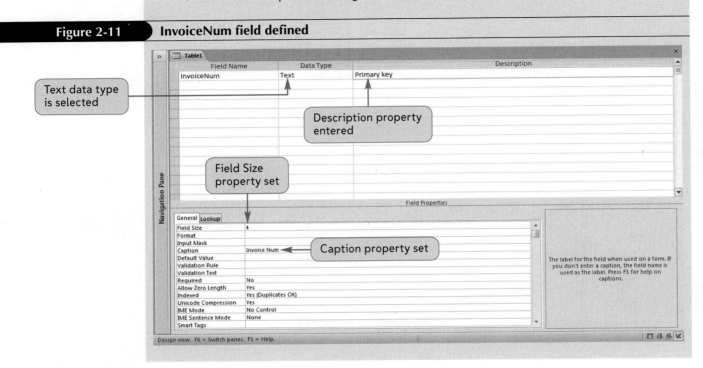

Oren's Invoice table design (Figure 2-9) shows ContractNum as the second field. Because Oren and other staff members want to relate information about invoices to the contract data in the Contract table, the Invoice table must include the ContractNum field, which is the Contract table's primary key. Recall that when you include the primary key from one table as a field in a second table to connect the two tables, the field is a foreign key in the second table. The field must be defined in the same way in both tables.

Next, you will define ContractNum as a Text field with a field size of 4. Later in this session, you'll change the Field Size property for the ContractNum field in the Contract table to 4 so that the field definition is the same in both tables.

To define the ContractNum field:

> **1.** In the Table Design grid, click the second row's Field Name box, type **ContractNum** in the box, and then press the **Tab** key to advance to the Data Type box.

> **2.** Press the **Tab** key to accept Text as the field's data type. Because the ContractNum field is a foreign key to the Contract table, you'll enter "Foreign key" in the Description box to help users of the database understand the purpose of this field.

> **3.** Type **Foreign key** in the Description box. Next, you'll change the Field Size property to 4.

> **4.** Press the **F6** key to move to the Field Properties pane. The current entry for the Field Size property, 255, is highlighted.

> **5.** Type **4** to set the Field Size property. Finally, you need to set the Caption property for this field.

> **6.** Press the **Tab** key three times to move to the Caption box, and then type **Contract Num**. You have completed the definition of the second field.

The third field in the Invoice table is the InvoiceAmt field, which will display currency values, similar to the ContractAmt field in the Contract table. However, for this field, Oren wants the values to appear with two decimal places because invoice amounts might include cents. He also wants the values to include dollar signs, so that the values will be formatted as currency when they are printed in reports sent to customers.

To define the InvoiceAmt field:

1. Click the third row's Field Name box, type **InvoiceAmt** in the box, and then press the **Tab** key to advance to the Data Type box.

2. Click the **Data Type** arrow, click **Currency** in the list, and then press the **Tab** key to advance to the Description box.

   According to Oren's design (Figure 2-9), you do not need to enter a description for this field. If you've assigned a descriptive field name and the field does not fulfill a special function (such as primary key), you usually do not enter a value for the optional Description property. InvoiceAmt is a field that does not require a value for its Description property.

   Oren wants the InvoiceAmt field values to be displayed with two decimal places. The **Decimal Places property** specifies the number of decimal places that are displayed to the right of the decimal point.

TIP

You can display the arrow and the list simultaneously by clicking the right side of a box.

3. In the Field Properties pane, click the **Decimal Places** box to position the insertion point there. An arrow appears on the right side of the Decimal Places box. When you position the insertion point or select text in many Access boxes, Access displays an arrow, which you can click to display a list with options.

4. Click the **Decimal Places** arrow, and then click **2** in the list to specify two decimal places for the InvoiceAmt field values.

5. Press the **Tab** key twice to move to the Caption box, and then type **Invoice Amt**. The definition of the third field is now complete. See Figure 2-12.

Figure 2-12   Table window after defining the first three fields

The next field you'll define in the Invoice table is InvoiceDate. This field will contain the dates on which invoices are generated for Belmont Landscapes customers. When Belmont Landscapes first draws up contracts with its customers, the firm establishes invoice dates based on the different phases of the projects. For long-term projects with multiple phases, some of these dates are months or years in the future. You'll define the InvoiceDate field using the Date/Time data type. Also, according to Oren's design (Figure 2-9), the date values should be displayed in the format mm/dd/yyyy, which is a two-digit month, a two-digit day, and a four-digit year.

To define the InvoiceDate field:

1. Click the fourth row's Field Name box, type **InvoiceDate**, and then press the **Tab** key to advance to the Data Type box.

   You can select a value from the Data Type list as you did for the InvoiceAmt field. Alternately, you can type the property value in the box or type just the first character of the property value.

2. Type **d**. The value in the fourth row's Data Type box changes to "date/Time," with the letters "ate/Time" highlighted. See Figure 2-13.

Figure 2-13	Selecting a value for the Data Type property

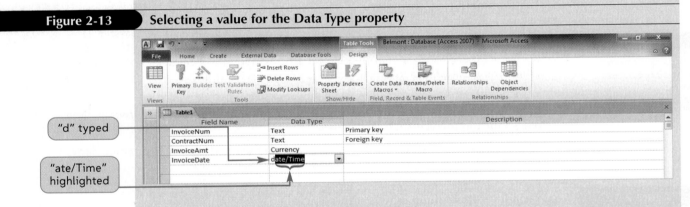

"d" typed

"ate/Time" highlighted

3. Press the **Tab** key to advance to the Description box. Note that Access changes the value for the Data Type property to "Date/Time."

   Oren wants the values in the InvoiceDate field to be displayed in a format showing the month, the day, and a four-digit year, as in the following example: 03/11/2013. You use the Format property to control the display of a field value.

4. In the Field Properties pane, click the right side of the **Format** box to display the list of predefined formats for Date/Time fields. As noted in the right side of the Field Properties pane, you can either choose a predefined format or enter a custom format.

   Trouble? If you see an arrow instead of a list of predefined formats, click the arrow to display the list.

   None of the predefined formats matches the exact layout Oren wants for the InvoiceDate values, so you need to create a custom date format. Figure 2-14 shows some of the symbols available for custom date and time formats.

TIP

A complete description of all the custom formats is available in Access Help.

Figure 2-14   **Symbols for some custom date formats**

Symbol	Description
/	date separator
d	day of the month in one or two numeric digits, as needed (1 to 31)
dd	day of the month in two numeric digits (01 to 31)
ddd	first three letters of the weekday (Sun to Sat)
dddd	full name of the weekday (Sunday to Saturday)
w	day of the week (1 to 7)
ww	week of the year (1 to 53)
m	month of the year in one or two numeric digits, as needed (1 to 12)
mm	month of the year in two numeric digits (01 to 12)
mmm	first three letters of the month (Jan to Dec)
mmmm	full name of the month (January to December)
yy	last two digits of the year (01 to 99)
yyyy	full year (0100 to 9999)

Oren wants the dates to be displayed with a two-digit month (mm), a two-digit day (dd), and a four-digit year (yyyy). You'll enter this custom format now.

5. Click the **Format** arrow to close the list of predefined formats, and then type **mm/dd/yyyy** in the Format box.

6. Press the **Tab** key twice to move to the Caption box, and then type **Invoice Date**. See Figure 2-15.

Figure 2-15   **Specifying the custom date format**

current field

custom date format entered

Caption property entered

The fifth, and final, field to be defined in the Invoice table is InvoicePaid. This field will be a Yes/No field to indicate the payment status of each invoice record stored in the Invoice table. Recall that the Yes/No data type is used to define fields that store true/false, yes/no, and on/off field values. When you create a Yes/No field in a table, the default Format property is set to True/False. After setting the data type, you'll set the Format property for the InvoicePaid field to Yes/No.

To define the InvoicePaid field:

▶ 1. Click the fifth row's Field Name box, type **InvoicePaid**, and then press the **Tab** key to advance to the Data Type box.

▶ 2. Type **y**. Access completes the data type as "yes/No."

▶ 3. Press the **Tab** key to select the Yes/No data type and move to the Description box.

▶ 4. Click the **Format** box, click the **arrow** on its right side, and then click **Yes/No** to set the Format property.

▶ 5. Press the **Tab** key to move to the Caption box, and then type **Invoice Paid**.

You've finished defining the fields for the Invoice table. Next, you need to specify the primary key for the table.

Specifying the Primary Key

As you learned in Tutorial 1, the primary key for a table uniquely identifies each record in a table.

Understanding the Importance of the Primary Key

Although Access does not require a table to have a primary key, including a primary key offers several advantages:

- A primary key uniquely identifies each record in a table.
- Access does not allow duplicate values in the primary key field. For example, if a record already exists in the Contract table with a ContractNum value of 3020, Access prevents you from adding another record with this same value in the ContractNum field. Preventing duplicate values ensures the uniqueness of the primary key field.
- When a primary key has been specified, Access forces you to enter a value for the primary key field in every record in the table. This is known as **entity integrity**. If you do not enter a value for a field, you have actually given the field a **null value**. You cannot give a null value to the primary key field because entity integrity prevents Access from accepting and processing that record.
- Access stores records on disk as you enter them. You can enter records in any order, but Access displays them by default in order by the field values of the primary key. If you enter records in no specific order, you are ensured that you will later be able to work with them in a more meaningful, primary key sequence.
- Access responds faster to your requests for specific records based on the primary key.

REFERENCE

Specifying a Primary Key in Design View

- Display the table in Design view.
- Click in the row for the field you've chosen to be the primary key to make it the active field. If the primary key will consist of two or more fields, click the row selector for the first field, press and hold down the Ctrl key, and then click the row selector for each additional primary key field.
- In the Tools group on the Design tab, click the Primary Key button.

According to Oren's design, you need to specify InvoiceNum as the primary key for the Invoice table. You can do so while the table is in Design view.

TIP

The Primary Key button works as a toggle; you can click it to remove the key symbol if you want to specify a different field as the primary key.

To specify InvoiceNum as the primary key:

1. Click in the row for the InvoiceNum field to make it the current field.

2. In the Tools group on the Design tab, click the **Primary Key** button. A key symbol appears in the row selector for the first row, indicating that the InvoiceNum field is the table's primary key. See Figure 2-16.

Figure 2-16   **InvoiceNum field selected as the primary key**

Primary Key button

key symbol indicates the table's primary key

Saving the Table Structure

The last step in creating a table is to name the table and save the table's structure. When you save a table structure, the table is stored in the database file (in this case, the Belmont database file). Once the table is saved, you can use it to enter data in the table. According to Oren's plan, you need to save the table you've defined as "Invoice."

To name and save the Invoice table:

1. Click the **Save** button on the Quick Access Toolbar. The Save As dialog box opens.

2. Type **Invoice** in the Table Name box, and then press the **Enter** key. Access saves the Invoice table in the Belmont database. Notice that the tab for the table now displays the name "Invoice" instead of "Table1."

Modifying the Structure of an Access Table

Even a well-designed table might need to be modified. Some changes that you can make to a table's structure in Design view are changing the order of fields, adding and deleting fields, and changing field properties.

After meeting with Sarah Fisher, the office manager at Belmont Landscapes, and reviewing the structure of the Invoice table, Oren has changes he wants you to make to the table. First, he wants the InvoiceAmt field to be moved so that it appears right before the InvoicePaid field. Then, he wants you to add a new Text field, named InvoiceItem, to the table to include information about what the invoice is for, such as schematic landscape plans, construction documents, and so on. Oren would like the InvoiceItem field to be inserted between the InvoiceDate and InvoiceAmt fields.

Moving a Field

To move a field, you use the mouse to drag it to a new location in the Table Design grid. Next, you'll move the InvoiceAmt field so that it is before the InvoicePaid field.

To move the InvoiceAmt field:

1. Position the pointer on the row selector for the InvoiceAmt field until the pointer changes to a ➡ shape.

2. Click the **row selector** to select the entire InvoiceAmt row.

3. Place the pointer on the row selector for the InvoiceAmt field, click the ⌖ pointer, and then drag the ⌖ pointer to the row selector for the InvoicePaid field. See Figure 2-17.

Figure 2-17	Moving the InvoiceAmt field in the table structure

black line indicates the new position for the field being moved

selected field

move pointer

4. Release the mouse button. The InvoiceAmt field now appears between the InvoiceDate and InvoicePaid fields in the table structure.

   Trouble? If the InvoiceAmt field did not move, repeat Steps 1 through 4, making sure you hold down the mouse button during the drag operation.

Adding a Field

To add a new field between existing fields, you must insert a row. You begin by selecting the row below where you want the new field to be inserted.

Adding a Field Between Two Existing Fields

- In the Table window in Design view, select the row below where you want the new field to be inserted.
- In the Tools group on the Design tab, click the Insert Rows button.
- Define the new field by entering the field name, data type, optional description, and any property specifications.

Next, you need to add the InvoiceItem field to the Invoice table structure between the InvoiceDate and InvoiceAmt fields.

To add the InvoiceItem field to the Invoice table:

1. Click the **InvoiceAmt** Field Name box. You need to establish this field as the current field so that the row for the new record will be inserted above this field.

2. In the Tools group on the Design tab, click the **Insert Rows** button. Access adds a new, blank row between the InvoiceDate and InvoiceAmt fields. The insertion point is positioned in the Field Name box for the new row, ready for you to type the name for the new field. See Figure 2-18.

| Figure 2-18 | Table structure after inserting a row |

Trouble? If you selected the InvoiceAmt field's row selector and then inserted the new row, you need to click the new row's Field Name box to position the insertion point in it.

You'll define the InvoiceItem field in the new row of the Invoice table. This field will be a Text field with a field size of 40, and you need to set the Caption property to include a space between the words in the field name.

3. Type **InvoiceItem**, press the **Tab** key to move to the Data Type property, and then press the **Tab** key again to accept the default Text data type.

4. Press the **F6** key to move to the Field Size box and to select the default field size, and then type **40**.

5. Press the **Tab** key three times to move to the Caption box, and then type **Invoice Item**. The definition of the new field is complete. See Figure 2-19.

Figure 2-19

InvoiceItem field added to the Invoice table

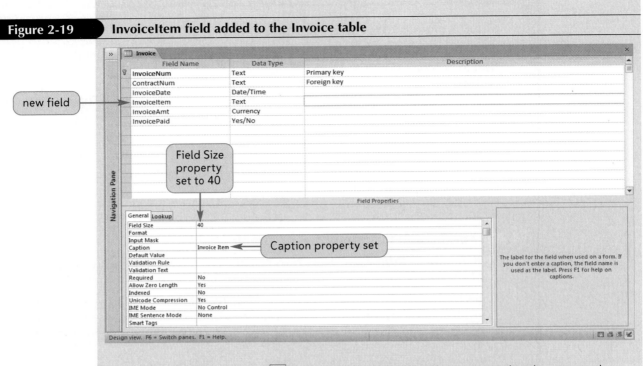

6. Click the **Save** button 🔲 on the Quick Access Toolbar to save the changes to the Invoice table structure.

Changing Field Properties

With the Invoice table design complete, you can now go back and modify the Field Size property for the three Text fields in the Contract table. Recall that each of these fields still has the default field size of 255, which is too large for the data contained in these fields. You'll also set the Caption property for each field to include a space between the words in the field name.

To modify the Contract table's field properties:

1. Click the **Close 'Invoice'** button ✕ on the object tab to close the Invoice table.

2. On the Navigation Pane, click the **Shutter Bar Open/Close Button** ≫ to open the pane. Notice that the Invoice table is listed below the Contract table in the Tables section of the pane.

3. Double-click **Contract** to open the Contract table in Datasheet view. To change the Field Size property and set the Caption property, you need to display the table in Design view.

4. In the Views group on the Home tab, click the **View** button. The table is displayed in Design view with the ContractNum field selected. You need to change the Field Size property for this field to 4 because each contract number at Belmont Landscapes consists of four digits.

5. Press the **F6** key to move to and select the default setting of 255 for the Field Size property, and then type **4**. Next you need to set the Caption property for this field.

6. Press the **Tab** key three times to move to the Caption box, and then type **Contract Num**.

Next you need to set the CustomerID Field Size property to 5 because each CustomerID number at Belmont Landscapes consists of five digits. You also need to set this field's Caption property.

▶ 7. Click the **CustomerID** Field Name box to make this the active field, press the **F6** key, type **5**, press the **Tab** key three times, and then type **Customer ID** in the Caption box.

Next you'll set the Caption property for the ContractAmt and SigningDate fields.

▶ 8. Click the **ContractAmt** Field Name box, click the **Caption** box, type **Contract Amt**; then click the **SigningDate** Field Name box, click the **Caption** box, and then type **Signing Date**.

Finally, for the ContractType field, you will set the Field Size property to 75. This size can accommodate the longer values in the ContractType field. You'll also set this field's Caption property.

▶ 9. Click the **ContractType** Field Name box, press the **F6** key, type **75**, press the **Tab** key three times, and then type **Contract Type**. Now you can save the modified table.

▶ 10. Click the **Save** button 🖫 on the Quick Access Toolbar. A dialog box opens informing you that some data may be lost because you decreased the field sizes. Because you know that all of the values in the ContractNum, CustomerID, and ContractType fields include fewer characters than the new Field Size properties that you set for each field, you can ignore this message.

▶ 11. Click the **Yes** button, and then close the Contract table.

▶ 12. If you are not continuing to Session 2.2, click the **File** tab, and then click **Close Database** in the navigation bar to close the Belmont database.

You have created the Invoice table and made modifications to its design. In the next session, you'll add records to the Invoice table and create the Customer table in the Belmont database.

Session 2.1 Quick Check

REVIEW

1. What guidelines should you follow when designing a database?
2. What is the purpose of the Data Type property for a field?
3. The _____ property specifies how a field's name is displayed in database objects, including table and query datasheets, forms, and reports.
4. For which three types of fields can you assign a field size?
5. The default Field Size property setting for a Text field is _____.
6. In Design view, which key do you press to move from the Table Design grid to the Field Properties pane?
7. A(n) _____ value, which results when you do not enter a value for a field, is not permitted for a primary key.

SESSION 2.2 VISUAL OVERVIEW

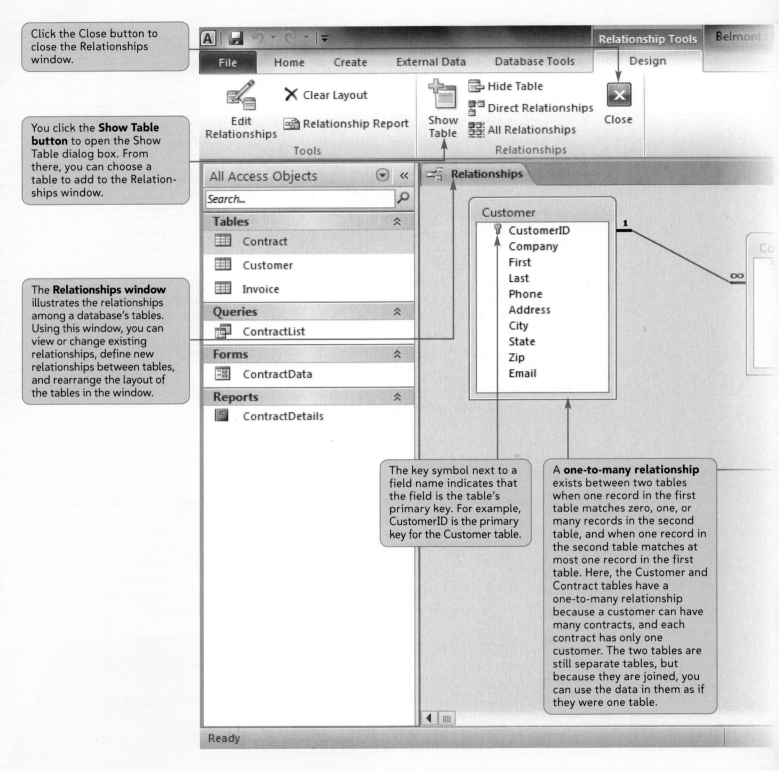

Click the Close button to close the Relationships window.

You click the **Show Table button** to open the Show Table dialog box. From there, you can choose a table to add to the Relationships window.

The **Relationships window** illustrates the relationships among a database's tables. Using this window, you can view or change existing relationships, define new relationships between tables, and rearrange the layout of the tables in the window.

The key symbol next to a field name indicates that the field is the table's primary key. For example, CustomerID is the primary key for the Customer table.

A **one-to-many relationship** exists between two tables when one record in the first table matches zero, one, or many records in the second table, and when one record in the second table matches at most one record in the first table. Here, the Customer and Contract tables have a one-to-many relationship because a customer can have many contracts, and each contract has only one customer. The two tables are still separate tables, but because they are joined, you can use the data in them as if they were one table.

TABLE RELATIONSHIPS

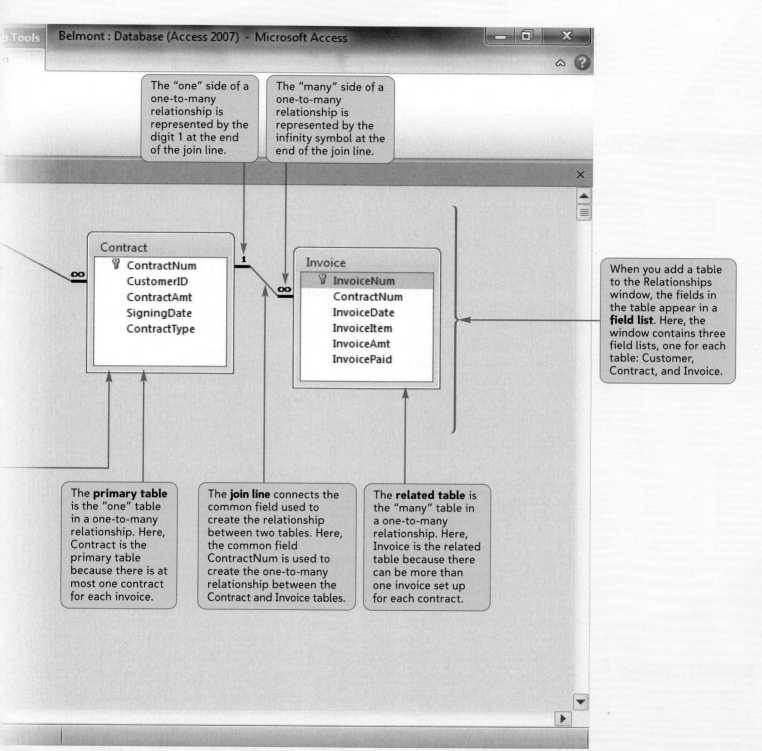

Belmont : Database (Access 2007) - Microsoft Access

The "one" side of a one-to-many relationship is represented by the digit 1 at the end of the join line.

The "many" side of a one-to-many relationship is represented by the infinity symbol at the end of the join line.

When you add a table to the Relationships window, the fields in the table appear in a **field list**. Here, the window contains three field lists, one for each table: Customer, Contract, and Invoice.

Contract
- ContractNum
- CustomerID
- ContractAmt
- SigningDate
- ContractType

Invoice
- InvoiceNum
- ContractNum
- InvoiceDate
- InvoiceItem
- InvoiceAmt
- InvoicePaid

The **primary table** is the "one" table in a one-to-many relationship. Here, Contract is the primary table because there is at most one contract for each invoice.

The **join line** connects the common field used to create the relationship between two tables. Here, the common field ContractNum is used to create the one-to-many relationship between the Contract and Invoice tables.

The **related table** is the "many" table in a one-to-many relationship. Here, Invoice is the related table because there can be more than one invoice set up for each contract.

Before you can begin to define the table relationships, as illustrated in the Session 2.2 Visual Overview, you need to finish creating the tables in the Belmont database.

Adding Records to a New Table

The Invoice table design is complete. Now, Oren would like you to add records to the table so it will contain the invoice data for Belmont Landscapes. You add records to a table in Datasheet view as you did in Tutorial 1, by typing the field values in the rows below the column headings for the fields. You'll begin by entering the records shown in Figure 2-20.

| Figure 2-20 | Records to be added to the Invoice table |

InvoiceNum	ContractNum	InvoiceDate	InvoiceItem	InvoiceAmt	InvoicePaid
2011	3011	03/23/2013	Schematic Plan	$1,500.00	Yes
2031	3020	04/19/2013	Schematic Plan	$1,500.00	Yes
2073	3023	09/21/2015	Construction Observation	$10,000.00	No
2062	3026	09/12/2014	Permitting	$10,000.00	No

To add the first record to the Invoice table:

1. If you took a break after the previous session, make sure that the Belmont database is open, and the Navigation Pane is open.

2. In the Tables section of the Navigation Pane, double-click **Invoice** to open the Invoice table in Datasheet view.

3. Close the Navigation Pane, and then use the ✛ pointer to resize each column so that the field names are completely visible.

> Be sure to type the numbers "0" and "1" and not the letters "O" and "l" in the field value.

4. In the Invoice Num column, type **2011**, press the **Tab** key, type **3011** in the Contract Num column, and then press the **Tab** key.

   Next you need to enter the invoice date. Recall that you specified a custom date format, mm/dd/yyyy, for the InvoiceDate field. You do not need to type each digit; for example, you can type just "3" instead of "03" for the month, and you can type "13" instead of "2013" for the year. Access will display the full value according to the custom date format.

5. Type **3/23/13**, press the **Tab** key, type **Schematic Plan** in the Invoice Item column, and then press the **Tab** key. Notice that Access displays the date "03/23/2013" in the Invoice Date column.

   Next you need to enter the invoice amount for the first record. This is a Currency field with the Currency format and two decimal places specified. Because of the field's set properties, you do not need to type the dollar sign, comma, or zeroes for the decimal places; Access will display these items automatically for you.

6. Type **1500** and then press the **Tab** key. Access displays the value as "$1,500.00."

   The last field in the table, InvoicePaid, is a Yes/No field. Notice the check box displayed in the column. By default, the value for any Yes/No field is "No;" therefore, the check box is initially empty. For Yes/No fields with check boxes, you press the Tab key to leave the check box unchecked, and you press the spacebar to insert a check mark in the check box. For the record you are entering in the Invoice table, the invoice has been paid, so you need to insert a check mark in the check box.

> **TIP**
>
> The spacebar works as a toggle for Yes/No fields; you press it to insert a check mark in an empty check box and to remove an existing check mark. You can also select or deselect a check box by clicking it.

7. Press the **spacebar** to insert a check mark, and then press the **Tab** key. The values for the first record are entered. See Figure 2-21.

Figure 2-21   **First record entered in the Invoice table**

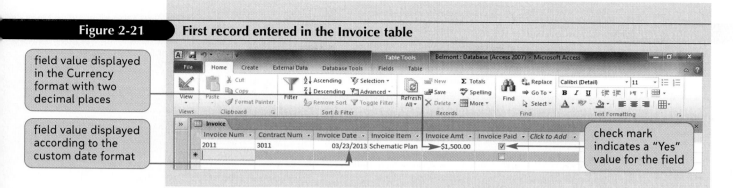

field value displayed in the Currency format with two decimal places

field value displayed according to the custom date format

check mark indicates a "Yes" value for the field

Now you can add the remaining three records. As you do, you'll learn a shortcut for inserting the value from the same field in the previous record.

To add the next three records to the Invoice table:

1. Refer to Figure 2-20 and enter the values in the second record's Invoice Num, Contract Num, and Invoice Date columns.

   Notice the value in the second record's Invoice Item column, "Schematic Plan." This value is the exact same value as in the first record. You can quickly insert the value from the same column in the previous record using the **Ctrl + '** (apostrophe) keyboard shortcut.

2. In the Invoice Item column, press the **Ctrl + '** keys. Access inserts the value "Schematic Plan" in the Invoice Item column for the second record.

3. Press the **Tab** key to move to the Invoice Amt column. Again, the value you need to enter in this column—$1,500.00—is the same as the value for this column in the previous record. So, you can use the keyboard shortcut again.

4. In the Invoice Amt column, press the **Ctrl + '** keys. Access inserts the value $1,500.00 in the Invoice Amt column for the second record.

5. Press the **Tab** key to move to the Invoice Paid column, press the **spacebar** to insert a check mark in the check box, and then press the **Tab** key. The second record is entered in the Invoice table.

6. Refer to Figure 2-20 to enter the values for the third and fourth records, using the Ctrl + ' keys to enter the value in the fourth record's Invoice Amt column. Also, for both records, the invoices have not been paid. Therefore, be sure to press the Tab key to leave the Invoice Paid column values unchecked (signifying "No").

7. Resize the columns, as necessary, so that all field values are completely visible. Then click the **Invoice Num** column for the next new record. Your table should look like the one in Figure 2-22.

| Figure 2-22 | Invoice table with four records added |

To finish entering records in the Invoice table, you'll use a method that allows you to import the data.

Importing Data from an Excel Worksheet

Often, the data you want to add to an Access table exists in another file, such as a Word document or an Excel workbook. You can bring the data from other files into Access in different ways. For example, you can copy and paste the data from an open file, or you can **import** the data, which is a process that allows you to copy the data from a source without having to open the source file.

Oren had been using Excel to track invoice data for Belmont Landscapes and already created a worksheet, named "Invoices," containing this data. You'll import this Excel worksheet into your Invoice table to complete the entry of data in the table. To use the import method, the columns in the Excel worksheet must match the names and data types of the fields in the Access table.

INSIGHT

Caption Property Values and the Import Process

When you want to import data from an Excel worksheet into an Access table, any Caption property values set for the fields in the table are not considered in the import process. For example, your Access table could have fields such as InvoiceDate and InvoiceAmt with Caption property values of Invoice Date and Invoice Amt, respectively. If the Excel worksheet you are importing has column headings such as Invoice Date and Invoice Amt, you might think that the data matches and you can proceed with the import. However, if the underlying field names in the Access table do not match the Excel worksheet column headings exactly, the import process will fail. It's a good idea to double-check to make sure that the actual Access field names—and not just the column headings displayed in a table datasheet (as specified by the Caption property)—match the Excel worksheet column headings. If there are differences, you can change the column headings in the Excel worksheet to match the Access table field names before you import the data, ensuring that the process will work correctly.

The Invoices worksheet contains the following columns: InvoiceNum, ContractNum, InvoiceDate, InvoiceItem, InvoiceAmt, and InvoicePaid. These column headings match the field names in the Invoice table exactly, so you can import the data. Before you import data into a table, you need to close the table.

To import the Invoices worksheet into the Invoice table:

1. Click the **Close 'Invoice'** button ⊠ on the object tab to close the Invoice table. A dialog box opens asking if you want to save the changes to the table layout. This dialog box opens because you resized the table columns.

2. Click the **Yes** button in the dialog box.

3. Click the **External Data** tab on the Ribbon.

4. In the Import & Link group on the External Data tab, click the **Excel** button. The Get External Data - Excel Spreadsheet dialog box opens. See Figure 2-23.

Figure 2-23 | Get External Data - Excel Spreadsheet dialog box

The dialog box provides options for importing the entire worksheet as a new table in the current database, adding the data from the worksheet to an existing table, or linking the data in the worksheet to the table. You need to add, or append, the worksheet data to the Invoice table.

5. Click the **Browse** button. The File Open dialog box opens. The Excel workbook file is named "Invoices" and is located in the Access1\Tutorial folder provided with your Data Files.

6. Navigate to the **Access1\Tutorial** folder, where your starting Data Files are stored, and then double-click the **Invoices** Excel file. You return to the dialog box.

7. Click the **Append a copy of the records to the table** option button. The box to the right of this option becomes active. Next, you need to select the table to which you want to add the data.

8. Click the **arrow** on the box, and then click **Invoice**.

9. Click the **OK** button. The first Import Spreadsheet Wizard dialog box opens. See Figure 2-24.

Figure 2-24 **First Import Spreadsheet Wizard dialog box**

selected check box confirms that the first row contains column headings

data from the worksheet to be imported

The dialog box confirms that the first row of the worksheet you are importing contains column headings. The bottom section of the dialog box displays some of the data contained in the worksheet.

10. Click the **Next** button. The second, and final, Import Spreadsheet Wizard dialog box opens. Notice that the Import to Table box shows that the data from the spreadsheet will be imported into the Invoice table.

11. Click the **Finish** button. A dialog box opens asking if you want to save the import steps. If you needed to repeat this same import procedure many times, it would be a good idea to save the steps for the procedure. However, you don't need to save these steps because you'll be importing the data only one time. Once the data is in the Invoice table, Oren will no longer use Excel to track invoice data.

12. Click the **Close** button in the dialog box to close it without saving the steps.

The data from the Invoices worksheet has been added to the Invoice table. Next, you'll open the table to view the new records.

To open the Invoice table and view the imported data:

1. Open the Navigation Pane, and then double-click **Invoice** in the Tables section to open the table in Datasheet view.

2. Resize the Invoice Item column so that all field values are fully displayed, being sure to scroll down through the entire datasheet and repeat the resizing as necessary. When you resize a column by double-clicking the pointer on the column dividing line, you are sizing the column to its **best fit**—that is, so the column is just wide enough to display the longest visible value in the column, including the field name.

3. Press the **Ctrl+Home** keys to scroll to the top of the datasheet. Notice that the table now contains a total of 176 records—four records you entered plus 172 records imported from the Invoices worksheet. The records are displayed in primary key order by the values in the Invoice Num column. See Figure 2-25.

Figure 2-25	Invoice table after importing data from Excel

TIP

When you resize a column to its best fit, only the visible field values are affected. You must scroll down the datasheet to make sure all field values for the entire column are fully displayed, resizing as you scroll, if necessary.

records are displayed in order by the values in the Invoice Num column

table contains a total of 176 records

4. Save and close the Invoice table, and then close the Navigation Pane.

Two of the tables—Contract and Invoice—are now complete. According to Oren's plan for the Belmont database, you need to create a third table, named "Customer," to track data about Belmont Landscapes' residential and commercial customers. You'll use a different method to create this table.

Creating a Table by Importing an Existing Table Structure

If another Access database contains a table—or even just the design, or structure, of a table—that you want to include in your database, you can easily import the table and any records it contains or import only the table structure into your database.

Oren documented the design for the new Customer table by listing each field's name; data type; and size, description, and caption (if applicable), as shown in Figure 2-26. Note that each field in the Customer table will be a Text field, and the CustomerID field will be the table's primary key.

Figure 2-26   **Design for the Customer table**

Field Name	Data Type	Field Size	Description	Caption
CustomerID	Text	5	Primary key	Customer ID
Company	Text	50		
Last	Text	25	Contact's last name	Last Name
First	Text	20	Contact's first name	First Name
Phone	Text	14		
Address	Text	35		
City	Text	25		
State	Text	2		
Zip	Text	10		
Email	Text	50		

Sarah already created an Access database containing a Customer table design. She never entered any records into the table because she wasn't sure if the table design was complete or correct. After reviewing the table design, both Sarah and Oren agree that it contains some of the fields Oren wants to track, but that some changes are needed. So, you can import the table structure in Sarah's database to create the Customer table in the Belmont database, and then modify the imported table to produce the final table structure Oren wants.

To create the Customer table by importing the structure of another table:

1. Make sure the External Data tab is the active tab on the Ribbon.

2. In the Import & Link group, click the **Access** button. The Get External Data - Access Database dialog box opens. This dialog box is similar to the one you used earlier when importing the Excel spreadsheet.

3. Click the **Browse** button. The File Open dialog box opens. The Access database file from which you need to import the table structure is named "Sarah" and is located in the Access1\Tutorial folder provided with your Data Files.

4. Navigate to the **Access1\Tutorial** folder, where your starting Data Files are stored, and then double-click the **Sarah** database file. You return to the dialog box.

5. Make sure the **Import tables, queries, forms, reports, macros, and modules into the current database** option button is selected, and then click the **OK** button. The Import Objects dialog box opens. The dialog box contains tabs for importing all the different types of Access database objects—tables, queries, forms, and so on. The Tables tab is the current tab.

6. Click the **Options** button in the dialog box to see all the options for importing tables. See Figure 2-27.

Figure 2-27 Import Objects dialog box

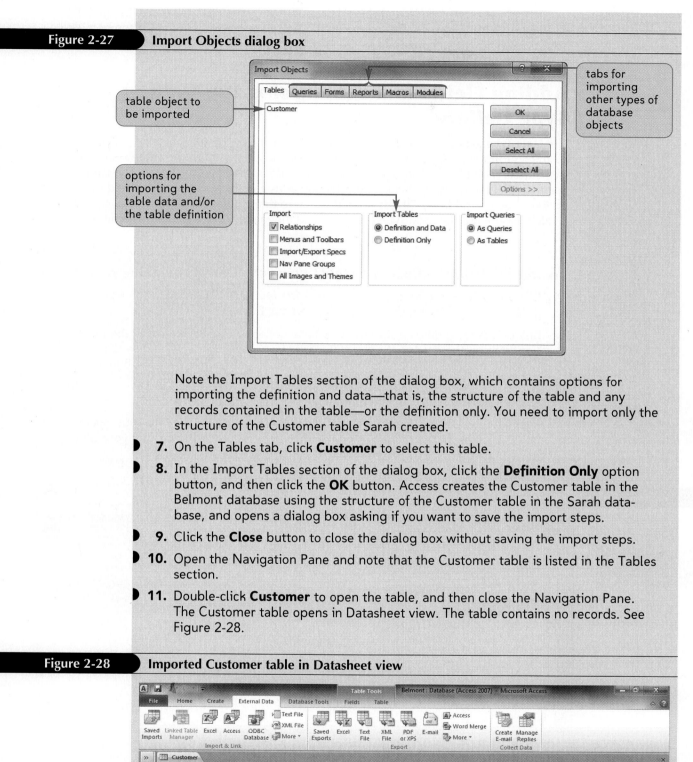

table object to
be imported

options for
importing the
table data and/or
the table definition

tabs for
importing
other types of
database
objects

Note the Import Tables section of the dialog box, which contains options for importing the definition and data—that is, the structure of the table and any records contained in the table—or the definition only. You need to import only the structure of the Customer table Sarah created.

7. On the Tables tab, click **Customer** to select this table.

8. In the Import Tables section of the dialog box, click the **Definition Only** option button, and then click the **OK** button. Access creates the Customer table in the Belmont database using the structure of the Customer table in the Sarah database, and opens a dialog box asking if you want to save the import steps.

9. Click the **Close** button to close the dialog box without saving the import steps.

10. Open the Navigation Pane and note that the Customer table is listed in the Tables section.

11. Double-click **Customer** to open the table, and then close the Navigation Pane. The Customer table opens in Datasheet view. The table contains no records. See Figure 2-28.

Figure 2-28 Imported Customer table in Datasheet view

The table structure you imported contains some of the fields Oren wants, but not all (see Figure 2-26); it also contains some fields Oren does not want in the Customer table. You can add the missing fields using the Data Type gallery.

Adding Fields to a Table Using the Data Type Gallery

The **Data Type gallery**, available in the Add & Delete group on the Fields tab, allows you to add a group of related fields to a table at the same time, rather than adding each field to the table individually. The group of fields you add is called a **Quick Start selection**. For example, the Address Quick Start selection adds a collection of fields related to an address, such as Address, City, State, and so on, to the table at one time.

Next, you'll use the Data Type gallery to add the missing fields to the Customer table.

To add fields to the Customer table using the Data Type gallery:

1. Click the **Fields** tab on the Ribbon. Note the More Fields button in the Add & Delete group. Clicking this button displays the Data Type gallery.

   Before inserting fields from the Data Type gallery, you need to place the insertion point in the field to the right of where you want to insert the new fields. According to Oren's design, the Address field should come after the Phone field, so you need to make the next field, FaxNumber, the active field.

   Make sure the correct field is active before adding new fields.

2. Click the first row in the **FaxNumber** field to make it the active field.

3. In the Add & Delete group, click the **More Fields** button. The Data Type gallery opens and displays options for different types of fields you can add to your table.

4. Scroll the gallery down so the Quick Start section is visible. See Figure 2-29.

Figure 2-29	Customer table with the Data Type gallery displayed

The Quick Start section provides options that will add multiple, related fields to the table at one time. The new fields will be inserted to the left of the current field.

5. In the Quick Start section, click **Address**. Access adds five fields to the table: Address, City, State Province, ZIP Postal, and Country Region. See Figure 2-30.

| Figure 2-30 | Customer table after adding fields from the Data Type gallery |

five fields added with Address Quick Start selection

Modifying the Imported Table

Refer back to Oren's design for the Customer table (Figure 2-26). To finalize the table design, you need to modify the imported table by deleting fields, renaming fields, changing field data types, and moving some fields. You'll begin by deleting fields.

Deleting Fields from a Table Structure

After you've created a table, you might need to delete one or more fields. When you delete a field, you also delete all the values for that field from the table. So, before you delete a field you should make sure that you want to do so and that you choose the correct field to delete. You can delete fields from either Datasheet view or Design view.

REFERENCE

Deleting a Field from a Table Structure

- In Datasheet view, click the column heading for the field you want to delete.
- In the Add & Delete group on the Fields tab, click the Delete button.
or
- In Design view, click the Field Name box for the field you want to delete.
- In the Tools group on the Design tab, click the Delete Rows button.

The Address Quick Start selection added a field named "Country Region" to the Customer table. Oren doesn't need a field to store country data because all Belmont Landscapes customers are located in the United States. You'll begin to modify the Customer table structure by deleting the Country Region field.

To delete the Country Region field from the table in Datasheet view:

1. Click the first row in the **Country Region** field (if necessary).

2. In the Add & Delete group on the Fields tab, click the **Delete** button. The Country Region field is removed and the first field, CustomerID, is now the active field.

You can also delete fields from a table structure in Design view. You'll switch to Design view to delete the other unnecessary fields.

To delete the fields in Design view:

1. In the Views group on the Fields tab, click the **View** button. The Customer table opens in Design view. See Figure 2-31.

Figure 2-31 | **Customer table in Design view**

2. Click the **FaxNumber** Field Name box to make it the current field.

3. In the Tools group on the Design tab, click the **Delete Rows** button. The FaxNumber field is removed from the Customer table structure.

   You'll delete the County, Web Page, and Notes fields next. Instead of deleting these fields individually, you'll select and delete them at the same time.

4. Click and hold down the mouse button on the row selector for the **County** field, and then drag the mouse to select the **Web Page** and **Notes** fields.

5. Release the mouse button. The rows for the three fields are outlined in an orange box, meaning all three fields are selected.

6. In the Tools group, click the **Delete Rows** button. See Figure 2-32.

Figure 2-32 | **Customer table after deleting fields**

Renaming Fields in Design View

To match Oren's design for the Customer table, you need to rename the StateProvince and ZIPPostal fields. In Tutorial 1, you renamed the default primary key field, ID, in Datasheet view. You can also rename fields in Design view by simply editing the names in the Table Design grid.

To rename the fields in Design view:

1. Click to position the insertion point to the right of the word **StateProvince** in the eighth row's Field Name box, and then press the **Backspace** key eight times to delete the word "Province." The name of the eighth field is now State.

   You can also select an entire field name and then type new text to replace it.

2. In the ninth row's Field Name box, drag to select the text **ZIPPostal**, and then type **Zip**. The text you type replaces the original text. See Figure 2-33.

Figure 2-33   **Customer table after renaming fields**

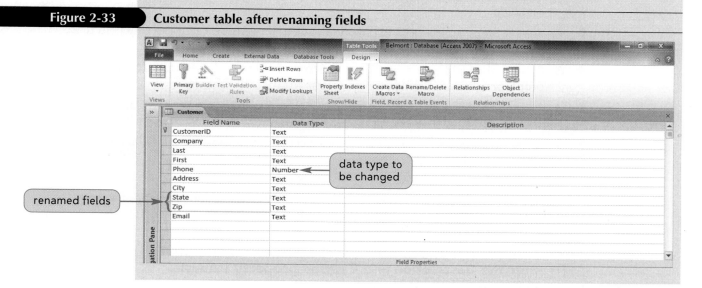

Changing the Data Type for a Field in Design View

According to Oren's plan, all of the fields in the Customer table should be Text fields. The table structure you imported specifies the Number data type for the Phone field. In Tutorial 1, you used an option in Datasheet view to change a field's data type. You can also change the data type for a field in Design view.

To change the data type of the Phone field in Design view:

1. Click the right side of the **Data Type** box for the Phone field to display the list of data types.

2. Click **Text** in the list. The Phone field is now a Text field. Note that, by default, the Field Size property is set to 255. According to Oren's plan, the Phone field should have a Field Size property of 14. You'll make this change next.

3. Press the **F6** key to move to and select the default Field Size property, and then type **14**.

Each of the remaining fields you added using the Address Quick Start selection—Address, City, State, and Zip—also has the default field size of 255. You need to change the Field Size property for these fields to match Oren's design. You'll also delete any Caption property values for these fields because the field names match how Oren wants them displayed.

To change the Field Size and Caption properties for the fields:

1. Click the **Address** Field Name box to make it the current field.

2. Press the **F6** key to move to and select the default Field Size property, and then type **35**.

   Note that the Caption property setting for this field is the same as the field name. This field doesn't need a caption, so you can delete this value.

3. Press the **Tab** key three times to move to and select the word Address in the Caption box, and then press the **Delete** key. The Caption property value is removed.

4. Repeat Steps 1 through 3 to change the Field Size property for the City field to **25** and to delete its Caption property value.

5. Change the Field Size property for the State field to **2** and delete its Caption property value.

6. Change the Field Size property for the Zip field to **10** and delete its Caption property value.

7. Click the **Save** button 🖫 on the Quick Access Toolbar to save your changes to the Customer table.

Finally, Oren would like you to set the Description and Caption properties for the CustomerID, Last, and First fields. You'll make these changes now.

To enter the Description and Caption property values:

1. Click the **CustomerID** Description box, and then type **Primary key**.

2. In the Field Properties pane, click the **Caption** box.

   After you leave the Description box, a Property Update Options button 🗷 appears below the Description box for the CustomerID field. When you change a field's property in Design view, you can use this button to update the corresponding property on forms and reports that include the modified field. For example, if the Belmont database included a form that contained the CustomerID field, you could choose to **propagate**, or update, the modified Description property in the form by clicking the Property Update Options button, and then choosing the option to make the update everywhere the field is used. The text on the Property Update Options button varies depending on the task; in this case, if you click the button, the option is "Update Status Bar Text everywhere CustomerID is used."

   Because the Belmont database does not include any forms or reports that are based on the Customer table, you do not need to update the properties, so you can ignore the button for now.

3. In the Caption box for the CustomerID field, type **Customer ID**.

4. Click the **Description** box for the Last field, and then type **Contact's last name**.

▶ **5.** Click the **Caption** box, and then type **Last Name**.

▶ **6.** Click the **Description** box for the First field, and then type **Contact's first name**.

▶ **7.** Click the **Caption** box, and then type **First Name**. See Figure 2-34.

| Figure 2-34 | Customer table after entering descriptions and captions |

Description property values entered

data type changed to Text

Caption property entered

▶ **8.** Click the **Save** button 🖫 on the Quick Access Toolbar to save your changes to the Customer table.

▶ **9.** In the Views group on the Design tab, click the **View** button to display the table in Datasheet view.

▶ **10.** Use the ↔ pointer to resize each column so that more fields are visible in the datasheet. Then click in the first row for the **Customer ID** column. See Figure 2-35.

| Figure 2-35 | Modified Customer table in Datasheet view |

After viewing the Customer table datasheet, Oren decides that he would like the First field to appear before the Last field. Earlier in this tutorial, when you created the Invoice table, you learned how to change the order of fields in Design view. Although you can move fields in Datasheet view by dragging a field's column heading to a new location, doing so rearranges only the *display* of the table's fields; the table structure is not changed. To move a field permanently, you must display the table in Design view.

To move the Last field to follow the First field:

▶ 1. In the Views group on the Home tab, click the **View** button. The Customer table opens in Design view.

▶ 2. Point to the row selector for the Last field so the pointer changes to a ➡ shape.

▶ 3. Click the **row selector** to select the entire row for the Last field.

▶ 4. Place the pointer on the row selector for the Last field, click the ⬚ pointer, and then drag the ⬚ pointer down to the line below the row selector for the First field.

▶ 5. Release the mouse button. The Last field now appears below the First field.

▶ 6. Click the **Save** button 🖫 on the Quick Access Toolbar to save the table, and then display the table in Datasheet view.

   Trouble? If the fields in the datasheet do not appear in the same order as they did in Design view, close the Customer table, reopen it in Datasheet view, and then close the Navigation Pane. If a field that you deleted (FaxNumber, County, Web Page, or Notes) still appears in the table, close the table, open it in Design view, delete the field(s), save and close the table, open the table in Datasheet view, and then close the Navigation Pane.

With the Customer table design set, you can now enter records in it. You'll begin by entering two records, and then you'll use a different method to add the remaining records. *Note: Be sure to enter your first name and last name where indicated.*

To add two records to the Customer table:

▶ 1. Enter the following values in the columns in the first record (these values are for a residential customer with no company name):

   Customer ID = **11001**
   Company = [do not enter a value; leave blank]
   First Name = **[student's first name]**
   Last Name = **[student's last name]**
   Phone = **616-866-3901**
   Address = **49 Blackstone Dr**
   City = **Rockford**
   State = **MI**
   Zip = **49341**
   Email = **student2@milocal123.com**

▶ 2. Enter the following values in the columns in the second record, for a commercial customer:

   Customer ID = **11012**
   Company = **Grand Rapids Engineering Dept.**
   First Name = **Anthony**
   Last Name = **Rodriguez**
   Phone = **616-454-9801**
   Address = **225 Summer St**
   City = **Grand Rapids**
   State = **MI**
   Zip = **49503**
   Email = **arod24@gred11.gov**

▶ 3. Close the Customer table.

Before Belmont Landscapes decided to store data using Access, Sarah managed the company's customer data in a different system. She exported that data into a text file and now asks you to import it into the new Customer table. You can import the data contained in this text file to add the remaining records to the Customer table.

Adding Data to a Table by Importing a Text File

There are many ways to import data into an Access database. So far, you've learned how to add data to an Access table by importing an Excel spreadsheet, and you've created a new table by importing the structure of an existing table. You can also import data contained in text files.

To complete the entry of records in the Customer table, you'll import the data contained in Sarah's text file. The file is named "Customer" and is located in the Access1\Tutorial folder provided with your Data Files.

To import the data contained in the Customer text file:

▶ **1.** Click the **External Data** tab on the Ribbon.

▶ **2.** In the Import & Link group, click the **Text File** button. The Get External Data - Text File dialog box opens. This dialog box is similar to the one you used earlier when importing the Excel spreadsheet and the Access table structure.

▶ **3.** Click the **Browse** button. The File Open dialog box opens.

▶ **4.** Navigate to the **Access1\Tutorial** folder, where your starting Data Files are stored, and then double-click the **Customer** file. You return to the dialog box.

▶ **5.** Click the **Append a copy of the records to the table** option button. The box to the right of this option becomes active. Next, you need to select the table to which you want to add the data.

▶ **6.** Click the **arrow** on the box, and then click **Customer**.

▶ **7.** Click the **OK** button. The first Import Text Wizard dialog box opens. The dialog box indicates that the data to be imported is in a delimited format. A **delimited** text file is one in which fields of data are separated by a character such as a comma or a tab. In this case, the dialog box shows that data is separated by the comma character in the text file.

▶ **8.** Make sure the **Delimited** option button is selected in the dialog box, and then click the **Next** button. The second Import Text Wizard dialog box opens. See Figure 2-36.

Figure 2-36 Second Import Text Wizard dialog box

fields in the text file are separated by commas

preview of the data being imported

This dialog box asks you to confirm the delimiter character that separates the fields in the text file you're importing. Access detects that the comma character is used in the Customer text file and selects this option. The bottom area of the dialog box provides a preview of the data you're importing.

9. Make sure the **Comma** option button is selected, and then click the **Next** button. The third, and final, Import Text Wizard dialog box opens. Notice that the Import to Table box shows that the data will be imported into the Customer table.

10. Click the **Finish** button. A dialog box opens asking if you want to save the import steps. You'll only import the customer data once, so you can close the dialog box without saving the import steps.

11. Click the **Close** button in the dialog box to close it without saving the import steps.

Oren asks you to open the Customer table in Datasheet view so he can see the results of importing the text file.

To view the Customer table datasheet:

1. Open the Navigation Pane, and then double-click **Customer** to open the Customer table in Datasheet view. The Customer table contains a total of 40 records.

2. Close the Navigation Pane.

> **3.** Resize all the columns to their best fit, scrolling the table datasheet as necessary. When finished, scroll back to display the first fields in the table. See Figure 2-37.

Figure 2-37	**Customer table after importing data from the text file**

> **4.** Save and close the Customer table, and then open the Navigation Pane.

The Belmont database now contains three tables—Contract, Customer, and Invoice—and the tables contain all the necessary records. Your final task is to complete the database design by defining the necessary relationships between its tables.

Defining Table Relationships

One of the most powerful features of a relational database management system is its ability to define relationships between tables. You use a common field to relate one table to another. The process of relating tables is often called performing a **join**. When you join tables that have a common field, you can extract data from them as if they were one larger table. For example, you can join the Customer and Contract tables by using the CustomerID field in both tables as the common field. Then you can use a query, form, or report to extract selected data from each table, even though the data is contained in two separate tables, as shown in Figure 2-38. In the CustomerContracts query shown in Figure 2-38, the CustomerID, Company, First, and Last fields are from the Customer table, and the ContractNum and ContractAmt fields are from the Contract table. The joining of records is based on the common field of CustomerID. The Customer and Contract tables have a type of relationship called a one-to-many relationship.

| Figure 2-38 | One-to-many relationship and sample query |

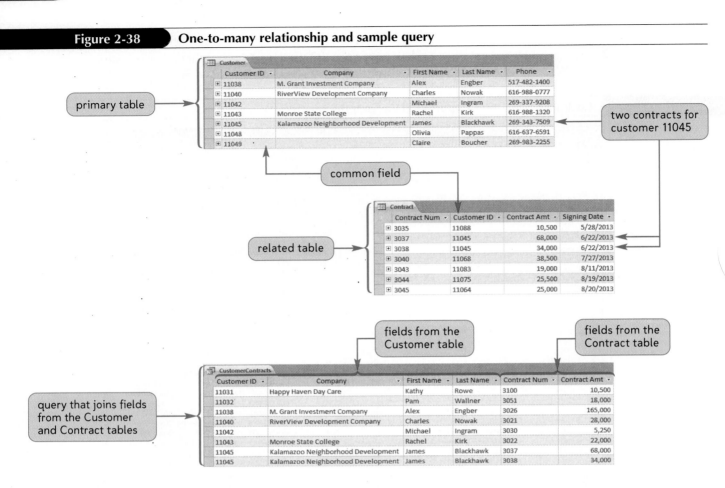

One-to-Many Relationships

As shown earlier in the Session 2.2 Visual Overview, a one-to-many relationship exists between two tables when one record in the first table matches zero, one, or many records in the second table, and when one record in the second table matches at most one record in the first table. For example, as shown in Figure 2-38, customer 11045 has two contracts in the Contract table. Other customers have one or more contracts. Every contract has a single matching customer.

Access refers to the two tables that form a relationship as the primary table and the related table. The primary table is the "one" table in a one-to-many relationship; in Figure 2-38, the Customer table is the primary table because there is only one customer for each contract. The related table is the "many" table; in Figure 2-38, the Contract table is the related table because a customer can have zero, one, or many contracts.

PROSKILLS

Problem Solving: Avoiding Inconsistent Data

Because related data is stored in two tables, inconsistencies between the tables can occur. Referring to Figure 2-38, consider the following three scenarios:

- Oren adds a record to the Contract table for a new customer, Taylor McNulty, using CustomerID 12050. Oren did not first add the new customer's information to the Customer table, so this contract does not have a matching record in the Customer table. The data is inconsistent, and the contract record is considered to be an **orphaned record**.
- In another situation, Oren changes the CustomerID in the Customer table for Kalamazoo Neighborhood Development from 11045 to 12090. Because there is no longer a customer with the CustomerID 11045 in the Customer table, this change creates two orphaned records in the Contract table, and the database is inconsistent.
- In a third scenario, Oren deletes the record for Kalamazoo Neighborhood Development, customer 11045, from the Customer table because this customer no longer does business with Belmont Landscapes. The database is again inconsistent; two records for customer 11045 in the Contract table have no matching record in the Customer table.

You can avoid these types of problems and avoid having inconsistent data in your database by specifying referential integrity (discussed next) between tables when you define their relationships.

Referential Integrity

Referential integrity is a set of rules that Access enforces to maintain consistency between related tables when you update data in a database. Specifically, the referential integrity rules are as follows:

- When you add a record to a related table, a matching record must already exist in the primary table, thereby preventing the possibility of orphaned records.
- If you attempt to change the value of the primary key in the primary table, Access prevents this change if matching records exist in a related table. However, if you choose the **Cascade Update Related Fields option**, Access permits the change in value to the primary key and changes the appropriate foreign key values in the related table, thereby eliminating the possibility of inconsistent data.
- When you attempt to delete a record in the primary table, Access prevents the deletion if matching records exist in a related table. However, if you choose the **Cascade Delete Related Records option**, Access deletes the record in the primary table and also deletes all records in related tables that have matching foreign key values.

INSIGHT

Understanding the Cascade Delete Related Records Option

Although there are advantages to using the Cascade Delete Related Records option for enforcing referential integrity, its use does present risks as well. You should rarely select the Cascade Delete Related Records option because setting this option might cause you to inadvertently delete records you did not intend to delete. It is best to use other methods for deleting records that give you more control over the deletion process.

Defining a Relationship Between Two Tables

When two tables have a common field, you can define a relationship between them in the Relationships window (see the Session 2.2 Visual Overview). Next, you need to define a one-to-many relationship between the Customer and Contract tables, with

Customer as the primary table and Contract as the related table, and with CustomerID as the common field (the primary key in the Customer table and a foreign key in the Contract table). You'll also define a one-to-many relationship between the Contract and Invoice tables, with Contract as the primary table and Invoice as the related table, and with ContractNum as the common field (the primary key in the Contract table and a foreign key in the Invoice table).

To define the one-to-many relationship between the Customer and Contract tables:

1. Click the **Database Tools** tab on the Ribbon.

2. In the Relationships group on the Database Tools tab, click the **Relationships** button. The Show Table dialog box opens. See Figure 2-39.

Figure 2-39 | Show Table dialog box

add these two tables to the Relationships window

You must add each table participating in a relationship to the Relationships window. Because the Customer table is the primary table in the relationship, you'll add it first.

TIP

You can also double-click a table in the Show Table dialog box to add it to the Relationships window.

3. Click **Customer**, and then click the **Add** button. The Customer table's field list is added to the Relationships window.

4. Click **Contract**, and then click the **Add** button. The Contract table's field list is added to the Relationships window.

5. Click the **Close** button in the Show Table dialog box to close it.

So that you can view all the fields and complete field names, you'll resize the Customer table field list.

6. Use the ↕ pointer to drag the bottom of the Customer table field list to lengthen it until the vertical scroll bar disappears and all the fields are visible.

To form the relationship between the two tables, you drag the common field of CustomerID from the primary table to the related table. Then Access opens the Edit Relationships dialog box, in which you select the relationship options for the two tables.

7. Click **CustomerID** in the Customer field list, and then drag it to **CustomerID** in the Contract field list. When you release the mouse button, the Edit Relationships dialog box opens. See Figure 2-40.

Figure 2-40 ❯ **Edit Relationships dialog box**

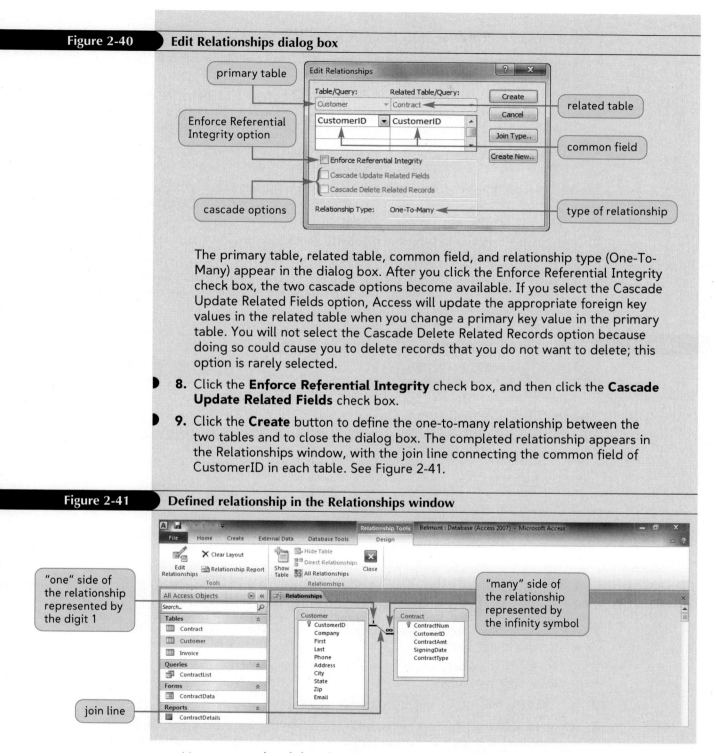

The primary table, related table, common field, and relationship type (One-To-Many) appear in the dialog box. After you click the Enforce Referential Integrity check box, the two cascade options become available. If you select the Cascade Update Related Fields option, Access will update the appropriate foreign key values in the related table when you change a primary key value in the primary table. You will not select the Cascade Delete Related Records option because doing so could cause you to delete records that you do not want to delete; this option is rarely selected.

❯ **8.** Click the **Enforce Referential Integrity** check box, and then click the **Cascade Update Related Fields** check box.

❯ **9.** Click the **Create** button to define the one-to-many relationship between the two tables and to close the dialog box. The completed relationship appears in the Relationships window, with the join line connecting the common field of CustomerID in each table. See Figure 2-41.

Figure 2-41 ❯ **Defined relationship in the Relationships window**

Now you need to define the one-to-many relationship between the Contract and Invoice tables. In this relationship, Contract is the primary ("one") table because there is at most one contract for each invoice. Invoice is the related ("many") table because there are zero, one, or many invoices set up for each contract, depending on how many project phases are involved for each contract.

To define the relationship between the Contract and Invoice tables:

1. In the Relationships group on the Design tab, click the **Show Table** button. The Show Table dialog box opens.

2. Click **Invoice** on the Tables tab, click the **Add** button, and then click the **Close** button to close the Show Table dialog box. The Invoice table's field list appears in the Relationships window to the right of the Contract table's field list.

   Because the Contract table is the primary table in this relationship, you need to drag the ContractNum field from the Contract field list to the Invoice field list.

3. Click and drag the **ContractNum** field in the Contract field list to the **ContractNum** field in the Invoice field list. When you release the mouse button, the Edit Relationships dialog box opens.

4. Click the **Enforce Referential Integrity** check box, and then click the **Cascade Update Related Fields** check box.

5. Click the **Create** button to define the one-to-many relationship between the two tables and to close the dialog box. The completed relationship appears in the Relationships window. See Figure 2-42.

Figure 2-42 | **Both relationships defined**

With both relationships defined, you have connected the data among the three tables in the Belmont database.

6. Click the **Save** button 🖫 on the Quick Access Toolbar to save the layout in the Relationships window.

7. In the Relationships group on the Design tab, click the **Close** button to close the Relationships window.

8. Click the **File** tab on the Ribbon to display Backstage view.

9. Make sure the Info tab is selected in the navigation bar, and then click the **Compact & Repair Database** button. Access compacts and repairs the Belmont database.

10. Click the **File** tab, and then click **Close Database** to close the Belmont database.

Session 2.2 Quick Check

1. To insert a check mark in an empty check box for a Yes/No field, you press the _____.

2. What is the keyboard shortcut for inserting the value from the same field in the previous record into the current record?

3. _____ data is a process that allows you to copy the data from a source without having to open the source file.

4. The _____ gallery allows you to add a group of related fields to a table at the same time, rather than adding each field to the table individually.

5. What is the effect of deleting a field from a table structure?

6. A(n) _____ text file is one in which fields of data are separated by a character such as a comma or a tab.

7. The _____ is the "one" table in a one-to-many relationship, and the _____ is the "many" table in the relationship.

8. _____ is a set of rules that Access enforces to maintain consistency between related tables when you update data in a database.

PRACTICE

ctice the skills
ou learned in
the tutorial using
the same case
scenario.

Review Assignments

Data Files needed for the Review Assignments: Supplier.accdb (*cont. from Tutorial 1*) and Goods.xlsx

In addition to tracking information about the suppliers Belmont Landscapes works with, Oren also wants to track information about their products. He asks you to create a new table in the Supplier database by completing the following steps:

1. Open the **Supplier** database, which you created and stored in the Access1\Review folder in Tutorial 1.
2. Open the **Company** table in Design view, and set the field properties as shown in Figure 2-43.

Figure 2-43   Field properties for the Company table

Field Name	Data Type	Description	Field Size	Other
CompanyID	Text	Primary key	6	Caption = Company ID
Company	Text		50	Caption = Company Name
Product	Text		40	Caption = Product Type
Address	Text		35	
City	Text		25	
State	Text		2	
Zip	Text		10	
Phone	Text		14	
ContactFirst	Text		20	Caption = Contact First Name
ContactLast	Text		25	Caption = Contact Last Name
InitialContact	Date/Time			Format = Short Date
				Caption = Initial Contact Date

3. Save and close the Company table. Click the Yes button when a message appears indicating some data might be lost. Switch to Datasheet view and resize columns, as necessary, to their best fit. Then save and close the Company table.
4. Create a new table in Design view, using the table design shown in Figure 2-44.

Figure 2-44   Design for the Product table

Field Name	Data Type	Description	Field Size	Other
ProductID	Text	Primary key	4	Caption = Product ID
CompanyID	Text	Foreign key	6	Caption = Company ID
ProductType	Text		35	Caption = Product Type
Price	Currency			Format = Standard
				Decimal Places = 2
Color	Text		15	
Size	Text		15	
Material	Text		30	
Weight	Number		Single	Caption = Weight in Lbs
Discount	Yes/No			Caption = Discount Offered
				Format = Yes/No

5. Specify ProductID as the primary key, and then save the table as **Product**.
6. Modify the table structure by adding a new field named **Unit** (data type: Text, field size: **15**) between the Price and Color fields. Move the Size field so that it follows the Material field.
7. Enter the records shown in Figure 2-45 in the Product table. When finished, close the Product table.

Figure 2-45 | **Records for the Product table**

Product ID	Company ID	Product Type	Price	Unit	Color	Material	Size	Weight in Lbs	Discount Offered
5306	GEN359	Pine mulch	23.35	Cubic yard	Dark brown	Softwoods-pine			Y
5013	HOL207	Small bench	712.00	Each	Green	Steel and cast iron	8 x 2 feet	266	N

---

8. Use the Import Spreadsheet Wizard to add data to the Product table. The data you need to import is contained in the Goods workbook, which is an Excel file located in the Access1\Review folder provided with your Data Files.

   a. Specify the Goods workbook as the source of the data.

   b. Select the option for appending the data.

   c. Select Product as the table.

   d. In the Import Spreadsheet Wizard dialog boxes, make sure Access confirms that the first row contains column headings, and import to the Product table. Do not save the import steps.

9. Open the **Product** table in Datasheet view and resize all columns to their best fit. Then save and close the Product table.

10. Define a one-to-many relationship between the primary Company table and the related Product table. Select the referential integrity option and the cascade updates option for the relationship.

11. Save the changes to the Relationships window and close it, compact and repair the Supplier database, and then close the database.

Case Problem 1

If you have a SAM 2010 user profile, your instructor may have assigned an autogradable version of this assignment. If so, log into the SAM 2010 Web site at www.cengage.com/sam2010 to download the instructions and start files.

APPLY

Data Files needed for this Case Problem: Pinehill.accdb (*cont. from Tutorial 1*), **Music.accdb, Lessons.xlsx, and Student.txt**

Pine Hill Music School Yuka Koyama uses the Pinehill database to maintain information about the students, teachers, and contracts for her music school. Yuka asks you to help her build the database by updating one table and creating two new tables. Complete the following steps:

1. Open the **Pinehill** database, which you created and stored in the Access1\Case1 folder in Tutorial 1.

2. Open the **Teacher** table in Design view, and set the field properties as shown in Figure 2-46.

Figure 2-46 | **Field properties for the Teacher table**

Field Name	Data Type	Description	Field Size	Other
TeacherID	Text	Primary key	7	Caption = Teacher ID
FirstName	Text		20	Caption = First Name
LastName	Text		25	Caption = Last Name
Degree	Text		3	
School	Text		50	
HireDate	Date/Time			Format = Short Date
				Caption = Hire Date

---

3. Add a new field as the last field in the Teacher table with the field name **Beginners**, the Yes/No data type, a Format property of Yes/No, and a Caption property of **Takes Beginners**.

4. Save the Teacher table. Click the Yes button when a message appears indicating some data might be lost.

5. In the datasheet, resize the Takes Beginners column to best fit, and then specify that the following teachers can take beginners: Schwartz, Eberle, Norris, Tanaka, Culbertson, and Mueller.

6. Save and close the Teacher table.

7. Yuka created a table named Student in the Music database that is located in the Access1\Case1 folder provided with your Data Files. Import the structure of the Student table in the Music database into a new table named Student in the Pinehill database. Do not save the import steps.

8. Open the **Student** table in Datasheet view, and then add the following two fields to the end of the table: **BirthDate** (Date/Time field) and **Gender** (Text field).

9. Use the Phone Quick Start selection in the Data Type gallery to add four fields related to phones between the Zip and BirthDate fields. (*Hint:* Be sure to make the BirthDate field the active field before adding the new fields.)

10. Display the Student table in Design view, delete the BusinessPhone and FaxNumber fields, and then save and close the Student table.

11. Modify the design of the Student table so that it matches the design in Figure 2-47, including the revised field names and data types.

Figure 2-47	Field properties for the Student table

Field Name	Data Type	Description	Field Size	Other
StudentID	Text	Primary key	7	Caption = Student ID
LastName	Text		25	Caption = Last Name
FirstName	Text		20	Caption = First Name
Address	Text		35	
City	Text		25	
State	Text		2	
Zip	Text		10	
HomePhone	Text		14	
MobilePhone	Text		14	
BirthDate	Date/Time			Format = Short Date
				Caption = Birth Date
Gender	Text	F(emale), M(ale)	1	

12. Move the LastName field so it follows the FirstName field.

13. Save your changes to the table design, add the records shown in Figure 2-48 to the Student table, and then close the Student table.

Figure 2-48	Records for the Student table

Student ID	First Name	Last Name	Address	City	State	Zip	Home Phone	Mobile Phone	Birth Date	Gender
APP7509	Sam	Applegate	15675 SW Greens Way	Portland	OR	97224	503-968-2245	503-968-0091	10/10/1996	M
BAR7544	Andrea	Barreau	7660 SW 135th Ave	Beaverton	OR	97008	503-579-2227	503-579-8754	11/28/1999	F

14. Yuka exported the student data that she was maintaining in another computer system to a text file, and she asks you to add this data to the Student table. The data you need to import is contained in the Student text file (located in the Access1\Case1 folder provided with your Data Files).
   a. Specify the Student text file as the source of the data.
   b. Select the option for appending the data to the table.

    c. Select Student as the table.

    d. In the Import Text Wizard dialog boxes, choose the option to import delimited data, to use a comma delimiter, and to import the data into the Student table. Do not save the import steps.

15. Open the **Student** table in Datasheet view, resize columns in the datasheet to their best fit (as necessary), and then save and close the table.

16. Create a new table in Design view, using the table design shown in Figure 2-49.

Figure 2-49 > **Design for the Contract table**

Field Name	Data Type	Description	Field Size	Other
ContractID	Text	Primary key	4	Caption = Contract ID
StudentID	Text	Foreign key	7	Caption = Student ID
TeacherID	Text	Foreign key	7	Caption = Teacher ID
LessonType	Text		25	Caption = Lesson Type
LessonLength	Number	30 or 60 minutes	Integer	Caption = Lesson Length
LessonCost	Currency			Format = Currency Decimal Places = 0 Caption = Lesson Monthly Cost
RentalCost	Currency	Monthly rental charge for instrument		Format = Currency Decimal Places = 0 Caption = Monthly Rental Cost

17. Specify ContractID as the primary key, and then save the table using the name **Contract**.

18. Switch to Datasheet view, and then use the Start and End Dates Quick Start selection in the Data Type gallery to add two Date/Time fields between the TeacherID and LessonType fields. (*Hint:* Be sure to make the LessonType field the active field before adding the new fields.)

19. Switch to Design view, specify the Short Date format for the StartDate and EndDate fields, change the field captions to **Contract Start Date** and **Contract End Date** (respectively), and then save and close the Contract table.

⊕ EXPLORE 20. Use the Import Spreadsheet Wizard to add data to the Contract table. The data you need to import is contained in the Lessons workbook, which is an Excel file located in the Access1\Case1 folder provided with your Data Files.

    a. Specify the Lessons workbook as the source of the data.

    b. Select the option for appending the data to the table.

    c. Select Contract as the table.

    d. In the Import Spreadsheet Wizard dialog boxes, choose the Sheet1 worksheet, make sure Access confirms that the first row contains column headings, and import to the Contract table. Do not save the import steps.

21. Open the **Contract** table and add the records shown in Figure 2-50. (*Hint:* Use the New button in the Records group on the Home tab to add a new record.)

Figure 2-50 > **Records for the Contract table**

Contract ID	Student ID	Teacher ID	Contract Start Date	Contract End Date	Lesson Type	Lesson Length	Lesson Monthly Cost	Monthly Rental Cost
3176	VAR7527	91-0178	3/21/2013	3/21/2014	Violin	30	$140	$35
3179	MCE7551	70-4490	6/1/2013	6/1/2014	Guitar	60	$200	$0

22. Resize columns in the datasheet to their best fit (as necessary), and then save and close the Contract table.

23. Define the one-to-many relationships between the database tables as follows: between the primary Student table and the related Contract table, and between the primary Teacher table and the related Contract table. Select the referential integrity option and the cascade updates option for each relationship.

24. Save the changes to the Relationships window and close it, compact and repair the Pinehill database, and then close the database.

Use the Import Spreadsheet Wizard to create a table to store data about fitness center members.

CHALLENGE

Case Problem 2

Data Files needed for this Case Problem: Fitness.accdb (*cont. from Tutorial 1*) and Center.xlsx

Parkhurst Health & Fitness Center   Martha Parkhurst uses the Fitness database to track information about members who join the center and the programs in which each member is enrolled. She asks you to help her maintain this database. Complete the following:

1. Open the **Fitness** database, which you created and stored in the Access1\Case2 folder in Tutorial 1.

2. Open the **Program** table in Design view, and change the following field properties:
   a. ProgramID: Enter **Primary key** for the description, change the field size to **3**, and enter **Program ID** for the caption.
   b. ProgramType: Change the field size to **40** and enter **Program Type** for the caption.
   c. MonthlyFee: Change the format to **Standard** and enter **Monthly Fee** for the caption.
   d. PhysicalRequired: Change the data type to Yes/No, the Format property to Yes/No, and enter **Physical Required** for the caption.

3. Save and close the Program table. Click the Yes button when a message appears indicating some data might be lost.

⊕ **EXPLORE**   4. Use the Import Spreadsheet Wizard to create a table in the Fitness database. As the source of the data, specify the Center workbook, located in the Access1\Case2 folder provided with your Data Files. Select the option to import the source data into a new table in the current database, and then click the OK button.

⊕ **EXPLORE**   5. Complete the Import Spreadsheet Wizard dialog boxes as follows:
   a. Select Sheet1 as the worksheet you want to import.
   b. Accept the option specifying that the first row contains column headings.
   c. Accept the field options the wizard suggests, and do not skip any fields.
   d. Choose MemberID as your own primary key.
   e. Import the data to a table named **Member**, and do not save your import steps.

6. Open the **Member** table in Design view, and then delete the InitiationFeeWaived field.

7. Modify the design of the Member table so that it matches the design shown in Figure 2-51. (*Hint*: For Text fields, delete any formats specified in the Format property boxes.)

Figure 2-51   **Design for the Member table**

Field Name	Data Type	Description	Field Size	Other
MemberID	Text	Primary key	4	Caption = Member ID
ProgramID	Text	Foreign key	3	Caption = Program ID
First	Text		18	Caption = First Name
Last	Text		18	Caption = Last Name
Street	Text		30	
City	Text		24	
State	Text		2	
Zip	Text		10	
Phone	Text		14	
DateJoined	Date/Time			Format = Short Date
				Caption = Date Joined
Expiration	Date/Time	Date when membership expires		Format = Short Date
				Caption = Expiration Date
Status	Text	Active, Inactive, or On Hold	8	Caption = Membership Status

8. Save the Member table. Click the Yes button when a message appears indicating some data might be lost.

✥ EXPLORE

9. The Default Value property for a field allows you to specify the value that should be entered, by default, for that field for each new record you enter in the table. Specifying a default value can save you time if most of the records you enter will include that value for the field. Set the Default Value property for the Status field to **"Active"** (including the quotation marks). Save and close the Member table.

10. Open the **Member** table in Datasheet view and confirm that the InitiationFeeWaived field was removed from the table. If not, open the table in Design view again, repeat the step to delete the InitiationFeeWaived field, and then save and close the table.

11. Add the records shown in Figure 2-52 to the Member table. (*Hint*: Use the New button in the Records group on the Home tab to add a new record.) Be sure to enter your first and last names in the appropriate fields for the first new record added. Note the default field value of "Active" in the Membership Status column as you enter the new records.

Figure 2-52   **Records for the Member table**

Member ID	Program ID	First Name	Last Name	Street	City	State	Zip	Phone	Date Joined	Expiration Date	Membership Status
1170	203	Student First	Student Last	40 Green Boulevard	Bon Air	VA	23235	804-323-6824	6/3/2013	12/3/2013	Active
1172	211	Ed	Curran	25 Fairway Drive	Richmond	VA	23220	804-674-0227	11/16/2013	11/16/2014	Active

12. Resize columns in the datasheet to their best fit (as necessary), and then save and close the table.

13. Define a one-to-many relationship between the primary Program table and the related Member table. Select the referential integrity option and the cascade updates option for this relationship.

14. Save the changes to the Relationships window and close it, compact and repair the Fitness database, and then close the database.

Use your skills to create and modify tables for a recycling agency.

APPLY

Case Problem 3

Data Files needed for this Case Problem: Agency.txt, Rossi.accdb (*cont. from Tutorial 1*), Gifts.xlsx, and Recycle.accdb

Rossi Recycling Group   Tom Rossi uses the Rossi database to maintain information about the donors, agencies, and donations to his not-for-profit agency. Tom asks you to help him maintain the database by updating one table and creating two new ones. Complete the following steps:

1. Open the **Rossi** database, which you created and stored in the Access1\Case3 folder in Tutorial 1.
2. Open the **Donor** table in Design view, and change the following field properties:
    a. DonorID: Enter **Primary key** for the description, change the field size to **5**, and enter **Donor ID** for the caption.
    b. Title: Change the field size to **4**.
    c. FirstName: Change the field size to **20** and enter **First Name** for the caption.
    d. LastName: Change the field size to **25** and enter **Last Name** for the caption.
    e. Phone: Change the field size to **14.**
3. Save and close the Donor table. Click the Yes button when a message appears indicating some data might be lost.
4. Tom created a table named Agency in the Recycle database that is located in the Access1\Case3 folder provided with your Data Files. Import the structure of the Agency table in the Recycle database into a new table named Agency in the Rossi database. Do not save the import steps.
5. Open the Agency table in Datasheet view, and then delete the following fields from the table: Fax Number, Mobile Phone, and Notes.
6. Rename the ID field to **AgencyID**, and change its data type to Text.
7. Use the Address Quick Start selection in the Data Type gallery to add five fields between the First Name and Phone fields. (*Hint:* Be sure to make the Phone field the active field before adding the new fields.)
8. Switch to Design view, and then modify the Agency table so that it matches the design shown in Figure 2-53, including the field names and their order. Make sure the AgencyID field is specified as the primary key. Also, be sure to delete the CountryRegion field from the table, and delete the Caption property values for the fields added with the Address Quick Start selection.

| Figure 2-53 | Design for the Agency table |

Field Name	Data Type	Description	Field Size	Other
AgencyID	Text	Primary key	3	Caption = Agency ID
Agency	Text		40	Caption = Agency Name
FirstName	Text		20	Caption = Contact First Name
LastName	Text		25	Caption = Contact Last Name
Address	Text		30	
City	Text		24	
State	Text		2	
Zip	Text		10	
Phone	Text		14	

9. Save your changes to the table design, add the records shown in Figure 2-54 to the Agency table, and then close the Agency table.

Figure 2-54   **Records for the Agency table**

Agency ID	Agency Name	Contact First Name	Contact Last Name	Address	City	State	Zip	Phone
K64	Community Development	Jerri	Clarkson	223 Penn Ave	Salina	KS	67401	785-309-3351
K82	SeniorCare Program	Todd	Groverman	718 N Walnut	McPherson	KS	67460	620-241-3668

10. Tom exported the agency data that he was maintaining in another computer system to a text file, and he asks you to add this data to the Agency table. The data you need to import is contained in the Agency text file (located in the Access1\Case3 folder provided with your Data Files).

    a. Specify the Agency text file as the source of the data.

    b. Select the option for appending the data to the table.

    c. Select Agency as the table.

    d. In the Import Text Wizard dialog boxes, choose the options to import delimited data, to use a comma delimiter, and to import the data into the Agency table. Do not save the import steps.

11. Resize columns in the Agency datasheet to their best fit (as necessary), and then save and close the table.

12. Use Design view to create a table using the table design shown in Figure 2-55.

Figure 2-55   **Design for the Donation table**

Field Name	Data Type	Description	Field Size	Other
DonationID	Text	Primary key	4	Caption = Donation ID
DonorID	Text	Foreign key	5	Caption = Donor ID
AgencyID	Text	Foreign key	3	Caption = Agency ID
DonationDate	Date/Time			Format = Short Date
				Caption = Donation Date
Description	Text		50	Caption = Donation Description
DonationValue	Currency	Cash amount donated or estimated value of goods donated		Format = Currency
				Decimal Places = 2
				Caption = Donation Value
Pickup	Yes/No			Caption = Pickup Required
				Format = Yes/No

13. Specify DonationID as the primary key, save the table as **Donation**, and then close the table.

EXPLORE   14. Use the Import Spreadsheet Wizard to add data to the Donation table. The data you need to import is contained in the Gifts workbook, which is an Excel file located in the Access1\Case3 folder provided with your Data Files.

    a. Specify the Gifts workbook as the source of the data.

    b. Select the option for appending the data to the table.

    c. Select Donation as the table.

    d. In the Import Spreadsheet Wizard dialog boxes, choose the Sheet1 worksheet, make sure Access confirms that the first row contains column headings, and import to the Donation table. Do not save the import steps.

15. Open the **Donation** table, and add the records shown in Figure 2-56. (*Hint:* Use the New button in the Records group on the Home tab to add a new record.)

			Figure 2-56		Records for the Donation table		

Donation ID	Donor ID	Agency ID	Donation Date	Donation Description	Donation Value	Pickup Required
2117	36012	K82	02/20/2013	Cash	$50.00	No
2122	36016	N33	03/22/2013	Cash	$35.00	No

16. Resize columns in the datasheet to their best fit (as necessary), and then save and close the table.

17. Define the one-to-many relationships between the database tables as follows: between the primary Donor table and the related Donation table, and between the primary Agency table and the related Donation table. Select the referential integrity option and the cascade updates option for each relationship.

18. Save the changes to the Relationships window and close it, compact and repair the Rossi database, and then close the database.

Explore some new skills to finish creating a database for a luxury rental company.

CHALLENGE

Case Problem 4

Data Files needed for this Case Problem: Bookings.txt, GEM.accdb (*cont. from Tutorial 1*), and Overseas.accdb

GEM Ultimate Vacations   Griffin and Emma MacElroy use the GEM database to track the data about the services they provide to the clients who book luxury vacations through their agency. They ask you to help them maintain this database. Complete the following steps:

1. Open the **GEM** database, which you created and stored in the Access1\Case4 folder in Tutorial 1.

2. Open the **Guest** table in Design view and change the following field properties:
   a. GuestID: Enter **Primary key** for the description, change the field size to **3**, and enter **Guest ID** for the caption.
   b. GuestFirst: Change the field size to **20** and enter **Guest First Name** for the caption.
   c. GuestLast: Change the field size to **25** and enter **Guest Last Name** for the caption.
   d. Address: Change the field size to **32**.
   e. City: Change the field size to **24**.
   f. State/Prov: Change the field size to **2**.
   g. PostalCode: Change the field size to **10** and enter **Postal Code** for the caption.
   h. Country: Change the field size to **15**.
   i. Phone: Change the field size to **14**.

3. Save the Guest table, click the Yes button when a message appears indicating some data might be lost, resize the Guest First Name and Guest Last Name columns in Datasheet view to their best fit, and then save and close the table.

⊕ EXPLORE

4. In addition to importing the structure of an existing Access table, you can also import both the structure and the data contained in a table to create a new table. Import the Rentals table structure and data from the Overseas database into a new table in the GEM database as follows:
   a. Click the External Data tab on the Ribbon, and then click the Access button in the Import & Link group.
   b. As the source of the data, specify the Overseas database, located in the Access1\Case4 folder provided with your Data Files.

c. Select the option button to import tables, queries, forms, reports, macros, and modules into the current database, and then click the OK button.

d. In the Import Objects dialog box, click Rentals, click the Options button, and then make sure that the correct option is selected to import the table's data and structure (definition).

e. Do not save your import steps.

⊕ EXPLORE

5. Right-click the Rentals table in the Navigation Pane, click Rename on the shortcut menu, and then enter **Property** as the new name for this table.

6. Open the **Property** table in Design view, delete the VIP Program field, and then move the PropertyType field so that it appears between the Sleeps and Description fields. Make sure that the PropertyID field is specified as the table's primary key.

7. Change the following properties:

a. PropertyID: Change the data type to Text, change the field size to **4**, and enter **Property ID** for the caption.

b. PropertyName: Enter **Property Name** for the caption.

c. NightlyRate: Enter **Nightly Rate** for the caption.

d. PropertyType: Enter **Property Type** for the caption.

8. Save the modified table and then display it in Datasheet view. Resize all datasheet columns to their best fit, and then save and close the table.

9. Use Design view to create a table using the table design shown in Figure 2-57.

Figure 2-57	Design for the Reservation table

Field Name	Data Type	Description	Field Size	Other
ReservationID	Text	Primary key	3	Caption = Reservation ID
GuestID	Text	Foreign key	3	Caption = Guest ID
PropertyID	Text	Foreign key	4	Caption = Property ID
StartDate	Date/Time			Caption = Start Date
EndDate	Date/Time			Caption = End Date
People	Number	Number of people in the party	Integer	
Rate	Currency	Rate per day; includes any discounts or promotions		Format = Currency
				Decimal Places = 0
				Caption = Rental Rate

10. Specify ReservationID as the primary key, and then save the table as **Reservation**.

⊕ EXPLORE

11. Refer back to Figure 2-14 to review the custom date formats. Change the Format property of the StartDate and EndDate fields to a custom format that displays dates in a format similar to 11/23/13. Save and close the Reservation table.

12. Griffin exported the reservation data that he was maintaining in another computer system to a text file, and he asks you to add this data to the Reservation table. The data you need to import is contained in the Bookings text file (located in the Access1\Case4 folder provided with your Data Files).

a. Specify the Bookings text file as the source of the data.

b. Select the option for appending the data to the table.

c. Select Reservation as the table.

d. In the Import Text Wizard dialog boxes, choose the option to import delimited data, to use a comma delimiter, and to import the data into the Reservation table.

e. Do not save the import steps.

13. Resize columns in the **Reservation** table datasheet to their best fit (as necessary), and then save and close the table.

14. Define the one-to-many relationships between the database tables as follows: between the primary Guest table and the related Reservation table, and between the primary Property table and the related Reservation table. Select the referential integrity option and the cascade updates option for each relationship.

15. Save the changes to the Relationships window and close it, compact and repair the GEM database, and then close the database.

SAM: Skills Assessment Manager

For current SAM information, including versions and content details, visit SAM Central (http://samcentral.course.com). If you have a SAM user profile, you may have access to hands-on instruction, practice, and assessment of the skills covered in this tutorial. Since various versions of SAM are supported throughout the life of this text, check with your instructor for the correct instructions and URL/Web site for accessing assignments.

ENDING DATA FILES

Access1 → Tutorial — Belmont.accdb

Review — Supplier.accdb

Case1 — Pinehill.accdb

Case2 — Fitness.accdb

Case3 — Rossi.accdb

Case4 — GEM.accdb

ACCESS

Session 3.1
- Find, modify, and delete records in a table
- Learn how to use the Query window in Design view
- Create, run, and save queries
- Update data using a query datasheet
- Create a query based on multiple tables
- Sort data in a query
- Filter data in a query

Session 3.2
- Specify an exact match condition in a query
- Change the font size and alternate row color in a datasheet
- Use a comparison operator in a query to match a range of values
- Use the And and Or logical operators in queries
- Create and format a calculated field in a query
- Perform calculations in a query using aggregate functions and record group calculations
- Change the display of database objects in the Navigation Pane

Maintaining and Querying a Database

Updating and Retrieving Information About Customers, Contracts, and Invoices

Case | *Belmont Landscapes*

At a recent meeting, Oren Belmont and his staff discussed the importance of maintaining accurate information about the firm's customers, contracts, and invoices, and regularly monitoring the business activities of Belmont Landscapes. For example, Sarah Fisher and the office staff need to make sure they have up-to-date contact information, such as phone numbers and email addresses, for all the firm's customers. They also must monitor the invoice activity to ensure that invoices are paid on time and in full. Taylor Sico, the marketing manager at Belmont Landscapes, and her marketing staff track customer activity to develop new strategies for promoting the services provided by Belmont Landscapes. In addition, Oren is interested in analyzing other aspects of the business related to contracts and finances. You can satisfy all these informational needs for Belmont Landscapes by updating data in the Belmont database and by creating and using queries that retrieve information from the database.

STARTING DATA FILES

Access1 →	Tutorial	Review	Case1	Case2	Case3	Case4
	Belmont.accdb *(cont.)*	Supplier.accdb *(cont.)*	Pinehill.accdb *(cont.)*	Fitness.accdb *(cont.)*	Rossi.accdb *(cont.)*	GEM.accdb *(cont.)*

SESSION 3.1 VISUAL OVERVIEW

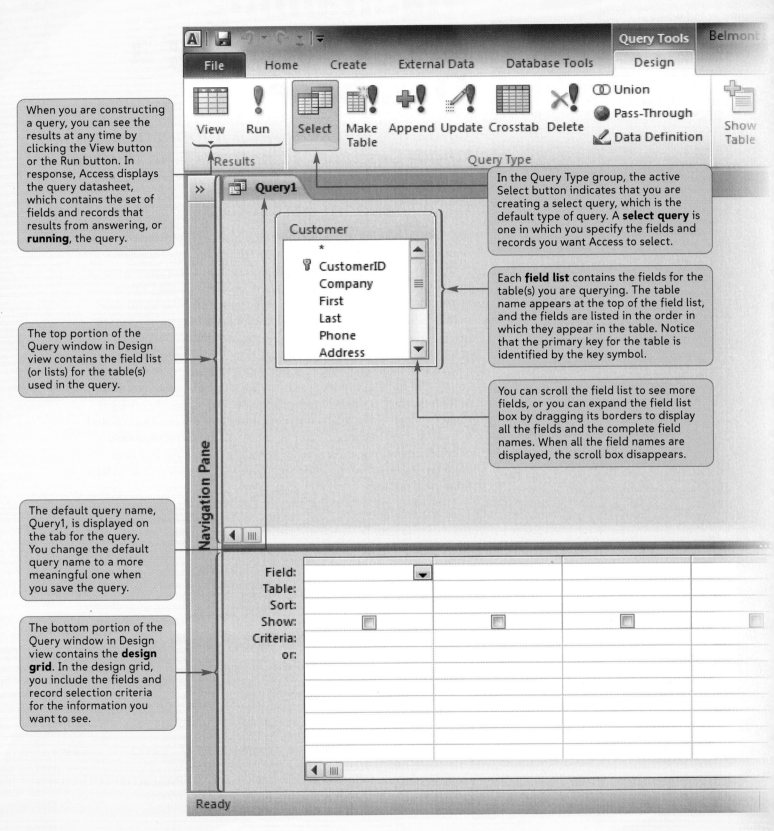

When you are constructing a query, you can see the results at any time by clicking the View button or the Run button. In response, Access displays the query datasheet, which contains the set of fields and records that results from answering, or **running**, the query.

In the Query Type group, the active Select button indicates that you are creating a select query, which is the default type of query. A **select query** is one in which you specify the fields and records you want Access to select.

Each **field list** contains the fields for the table(s) you are querying. The table name appears at the top of the field list, and the fields are listed in the order in which they appear in the table. Notice that the primary key for the table is identified by the key symbol.

The top portion of the Query window in Design view contains the field list (or lists) for the table(s) used in the query.

You can scroll the field list to see more fields, or you can expand the field list box by dragging its borders to display all the fields and the complete field names. When all the field names are displayed, the scroll box disappears.

The default query name, Query1, is displayed on the tab for the query. You change the default query name to a more meaningful one when you save the query.

The bottom portion of the Query window in Design view contains the **design grid**. In the design grid, you include the fields and record selection criteria for the information you want to see.

Ready

QUERY WINDOW IN DESIGN VIEW

: Database (Access 2007) – Microsoft Access

Insert Rows   **Insert Columns**   **Property Sheet**

Delete Rows   **Delete Columns**   **Table Names**

Builder   **Return:** All   Σ   **[?]**

Totals   Parameters

Query Setup   Show/Hide

The Ribbon displays the Query Tools Design tab with options for creating and running queries. Note the Query Type group on the Design tab; it provides buttons you can click to create various types of queries.

In Design view, you specify the data you want to view by constructing a query by example. When you use **query by example (QBE)**, you give Access an example of the information you are requesting. Access then retrieves the information that precisely matches your example.

Each column in the design grid contains specifications about a field you will use in the query. You can choose a single field for your query by double-clicking the field name to place it in the next available design grid column.

The view buttons on the status bar allow you to change to a different view; for example, you can click the Datasheet View button to run the query and display the results in Datasheet view.

Updating a Database

Updating, or **maintaining**, a database is the process of adding, modifying, and deleting records in database tables to keep them current and accurate. After reviewing the data in the Belmont database, Sarah identified some changes that need to be made to the data. She would like you to modify the field values in one record in the Customer table, and then to delete a record in the Contract table.

Modifying Records

To modify the field values in a record, you must first make the record the current record. Then you position the insertion point in the field value to make minor changes or select the field value to replace it entirely. In Tutorial 1, you used the mouse with the scroll bars and the navigation buttons to navigate the records in a datasheet. You can also use keystroke combinations and the F2 key to navigate a datasheet and to select field values. The **F2 key** is a toggle that you use to switch between navigation mode and editing mode:

- In **navigation mode**, Access selects an entire field value. If you type while you are in navigation mode, your typed entry replaces the highlighted field value.
- In **editing mode**, you can insert or delete characters in a field value based on the location of the insertion point.

Figure 3-1 shows some of the navigation mode and editing mode keystroke techniques.

| **Figure 3-1** | Navigation mode and editing mode keystroke techniques |

Press	To Move the Selection in Navigation Mode	To Move the Insertion Point in Editing Mode
←	Left one field value at a time	Left one character at a time
→	Right one field value at a time	Right one character at a time
Home	Left to the first field value in the record	To the left of the first character in the field value
End	Right to the last field value in the record	To the right of the last character in the field value
↑ or ↓	Up or down one record at a time	Up or down one record at a time and switch to navigation mode
Tab or Enter	Right one field value at a time	Right one field value at a time and switch to navigation mode
Ctrl+Home	To the first field value in the first record	To the left of the first character in the field value
Ctrl+End	To the last field value in the last record	To the right of the last character in the field value

The Customer table record Sarah wants you to change is for Walker Investment Company, one of Belmont Landscapes' commercial customers. The company recently moved its office from Grand Rapids to Battle Creek, so you need to update the Customer table record with the new address and phone information.

To open the Belmont database and modify the record:

▶ **1.** Start Access and open the **Belmont** database located in the Access1\Tutorial folder.

   Trouble? If the Security Warning is displayed below the Ribbon, click the Enable Content button next to the Security Warning.

▶ **2.** Open the **Customer** table in Datasheet view. The first value for the CustomerID field, 11001, is highlighted, indicating that the table is in navigation mode.

   The record you need to modify is near the end of the table and has a CustomerID field value of 11087.

▶ **3.** Press the **Ctrl+End** keys. Access displays records from the end of the table and selects the last field value in the last record, record 40. This field value is for the Email field.

▶ **4.** Press the **Home** key. The first field value in the last record is now selected. This field value is for the CustomerID field.

▶ **5.** Press the ↑ key. The CustomerID field value for the previous record, CustomerID 11087, is selected. This record is the one you need to change.

▶ **6.** Press the **Tab** key four times to move to the Phone field and select its field value, type **269-963-0190**, press the **Tab** key, type **1752 S Main St**, press the **Tab** key, type **Battle Creek**, press the **Tab** key twice, type **49014**, and then press the **Tab** key. The changes to the record are complete. See Figure 3-2.

Figure 3-2	Table after changing field values in a record

TIP

Access saves changes to field values when you move to a new field or another record, or when you close the table. You don't have to click the Save button to save changes to field values or records.

field values changed

⊞ Russell	616-940-3380	722 Beechwood Dr	East Grand Rapids	MI	49506	srussell3@dnd57.org
⊞ Van Dousen	616-392-4629	249 W 11th St	Holland	MI	49424	jvdousen2@tulips3.com
⊞ Williams	517-337-0990	1003 Albert Ave	East Lansing	MI	48823	jwilliams94@hsc7.edu
⊞ DeSantis	616-866-4882	78 Spring St	Rockford	MI	49341	cdesantis9@milocal123.com
⊞ Phillips	616-637-5408	39 Water St	South Haven	MI	49090	ephillips8@milocal123.com
⊞ Belanger	269-963-0190	1752 S Main St	Battle Creek	MI	49014	nbelanger4@wic88.com
⊞ Kervin	616-454-3327	333 Pearl St	Grand Rapids	MI	49503	skervin3@wcpf47.org

Record: ◄ ◄ 39 of 40 ► ►I ►* ☒ No Filter Search

Datasheet View

▶ **7.** Close the Customer table.

   The next update Sarah asks you to make is to delete a record in the Contract table. The customer who signed contract number 3101 owns a chain of small restaurants and had planned to renovate the landscaping at each restaurant site. His plans have changed for one of these sites and he has cancelled the contract, so the record needs to be deleted. When you are maintaining database tables, you first need to find the data to change.

Finding Data in a Table

Access provides options you can use to locate specific field values in a table. Instead of scrolling the Contract table datasheet to find the contract that you need to delete—the record for contract number 3101—you can use the Find command to find the record. The **Find command** allows you to search a table or query datasheet, or a form, to locate a specific field value or part of a field value. This feature is particularly useful when searching a table that contains a large number of records.

To search for the record in the Contract table:

▶ 1. Open the **Contract** table in Datasheet view. The first field value for the ContractNum field, 3011, is selected. You need to search the ContractNum field to find the record containing the value 3101, so the insertion point is already correctly positioned in the field you want to search.

▶ 2. In the Find group on the Home tab, click the **Find** button. The Find and Replace dialog box opens. See Figure 3-3.

Figure 3-3	Find and Replace dialog box

value selected in the table datasheet

specifies that the current field will be searched

specifies that Access will search for a match to the entire field value

specifies that all fields in the table will be searched

The field value 3011 appears in the Find What box because this value is selected in the table datasheet. The Look In box indicates that the current field will be searched for the value. The Match box indicates that the Find command will match the whole field value, which is correct for your search. You also can choose to search for only part of a field value, such as when you need to find all contract numbers that start with a certain value. The Search box indicates that all the records in the table will be searched for the value you want to find. You also can choose to search up or down from the currently selected record.

Trouble? Some of the settings in your dialog box might be different from those shown in Figure 3-3 depending on the last search performed on the computer you're using. If so, change the settings so that they match those in the figure.

▶ 3. Make sure the value 3011 is selected in the Find What box, type **3101** to replace the selected value, and then click the **Find Next** button. Access scrolls the datasheet to record 59 and selects the field value you specified.

▶ 4. Click the **Cancel** button to close the Find and Replace dialog box.

Deleting Records

To delete a record, you need to select the record in Datasheet view, and then delete it using the Delete button in the Records group on the Home tab, or the Delete Record option on the shortcut menu.

Deleting a Record

- With the table open in Datasheet view, click the row selector for the record you want to delete.
- In the Records group on the Home tab, click the Delete button (or right-click the row selector for the record, and then click Delete Record on the shortcut menu).
- In the dialog box asking you to confirm the deletion, click the Yes button.

Now that you have found the record with contract number 3101, you can delete it. To delete a record, you must first select the entire row for the record.

To delete the record:

1. Click the row selector for the record containing the ContractNum field value **3101**, which should still be highlighted. The entire row is selected.

2. In the Records group on the Home tab, click the **Delete** button. A dialog box opens and indicates that you cannot delete the record because the Invoice table contains records that are related to ContractNum 3101. Recall that you defined a one-to-many relationship between the Contract and Invoice tables and enforced referential integrity. When you try to delete a record in the primary table (Contract), Access prevents the deletion if matching records exist in the related table (Invoice). This protection helps to maintain the integrity of the data in the database.

   To delete the record in the Contract table, you first must delete the related records in the Invoice table.

3. Click the **OK** button in the dialog box to close it. Notice the plus sign that appears at the beginning of each record in the Contract table. The **plus sign** indicates that the Contract table is related to another table—in this case, the Invoice table.

4. Scroll the datasheet down until you see the rest of the records in the table, so that you have room to view the related records for the contract record.

5. Click the **plus sign** next to ContractNum 3101. Access displays the four related records from the Invoice table for this contract. See Figure 3-4.

Figure 3-4   **Related records from the Invoice table in the subdatasheet**

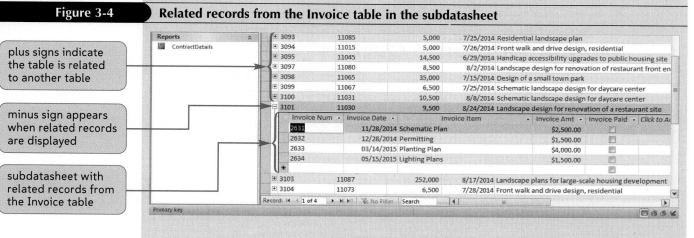

plus signs indicate the table is related to another table

minus sign appears when related records are displayed

subdatasheet with related records from the Invoice table

The related records from the Invoice table are displayed in a **subdatasheet**. When you first open a table that is the primary table in a one-to-many relationship, the subdatasheet containing the records from the related table is not displayed. You need to click the plus sign, also called the **expand indicator**, to display the related records in the subdatasheet. When the subdatasheet is open you can navigate and update it, just as you can using a table datasheet.

You need to delete the records in the Invoice table that are related to ContractNum 3101 before you can delete this contract record. The four Invoice table records are for invoices set up to be paid for future phases of the contract, which has now been cancelled. You could open the Invoice table and find the related records. However, an easier way is to delete them from the subdatasheet. The records will be deleted from the Invoice table automatically.

▶ 6. Click and hold the mouse button on the row selector for the first Invoice table record in the subdatasheet, drag the pointer down to select all four records, and then release the mouse button. With the four records selected, you can delete them all at the same time.

▶ 7. In the Records group on the Home tab, click the **Delete** button. Access opens a dialog box asking you to confirm the deletion of four records. Because the deletion of a record is permanent and cannot be undone, Access prompts you to make sure that you want to delete the records.

▶ 8. Click the **Yes** button to confirm the deletion and close the dialog box. The records are removed from the Invoice table, and the subdatasheet is now empty.

▶ 9. Click the **minus sign** next to ContractNum 3101 to close the subdatasheet.

Now that you have deleted all the related records in the Invoice table, you can delete the record for ContractNum 3101. You'll use the shortcut menu to do so.

Be sure to select the correct record before deleting it.

▶ 10. Right-click the row selector for the record for ContractNum **3101**. Access selects the record and displays the shortcut menu.

▶ 11. Click **Delete Record** on the shortcut menu, and then click the **Yes** button in the dialog box to confirm the deletion. The record is deleted from the table.

▶ 12. Close the Contract table.

You have finished updating the Belmont database by modifying and deleting records. Next, you'll retrieve specific data from the database to meet various requests for information about Belmont Landscapes.

Introduction to Queries

As you learned in Tutorial 1, a query is a question you ask about data stored in a database. For example, Oren might create a query to find records in the Customer table for only those customers located in a specific city. When you create a query, you tell Access which fields you need and what criteria Access should use to select the records. Access provides powerful query capabilities that allow you to do the following:

- Display selected fields and records from a table.
- Sort records.
- Perform calculations.
- Generate data for forms, reports, and other queries.
- Update data in the tables in a database.
- Find and display data from two or more tables.

Most questions about data are generalized queries in which you specify the fields and records you want Access to select. These common requests for information, such as "Which customers are located in Kalamazoo?" or "How many invoices have been paid?" are select queries. The answer to a select query is returned in the form of a datasheet. The result of a query is also referred to as a **recordset** because the query produces a set of records that answers your question.

Designing Queries vs. Using a Query Wizard

More specialized, technical queries, such as finding duplicate records in a table, are best formulated using a Query Wizard. A **Query Wizard** prompts you for information by asking a series of questions and then creates the appropriate query based on your answers. In Tutorial 1, you used the Simple Query Wizard to display only some of the fields in the Contract table; Access provides other Query Wizards for more complex queries. For common, informational queries, it is easier for you to design your own query than to use a Query Wizard.

Taylor wants you to create a query to display the customer ID, company, first name, last name, city, and email address for each record in the Customer table. Her marketing staff needs this information to complete an email campaign advertising a special promotion being offered to Belmont Landscapes customers. You'll open the Query window in Design view to create the query for Taylor.

To open the Query window in Design view:

1. Close the Navigation Pane so that more of the workspace is displayed.

2. Click the **Create** tab on the Ribbon. Access displays the options for creating different database objects.

3. In the Queries group, click the **Query Design** button. The Show Table dialog box opens on the Query window in Design view. See Figure 3-5.

| Figure 3-5 | Show Table dialog box |

The Show Table dialog box lists all the tables in the Belmont database. You can choose to base a query on one or more tables, on other queries, or on a combination of tables and queries. The query you are creating will retrieve data from the Customer table, so you need to add this table to the Query window.

4. Click **Customer** in the Tables list, click the **Add** button, and then click the **Close** button. Access places the Customer table's field list in the Query window and closes the Show Table dialog box.

Trouble? If you add the wrong table to the Query window, right-click the bar at the top of the field list containing the table name, and then click Remove Table on the shortcut menu. To add the correct table to the Query window, click the Show Table button in the Query Setup group on the Design tab to redisplay the Show Table dialog box, and then repeat Step 4.

Now you'll create and run Taylor's query to display selected fields from the Customer table.

Creating and Running a Query

The default table datasheet displays all the fields in the table in the same order as they appear in the table. In contrast, a query datasheet can display selected fields from a table, and the order of the fields can be different from that of the table, enabling those viewing the query results to see only the information they need and in the order they want.

Taylor wants the CustomerID, Company, First, Last, City, and Email fields from the Customer table to appear in the query results. You'll add each of these fields to the design grid. First you'll resize the Customer table field list to display all of the fields.

To select the fields for the query, and then run the query:

1. Position the pointer on the bottom border of the Customer field list until the pointer changes to a ↕ shape, and then click and drag the pointer down until the vertical scroll bar in the field list disappears and all fields in the Customer table are displayed.

TIP

You can also use the mouse to drag a field from the field list to a column in the design grid.

2. In the Customer field list, double-click **CustomerID** to place the field in the design grid's first column Field box. See Figure 3-6.

Figure 3-6   **Field added to the design grid**

field list resized to display all the fields in the table

field added from field list to the first column in the design grid

specifies the field is in the Customer table

indicates that the field will appear in the query datasheet

In the design grid's first column, the field name CustomerID appears in the Field box, the table name Customer appears in the Table box, and the check mark in the Show check box indicates that the field will be displayed in the datasheet when you run the query. Sometimes you might not want to display a field and its values in the query results. For example, if you are creating a query to list all customers located in Lansing, and you assign the name "LansingCustomers" to the query, you do not need to include the City field value for each record in the query results—the query design only lists customers with the City field value of "Lansing." Even if you choose not to display a field in the query results, you can still use the field as part of the query to select specific records or to specify a particular sequence for the records in the datasheet.

3. Double-click **Company** in the Customer field list. Access adds this field to the second column in the design grid.

4. Repeat Step 3 for the **First**, **Last**, **City**, and **Email** fields to add these fields to the design grid in that order.

   Trouble? If you double-click the wrong field and accidentally add it to the design grid, you can remove the field from the grid. Select the field's column by clicking the pointer ↓ on the field selector, which is the thin bar above the Field box, for the field you want to delete, and then press the Delete key (or in the Query Setup group on the Design tab, click the Delete Columns button).

   Having selected the six fields for Taylor's query, you can now run the query.

5. In the Results group on the Design tab, click the **Run** button. Access runs the query and displays the results in Datasheet view. See Figure 3-7.

| Figure 3-7 | Datasheet displayed after running the query |

The six fields you added to the design grid appear in the datasheet in the same order as they appear in the design grid. The records are displayed in primary key sequence by CustomerID. Access selected a total of 40 records for display in the datasheet. Taylor asks you to save the query as "CustomerEmail" so that she can easily retrieve the same data again.

6. Click the **Save** button 🖫 on the Quick Access Toolbar. The Save As dialog box opens.

7. Type **CustomerEmail** in the Query Name box, and then press the **Enter** key. Access saves the query with the specified name in the Belmont database and displays the name on the tab for the query.

Decision Making: Comparing Methods for Adding All Fields to the Design Grid

If the query you are creating includes every field from the specified table, you can use one of the following three methods to transfer all the fields from the field list to the design grid:

- Click and drag each field individually from the field list to the design grid. Use this method if you want the fields in your query to appear in an order that is different from the order in the field list.
- Double-click the asterisk at the top of the field list. Access places the table name followed by a period and an asterisk (as in "Customer.*") in the Field box of the first column in the design grid, which signifies that the order of the fields is the same in the query as it is in the field list. Use this method if you don't need to sort the query or specify conditions for the records you want to select. The advantage of using this method is that you do not need to change the query if you add or delete fields from the underlying table structure. Such changes are reflected automatically in the query.
- Double-click the field list title bar to highlight all the fields, and then click and drag one of the highlighted fields to the first column in the design grid. Access places each field in a separate column and arranges the fields in the order in which they appear in the field list. Use this method when you need to sort your query or include record selection criteria.

By choosing the most appropriate method to add all the table fields to the query design grid, you can work more efficiently and ensure that the query produces the results you want.

When viewing the query results, Taylor noticed that the contact person for the RiverView Development Company is incorrect. Charles Nowak recently retired from his position, so Taylor asks you to update the record with the first name, last name, and email address of the new contact.

Updating Data Using a Query

A query datasheet is temporary and its contents are based on the criteria in the query design grid; however, you can still update the data in a table using a query datasheet. In this case, Taylor has changes she wants you to make to a record in the Customer table. Instead of making the changes in the table datasheet, you can make them in the CustomerEmail query datasheet because the query is based on the Customer table. The underlying Customer table will be updated with the changes you make.

To update data using the CustomerEmail query datasheet:

1. Locate the record with CustomerID 11040, RiverView Development Company (record 13 in the datasheet).

2. In the First Name column for this record, double-click **Charles** to select the name, and then type **Susan**.

3. Press the **Tab** key to move to and select the value in the Last Name column, and then type **Darcy**.

4. Press the **Tab** key twice to move to and select the value in the Email column, type **sdarcy33@rvdc3.com**, and then press the **Tab** key.

5. Close the CustomerEmail query, and then open the Navigation Pane. Note that the CustomerEmail query is listed in the Queries section of the Navigation Pane.

   Now you'll check the Customer table to verify that the changes you made in the query datasheet were also made in the Customer table.

▸ **6.** Open the **Customer** table in Datasheet view, and then close the Navigation Pane.

▸ **7.** For the record with CustomerID 11040 (record 13), use the **Tab** key to move through the field values. Notice that the changes you made in the query datasheet to the First Name, Last Name, and Email columns were made to the record in the Customer table.

▸ **8.** Close the Customer table.

Query Datasheet vs. Table Datasheet

Although a query datasheet looks just like a table datasheet and appears in Datasheet view, a query datasheet is temporary, and its contents are based on the criteria you establish in the design grid. In contrast, a table datasheet shows the permanent data in a table. However, you can update data while viewing a query datasheet, just as you can when working in a table datasheet or form.

Sarah also wants to view specific information in the Belmont database. She would like to review the contract signing dates and amounts for customers while also viewing certain contact information for them. So, she needs to see data from both the Customer table and the Contract table at the same time.

Creating a Multitable Query

A multitable query is a query based on more than one table. If you want to create a query that retrieves data from multiple tables, the tables must have a common field. In Tutorial 2, you established a relationship between the Customer (primary) and Contract (related) tables based on the common CustomerID field that exists in both tables, so you can now create a query to display data from both tables at the same time. Specifically, Sarah wants to view the values in the City, Company, First, and Last fields from the Customer table and the SigningDate and ContractAmt fields from the Contract table.

To create the query using the Customer and Contract tables:

▸ **1.** Click the **Create** tab on the Ribbon.

▸ **2.** In the Queries group, click the **Query Design** button. Access opens the Show Table dialog box. You need to add the Customer and Contract tables to the Query window.

▸ **3.** Click **Customer** in the Tables list, click the **Add** button, click **Contract**, click the **Add** button, and then click the **Close** button. The Customer and Contract field lists appear in the Query window, and the Show Table dialog box closes.

▸ **4.** Use the ↕ pointer to resize the Customer field list so that all the fields in the table are displayed.

The one-to-many relationship between the two tables is shown in the Query window in the same way that Access indicates a relationship between two tables in the Relationships window. Note that the join line is thick at both ends; this signifies that you selected the option to enforce referential integrity. If you had not selected this option, the join line would be thin at both ends and neither the "1" nor the infinity symbol would appear, even though the tables have a one-to-many relationship.

You need to place the City, Company, First, and Last fields (in that order) from the Customer field list into the design grid, and then place the SigningDate and ContractAmt fields from the Contract field list into the design grid. This is the order in which Sarah wants to view the fields in the query results.

▶ **5.** In the Customer field list, double-click **City** to place this field in the design grid's first column Field box.

▶ **6.** Repeat Step 5 to add the **Company**, **First**, and **Last** fields from the Customer table to the second through fourth columns of the design grid.

▶ **7.** Repeat Step 5 to add the **SigningDate** and **ContractAmt** fields (in that order) from the Contract table to the fifth and sixth columns of the design grid. The query specifications are complete, so you can now run the query.

▶ **8.** In the Results group on the Design tab, click the **Run** button. Access runs the query and displays the results in Datasheet view. See Figure 3-8.

| Figure 3-8 | Datasheet for query based on the Customer and Contract tables |

fields from the Customer table

fields from the Contract table

City	Company	First Name	Last Name	Signing Date	Contract Amt
Rockford		Student First	Student Last	2/9/2013	4,000
Holland		Owen	Hawes	3/1/2013	1,500
Holland		Owen	Hawes	7/8/2013	2,250
Holland		Owen	Hawes	11/30/2013	4,000
Saint Joseph		Melissa	Caputo	4/7/2013	1,250
Grand Rapids	Grand Rapids Engineering Dept.	Anthony	Rodriguez	3/1/2013	2,250
Holland		Amol	Mehta	6/22/2013	6,500
South Haven		John	Weiss	8/27/2013	1,000
South Haven		John	Weiss	1/20/2014	1,750
South Haven		John	Weiss	7/26/2014	5,000
Battle Creek	Battle Creek Dental Partners	Harry	Billings	4/25/2014	13,750
Lansing		Karen	O'Brien	2/18/2013	300
Holland	Finn's on the Waterfront	Devin	Finnerty	9/23/2013	7,500
Holland	Finn's on the Waterfront	Devin	Finnerty	2/24/2014	15,750
Holland	Finn's on the Waterfront	Devin	Finnerty	4/14/2014	22,800
Grand Haven	Happy Haven Day Care	Kathy	Rowe	8/8/2014	10,500
Saugatuck		Pam	Wallner	10/5/2013	18,000
Lansing	M. Grant Investment Company	Alex	Engber	3/11/2013	165,000
Grand Rapids	RiverView Development Company	Susan	Darcy	5/3/2013	28,000
Kalamazoo		Michael	Ingram	6/11/2013	5,250
Grand Rapids	Monroe State College	Rachel	Kirk	4/14/2013	22,000
Kalamazoo	Kalamazoo Neighborhood Development	James	Blackhawk	6/22/2013	68,000
Kalamazoo	Kalamazoo Neighborhood Development	James	Blackhawk	6/22/2013	34,000
Kalamazoo	Kalamazoo Neighborhood Development	James	Blackhawk	6/29/2014	14,500
Kalamazoo	Kalamazoo Neighborhood Development	James	Blackhawk	8/2/2014	50,000

Record: 1 of 64 ▸ ▸▸ No Filter Search

Only the six selected fields from the Customer and Contract tables appear in the datasheet. The records are displayed in order according to the values in the CustomerID field because it is the primary key field in the primary table, even though this field is not included in the query datasheet.

Sarah plans on frequently tracking the data retrieved by the query, so she asks you to save it as "CustomerContracts."

▶ **9.** Click the **Save** button 🖫 on the Quick Access Toolbar. The Save As dialog box opens.

▶ **10.** Type **CustomerContracts** in the Query Name box, and then press the **Enter** key. Access saves the query and displays its name on the object tab.

Sarah decides she wants the records displayed in alphabetical order by city. Because the query displays data in order by the field values in the CustomerID field, which is the primary key for the Customer table, you need to sort the records by the City field to display the data in the order Sarah wants.

Sorting Data in a Query

Sorting is the process of rearranging records in a specified order or sequence. Sometimes you might need to sort data before displaying or printing it to meet a specific request. For example, Sarah might want to review contract information arranged by the SigningDate field because she needs to know which months are the busiest for Belmont Landscapes in terms of signings. Oren might want to view contract information arranged by the ContractAmt field because he monitors the financial aspects of the business.

When you sort data in a query, you do not change the sequence of the records in the underlying tables. Only the records in the query datasheet are rearranged according to your specifications.

To sort records, you must select the **sort field**, which is the field used to determine the order of records in the datasheet. In this case, Sarah wants the data sorted by city, so you need to specify City as the sort field. Sort fields can be Text, Number, Date/Time, Currency, AutoNumber, or Yes/No fields, but not Memo, OLE object, Hyperlink, or Attachment fields. You sort records in either ascending (increasing) or descending (decreasing) order. Figure 3-9 shows the results of each type of sort for some of these data types.

Figure 3-9	**Sorting results for different data types**

Data Type	Ascending Sort Results	Descending Sort Results
Text	A to Z	Z to A
Number	lowest to highest numeric value	highest to lowest numeric value
Date/Time	oldest to most recent date	most recent to oldest date
Currency	lowest to highest numeric value	highest to lowest numeric value
AutoNumber	lowest to highest numeric value	highest to lowest numeric value
Yes/No	yes (check mark in check box) then no values	no then yes values

Access provides several methods for sorting data in a table or query datasheet and in a form. One of the easiest ways is to use the AutoFilter feature for a field.

Using an AutoFilter to Sort Data

TIP

You can also use the Ascending and Descending buttons in the Sort & Filter group on the Home tab to quickly sort records based on the currently selected field in a datasheet.

As you've probably noticed when working in Datasheet view for a table or query, each column heading has an arrow to the right of the field name. This arrow gives you access to the **AutoFilter** feature, which enables you to quickly sort and display field values in various ways. When you click this arrow, a menu opens with options for sorting and displaying field values. The first two options on the menu enable you to sort the values in the current field in ascending or descending order. Unless you save the datasheet or form after you've sorted the records, the rearrangement of records is temporary.

Next, you'll use an AutoFilter to sort the CustomerContracts query results by the City field.

To sort the records using an AutoFilter:

▶ **1.** Click the **arrow** on the City column heading to display the AutoFilter menu. See Figure 3-10.

| Figure 3-10 | Using an AutoFilter to sort records in the datasheet |

sort buttons on the Ribbon

choose this option to specify an ascending sort order

City field will be sorted

menu displayed with AutoFilter options

Sarah wants the data sorted in ascending order by the values in the City field, so you need to select the first option in the menu.

2. Click **Sort A to Z**. The records are rearranged in ascending alphabetical order by city. A small, upward-pointing arrow appears on the right side of the City column heading. This arrow indicates that the values in the field have been sorted in ascending order. If you used the same method to sort the field values in descending order, a small downward-pointing arrow would appear there.

After viewing the query results, Sarah decides that she would also like to see the records arranged by the values in the ContractAmt field, so that she can identify the contracts with the largest amounts. She still wants the records to be arranged by the City field values as well. To produce the results Sarah wants, you need to sort using two fields.

Sorting Multiple Fields in Design View

Sort fields can be unique or nonunique. A sort field is **unique** if the value in the sort field for each record is different. The CustomerID field in the Customer table is an example of a unique sort field because each customer record has a different value in this primary key field. A sort field is **nonunique** if more than one record can have the same value for the sort field. For example, the City field in the Customer table is a nonunique sort field because more than one record can have the same City value.

When the sort field is nonunique, records with the same sort field value are grouped together, but they are not sorted in a specific order within the group. To arrange these grouped records in a specific order, you can specify a **secondary sort field**, which is a second field that determines the order of records that are already sorted by the **primary sort field** (the first sort field specified).

Access lets you select up to 10 different sort fields. When you use the buttons on the Ribbon to sort by more than one field, the sort fields must be in adjacent columns in the datasheet. (Note that you cannot use an AutoFilter to sort on more than one field. This method works for a single field only.) You can specify only one type of sort—either ascending or descending—for the selected columns in the datasheet. You highlight the adjacent columns, and Access sorts first by the first column and then by each remaining highlighted column in order from left to right.

TIP

The primary sort field is *not* the same as a table's primary key field. A table has at most one primary key, which must be unique, whereas any field in a table can serve as a primary sort field.

Sarah wants the records sorted first by the City field values, as they currently are, and then by the ContractAmt field values. The two fields are in the correct left-to-right order in the query datasheet, but they are not adjacent, so you cannot use the Ascending and Descending buttons on the Ribbon to sort them. You could move the City field to the left of the ContractAmt field in the query datasheet, but both columns would be sorted with the same sort order. This is not what Sarah wants—she wants the City field values sorted in ascending order so that they are in the correct alphabetical order, for ease of reference; and she wants the ContractAmt field values to be sorted in descending order, so that she can focus on the contracts with the largest amounts. To sort the City and ContractAmt fields with different sort orders, you must specify the sort fields in Design view.

In the Query window in Design view, Access first uses the sort field that is leftmost in the design grid. Therefore, you must arrange the fields you want to sort from left to right in the design grid, with the primary sort field being the leftmost. In Design view, multiple sort fields do not have to be adjacent to each other, as they do in Datasheet view; however, they must be in the correct left-to-right order.

REFERENCE

Sorting a Query Datasheet

- In the query datasheet, click the arrow on the column heading for the field you want to sort.
- In the menu that opens, click Sort A to Z for an ascending sort, or click Sort Z to A for a descending sort.

or

- In the query datasheet, select the column or adjacent columns on which you want to sort.
- In the Sort & Filter group on the Home tab, click the Ascending button or the Descending button.

or

- In Design view, position the fields serving as sort fields from left to right.
- Click the right side of the Sort box for the field you want to sort, and then click Ascending or Descending for the sort order.

To achieve the results Sarah wants, you need to modify the query in Design view to specify the sort order for the two fields.

To select the two sort fields in Design view:

TIP

In Design view, the sort fields do not have to be adjacent, and fields that are not sorted can appear between the sort fields.

1. In the Views group on the Home tab, click the **View** button to open the query in Design view. The fields are currently in the correct left-to-right order in the design grid, so you only need to specify the sort order for the two fields.

   First, you need to specify an ascending sort order for the City field. Even though the records are already sorted by the values in this field, you need to modify the query so that this sort order, and the sort order you will specify for the ContractAmt field, are part of the query's design. Any time the query is run, the records will be sorted according to these specifications.

2. Click the right side of the **City Sort** box to display the arrow and the sort options, and then click **Ascending**. You've selected an ascending sort order for the City field, which will be the primary sort field. The City field is a Text field, and an ascending sort order will display the field values in alphabetical order.

3. Click the right side of the **ContractAmt Sort** box, click **Descending**, and then click in one of the empty text boxes to the right of the ContractAmt field to deselect the setting. You've selected a descending sort order for the ContractAmt

field, which will be the secondary sort field because it appears to the right of the primary sort field (City) in the design grid. The ContractAmt field is a Currency field, and a descending sort order will display the field values with the largest amounts first. See Figure 3-11.

Figure 3-11   **Selecting two sort fields in Design view**

You have finished your query changes, so now you can run the query and then save the modified query with the same query name.

▶ 4. In the Results group on the Design tab, click the **Run** button. Access runs the query and displays the query datasheet. The records appear in ascending order based on the values in the City field. Within groups of records with the same City field value, the records appear in descending order by the values of the ContractAmt field. See Figure 3-12.

Figure 3-12   **Datasheet sorted on two fields**

When you save the query, all of your design changes—including the selection of the sort fields—are saved with the query. The next time Sarah runs the query, the records will appear sorted by the primary and secondary sort fields.

▶ 5. Click the **Save** button 🔒 on the Quick Access Toolbar to save the revised CustomerContracts query.

Sarah knows that Belmont Landscapes has seen an increase in business recently for customers located in the city of Grand Rapids. She would like to focus briefly on the information for customers in that city only. Also, she is interested in knowing how many contracts were signed in March because this month has sometimes been a slow month for Belmont Landscapes in terms of contract signings. Selecting only the records with a City field value of "Grand Rapids" and a SigningDate field value beginning with "3" (for the month of March) is a temporary change that Sarah wants in the datasheet, so you do not need to switch to Design view and change the query. Instead, you can apply a filter.

Filtering Data

A **filter** is a set of restrictions you place on the records in an open datasheet or form to *temporarily* isolate a subset of the records. A filter lets you view different subsets of displayed records so that you can focus on only the data you need. Unless you save a query or form with a filter applied, an applied filter is not available the next time you run the query or open the form.

The simplest technique for filtering records is Filter By Selection. **Filter By Selection** lets you select all or part of a field value in a datasheet or form, and then display only those records that contain the selected value in the field. You can also use the AutoFilter feature to filter records. When you click the arrow on a column heading, the menu that opens provides options for filtering the datasheet based on a field value or the selected part of a field value. Another technique for filtering records is to use **Filter By Form**, which changes your datasheet to display blank fields. Then you can select a value using the arrow that appears when you click any blank field to apply a filter that selects only those records containing that value.

REFERENCE

Using Filter By Selection

- In the datasheet or form, select part of the field value that will be the basis for the filter; or, if the filter will be based on the entire field value, click anywhere within the field value.
- In the Sort & Filter group on the Home tab, click the Selection button.
- Click the type of filter you want to apply.

For Sarah's request, you need to select a City field value of Grand Rapids, and then use Filter By Selection to display only those records with this value. Then you will filter the records further by selecting only those records with a SigningDate value that begins with "3" (for March).

To display the records using Filter By Selection:

1. In the query datasheet, locate the first occurrence of a City field containing the value **Grand Rapids**, and then click anywhere within that field value. (Note: Make sure you find a field value containing only "Grand Rapids," not "East Grand Rapids.")

2. In the Sort & Filter group on the Home tab, click the **Selection** button. A menu opens with options for the type of filter to apply. See Figure 3-13.

| Figure 3-13 | Using Filter By Selection |

options for the type of filter to apply

current field is the basis for the filter

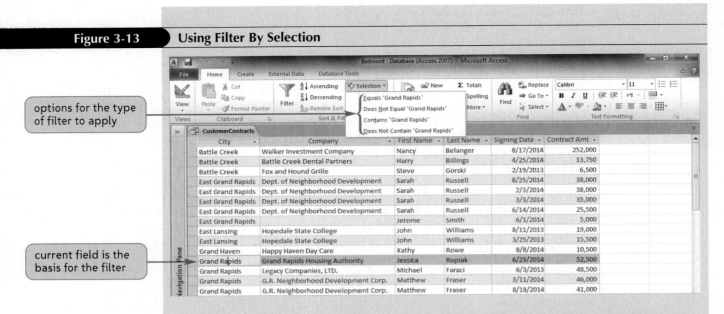

The menu provides options for displaying only those records with a City field value that equals the selected value (in this case, Grand Rapids); does not equal the value; contains the value somewhere within the field; or does not contain the value somewhere within the field. You want to display all the records whose City field value equals Grand Rapids.

3. In the Selection menu, click **Equals "Grand Rapids"**. Access displays the filtered results. Only the 13 records that have a City field value of Grand Rapids appear in the datasheet. See Figure 3-14.

| Figure 3-14 | Datasheet after applying the filter |

click to display more options for filtering the field

datasheet displays only records with a City value of Grand Rapids

City	Company	First Name	Last Name	Signing Date	Contract Amt
Grand Rapids	Grand Rapids Housing Authority	Jessica	Ropiak	6/23/2014	52,500
Grand Rapids	Legacy Companies, LTD.	Michael	Faraci	6/3/2013	48,500
Grand Rapids	G.R. Neighborhood Development Corp.	Matthew	Fraser	3/11/2014	46,000
Grand Rapids	G.R. Neighborhood Development Corp.	Matthew	Fraser	8/18/2014	41,000
Grand Rapids	Legacy Companies, LTD.	Michael	Faraci	3/22/2013	39,000
Grand Rapids	Grand Rapids Housing Authority	Jessica	Ropiak	7/27/2013	38,500
Grand Rapids	G.R. Neighborhood Development Corp.	Matthew	Fraser	3/11/2014	37,000
Grand Rapids	Legacy Companies, LTD.	Michael	Faraci	12/28/2013	30,800
Grand Rapids	RiverView Development Company	Susan	Darcy	5/3/2013	28,000
Grand Rapids	Monroe State College	Rachel	Kirk	4/14/2013	22,000
Grand Rapids	Weston Community Parks Foundation	Sam	Kervin	5/28/2013	10,500
Grand Rapids	Weston Community Parks Foundation	Sam	Kervin	5/28/2013	8,500
Grand Rapids	Grand Rapids Engineering Dept.	Anthony	Rodriguez	3/1/2013	2,250

indicate that a filter has been applied to the datasheet

Record: 1 of 13   Filtered   Search

Ready   Filtered

The button labeled "Filtered" to the right of the navigation buttons and the notation "Filtered" on the status bar both indicate that a filter has been applied to the datasheet. Also, notice that the Toggle Filter button in the Sort & Filter group on the Home tab is active; you can click this button or the Filtered button next to the navigation buttons to toggle between the filtered and unfiltered displays of the query datasheet. The City column heading also has a filter icon on it; you can click this icon to display additional options for filtering the field.

Next, Sarah wants to view only those records with a SigningDate value in the month of March to focus on contracts signed in that month for customers in Grand Rapids. So, you need to apply an additional filter to the datasheet.

▶ **4.** In any SigningDate field value beginning with the number "3" (for the month of March), select only the first digit **3**.

▶ **5.** In the Sort & Filter group, click the **Selection** button. Three filters are available based on your selection: to display only those records with a SigningDate field value that begins with 3; to display only those records with a SigningDate field value that does not begin with 3; and to display only those records with a SigningDate field value that is between two dates. If you choose the Between option, a dialog box opens in which you enter the date values that you want to use.

▶ **6.** Click **Begins With 3** in the Selection menu. The second filter is applied to the query datasheet, which now shows only the four records for customers located in Grand Rapids who signed contracts in the month of March.

Now you can redisplay all the query records by clicking the Toggle Filter button, which you use to switch between the filtered and unfiltered displays.

▶ **7.** In the Sort & Filter group on the Home tab, click the **Toggle Filter** button. Access removes the filter and redisplays all 64 records in the query datasheet.

▶ **8.** Close the CustomerContracts query. Access asks if you want to save your changes to the design of the query—in this case, the filtered display, which is still available through the Toggle Filter button. Sarah does not want the query saved with the filter because she doesn't need to view the filtered information on a regular basis.

▶ **9.** Click the **No** button to close the query without saving the changes.

▶ **10.** If you are not continuing to Session 3.2, click the **File** tab, and then click **Close Database** in the navigation bar to close the Belmont database.

Session 3.1 Quick Check

REVIEW

1. In Datasheet view, what is the difference between navigation mode and editing mode?
2. What is a select query?
3. Describe the field list and the design grid in the Query window in Design view.
4. How are a table datasheet and a query datasheet similar? How are they different?
5. For a Date/Time field, how do the records appear when sorted in ascending order?
6. True or False: When you define multiple sort fields in Design view, the sort fields must be adjacent to each other.
7. A(n) _____ is a set of restrictions you place on the records in an open datasheet or form to isolate a subset of records temporarily.

SESSION 3.2 VISUAL OVERVIEW

When creating queries in Design view, you can enter criteria so that Access will display only selected records in the query results.

Field:	CustomerID	Company	First	Last	City
Table:	Customer	Customer	Customer	Customer	Customer
Sort:					
Show:	☑	☑	☑	☑	☑
Criteria:					"Kalamazoo"
or:					

To define a condition for a field, you place the condition in the field's Criteria box in the design grid.

To tell Access which records you want to select, you must specify a condition as part of the query. A **condition** is a criterion, or rule, that determines which records are selected.

Field:	InvoiceNum	InvoiceDate	InvoiceAmt	
Table:	Invoice	Invoice	Invoice	
Sort:				
Show:	☑	☑	☑	☐
Criteria:			> 50000	
or:				

A condition usually consists of an operator, often a comparison operator, and a value. A **comparison operator** asks Access to compare the value in a field to the condition value and to select all the records for which the condition is true.

Field:	ContractNum	ContractAmt	SigningDate	ContractType
Table:	Contract	Contract	Contract	Contract
Sort:				
Show:	☑	☑	☑	☑
Criteria:			Between #9/1/2013# And #11/30/2013#	
or:				

Most comparison operators, such as Between...And..., ask Access to select records that match a range of values for the condition—in this case, all records with dates that fall within the range shown.

SELECTION CRITERIA IN QUERIES

The results of a query containing selection criteria include only the records that meet the specified criteria.

KalamazooCustomers

Customer ID	Company	First Name	Last Name	City
11042		Michael	Ingram	Kalamazoo
11045	Kalamazoo Neighborhood Development	James	Blackhawk	Kalamazoo
11072	Sierra Investment Company	Rodrigo	Valencia	Kalamazoo

The results of this query show only customers from Kalamazoo because the condition "Kalamazoo" in the City field's Criteria box specifies that Access should select records only with City field values of Kalamazoo. This type of condition is called an **exact match** because the value in the specified field must match the condition exactly in order for the record to be included in the query results.

LargeInvoiceAmts

Invoice Num	Invoice Date	Invoice Amt
2063	07/11/2015	$70,000.00
2453	05/05/2017	$85,000.00
2613	12/17/2017	$105,000.00
2614	09/30/2019	$77,000.00

The results of this query show only those invoices with amounts greater than $50,000 because the condition >50000, which uses the greater than comparison operator, specifies that Access should select records only with InvoiceAmt field values over $50,000.

FallSignings

Contract Num	Contract Amt	Signing Date	Contract Type
3046	300	9/2/2013	Consultation for back yard, residential
3048	7,500	9/23/2013	Landscape design for restaurant site
3051	18,000	10/5/2013	Site layout and landscape design for residential site
3053	375	9/15/2013	Consultation for front yard, residential
3056	32,500	9/30/2013	Handicap accessibility upgrades to public housing site
3057	15,500	9/30/2013	Handicap accessibility upgrades to public housing site
3060	4,000	11/30/2013	Front walk and drive design, residential

The results of this query show only those contracts that were signed in the fall of 2013 because the condition in the SigningDate's Criteria box specifies that Access should select records only with a signing date between 9/1/2013 and 11/30/2013.

Defining Record Selection Criteria for Queries

Oren wants to display customer and contract information for all customers who live in Holland, Oren's hometown. He is planning to do a special local promotion for Holland customers because Belmont Landscapes is located there, and Oren wants to increase his firm's presence in the community. For this request, you could create a query to select the correct fields and all records in the Customer and Contract tables, select a City field value of Holland in the query datasheet, and then click the Selection button and choose the appropriate filter option to filter the query results and display the information for only those customers in Holland. However, a faster way of displaying the data Oren needs is to create a query that displays the selected fields and only those records in the Customer and Contract tables that satisfy a condition.

Just as you can display selected fields from a database in a query datasheet, you can display selected records. To tell Access which records you want to select, you must specify a condition as part of the query, as illustrated in the Session 3.2 Visual Overview. A condition usually includes one of the comparison operators shown in Figure 3-15.

Figure 3-15	Access comparison operators

Operator	Meaning	Example
=	equal to (optional; default operator)	="Hall"
<>	not equal to	<>"Hall"
<	less than	<#1/1/99#
<=	less than or equal to	<=100
>	greater than	>"C400"
>=	greater than or equal to	>=18.75
Between ... And ...	between two values (inclusive)	Between 50 And 325
In ()	in a list of values	In ("Hall", "Seeger")
Like	matches a pattern that includes wildcards	Like "706*"

Specifying an Exact Match

For Oren's request, you need to create a query that will display only those records in the Customer table with the value Holland in the City field. This type of condition is an exact match because the value in the specified field must match the condition exactly in order for the record to be included in the query results. You'll create the query in Design view.

To create the query in Design view:

1. If you took a break after the previous session, make sure that the Belmont database is open and the Navigation Pane is closed.

2. Click the **Create** tab on the Ribbon.

3. In the Queries group, click the **Query Design** button. The Show Table dialog box opens. You need to add the Customer and Contract tables to the Query window.

4. Click **Customer** in the Tables list, click the **Add** button, click **Contract**, click the **Add** button, and then click the **Close** button.

5. Use the ↕ pointer to resize the Customer field list so that all the fields are displayed.

6. Add the following fields from the Customer table to the design grid in the order shown: **Company**, **First**, **Last**, **Phone**, **Address**, **City**, and **Email**.

Oren also wants information from the Contract table included in the query results.

7. Add the following fields from the Contract table to the design grid in the order shown: **ContractNum**, **ContractAmt**, **SigningDate**, and **ContractType**. See Figure 3-16.

Figure 3-16   **Design grid after adding fields from both tables**

The field lists for the Customer and Contract tables appear in the top portion of the window, and the join line indicating a one-to-many relationship connects the two tables. The fields you selected appear in the design grid; to see all of the fields, you need to scroll to the right using the horizontal scroll bar.

To display the information Oren wants, you need to enter the condition for the City field in its Criteria box. Oren wants to display only those records with a City field value of Holland.

To enter the exact match condition, and then save and run the query:

1. Click the **City Criteria** box, type **Holland**, and then press the **Enter** key. The condition changes to "Holland".

Access automatically enclosed the condition you typed in quotation marks. You must enclose Text values in quotation marks when using them as selection criteria. If you omit the quotation marks, however, Access will include them automatically.

2. Click the **Save** button 🖫 on the Quick Access Toolbar to open the Save As dialog box.

3. Type **HollandCustomers** in the Query Name box, and then press the **Enter** key. Access saves the query with the specified name and displays the name on the object tab.

4. In the Results group on the Design tab, click the **Run** button. Access runs the query and displays the selected field values for only those records with a City field value of Holland. A total of 12 records is selected and displayed in the datasheet. See Figure 3-17.

Figure 3-17	Datasheet displaying selected fields and records

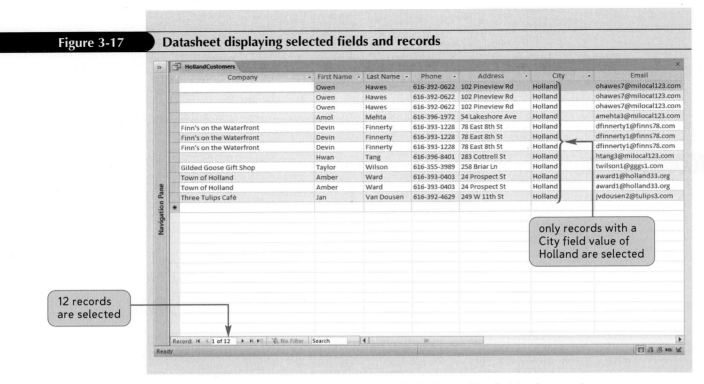

only records with a
City field value of
Holland are selected

12 records
are selected

Oren realizes that it's not necessary to include the City field values in the query results. The name of the query, HollandCustomers, indicates that the query design includes all customers that are located in Holland, so the City field values are unnecessary and repetitive. Also, he decides that he would prefer the query datasheet to show the fields from the Contract table first, followed by the Customer table fields. You need to modify the query to produce the results Oren wants.

Modifying a Query

After you create a query and view the results, you might need to make changes to the query if the results are not what you expected or require. First, Oren asks you to modify the HollandCustomers query to remove the City field values from the query results.

To remove the display of the City field values:

1. In the Views group on the Home tab, click the **View** button. The HollandCustomers query opens in Design view.

   You need to keep the City field as part of the query design because it contains the defined condition for the query. You only need to remove the display of the field's values from the query results.

2. Click the **City Show** check box to remove the check mark. The query will still find only those records with the value Holland in the City field, but the query results will not display these field values.

Next, you need to change the order of the fields in the query so that the contract information is listed first.

To move the Contract table fields to precede the Customer table fields:

1. Scroll the design grid to the right so you can see all four fields from the Contract table. You need to move the ContractNum field so it becomes the first field in the query design.

2. Position the pointer on the ContractNum field selector until the pointer changes to a ↓ shape, and then click to select the field. See Figure 3-18.

Figure 3-18 — Selected ContractNum field

ContractNum field selector

Show check box cleared

entire column is selected

Field:	Address	City	Email	ContractNum	ContractAmt	SigningDate	ContractType	
Table:	Customer	Customer	Customer	Contract	Contract	Contract	Contract	
Sort:								
Show:	☑	☐	☑	☑	☑	☑	☑	☐
Criteria:		"Holland"						
or:								

Ready

3. Position the pointer on the ContractNum field selector, and then click and drag the pointer ↖ to the left, allowing the design grid to scroll back to the left, until the vertical line to the left of the Company field is highlighted. See Figure 3-19.

Figure 3-19 — Dragging the field in the design grid

line is highlighted

drag pointer to here

selected field being moved

Field:	Company	First	Last	Phone	Address	City	Email	ContractNum
Table:	Customer	Customer	Customer	Customer	Customer	Customer	Customer	Contract
Sort:								
Show:	☑	☑	☑	☑	☑	☐	☑	☑
Criteria:						"Holland"		
or:								

Ready

4. Release the mouse button. The ContractNum field moves to the left of the Company field.

   You can also select and move multiple fields at once.

5. Scroll back to the right to view the remaining fields in the design grid. Now you need to select and move the ContractAmt, SigningDate, and ContractType fields so that they follow the ContractNum field in the query design. To select multiple fields, you simply click and drag the mouse over the field selectors for the fields you want.

6. Click and hold the pointer ↓ on the ContractAmt field selector, drag the pointer to the right to select the SigningDate and ContractType fields, and then release the mouse button. All three fields are now selected. See Figure 3-20.

Figure 3-20   **Multiple fields selected to be moved**

> **7.** Position the pointer ⟨ anywhere near the top of the three selected fields, and then click and drag the pointer to the left until the vertical line to the left of the Company field is highlighted.

> **8.** Release the mouse button. The four fields from the Contract table are now the first four fields in the query design.

> You have finished making the modifications to the query Oren requested, so you can now run the query.

> **9.** In the Results group on the Design tab, click the **Run** button. Access displays the results of the modified query. See Figure 3-21.

Figure 3-21   **Results of the modified query**

Note that the City field values are no longer displayed in the query results (you need to scroll the datasheet to the right to verify this).

Oren would like to see more fields and records on the screen at one time. He asks you to change the datasheet's font size, and then to resize all the columns to their best fit.

Changing a Datasheet's Appearance

You can change the characteristics of a datasheet, including the font type and size of text in the datasheet, to improve its appearance or readability. As you learned in earlier tutorials, you can also resize the datasheet columns to view more columns on the screen at the same time. You'll change the font size from the default 11 points to 9, and then resize the datasheet columns.

To change the font size and resize the columns in the datasheet:

1. In the Text Formatting group on the Home tab, click the **Font Size** arrow, and then click **9**. The font size for the entire datasheet changes to 9 points.

   Next, you need to resize the columns to their best fit, so that each column is just wide enough to display the longest value in the column. Instead of resizing each column individually, you'll use the datasheet selector to select all the columns and resize them at the same time.

2. Click the **datasheet selector**, which is the box to the left of the Contract Num column heading (see Figure 3-21). All the columns in the datasheet are highlighted, indicating they are selected.

3. Position the pointer ⟷ at the right edge of any column in the datasheet, and then double-click the pointer. All the columns visible on the screen are resized to their best fit. Because only the visible columns are resized, you must scroll the datasheet to the right to make sure all field values for all columns are fully displayed, resizing as you scroll, if necessary.

4. Scroll the datasheet to the right and verify that all columns were resized to their best fit. If necessary, resize any individual column that might not have been resized to best fit the data it contains.

5. Scroll to the left, if necessary, so that the Contract Num column is visible, and then click any value in the Contract Num column to make it the current field. More columns are now visible in the datasheet.

TIP

Click a field value to deselect the columns before resizing an individual column.

Changing the Alternate Row Color in a Datasheet

Access uses themes to format the objects in a database. A **theme** is a predefined set of formats including colors, fonts, and other effects that enhance an object's appearance and usability. When you create a database, Access applies the Office theme to objects as you create them. By default, the Office theme formats every other row in a datasheet with a gray background color to distinguish one row from another, making it easier to view and read the contents of a datasheet. The gray alternate row color provides a subtle difference compared to the rows that have the default white row color. You can change the alternate row color in a datasheet to something more noticeable using the Alternate Row Color button in the Text Formatting group on the Home tab. Oren suggests that you change the alternate row color in the datasheet to see the effect of using this feature.

To change the alternate row color in the datasheet:

1. In the Text Formatting group on the Home tab, click the **Alternate Row Color** button arrow ▦ ▾ to display the gallery of color choices. See Figure 3-22.

Figure 3-22 Gallery of color choices for alternate row color

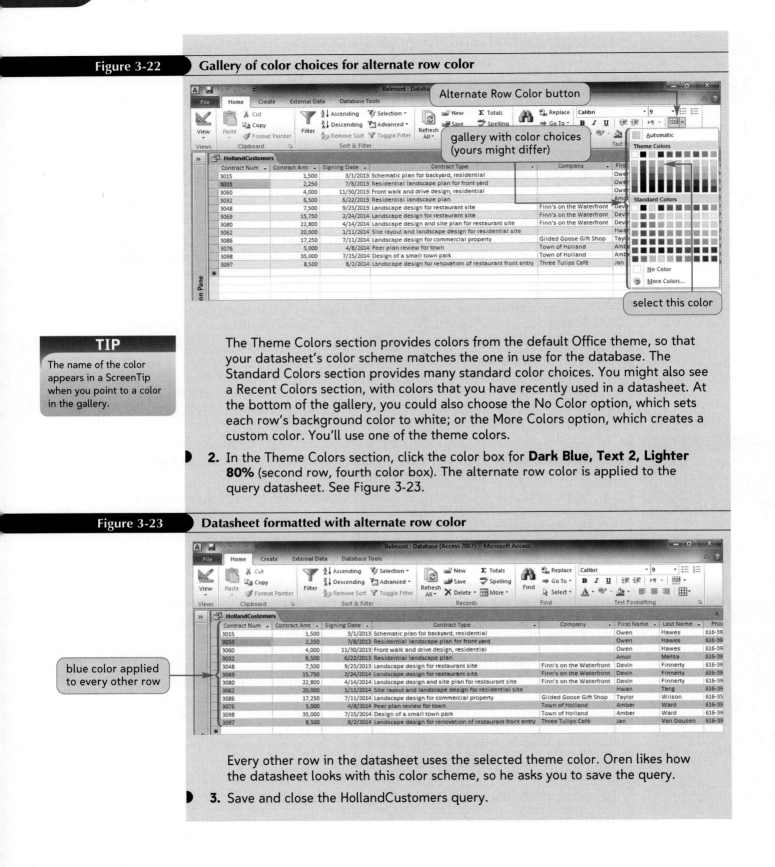

The Theme Colors section provides colors from the default Office theme, so that your datasheet's color scheme matches the one in use for the database. The Standard Colors section provides many standard color choices. You might also see a Recent Colors section, with colors that you have recently used in a datasheet. At the bottom of the gallery, you could also choose the No Color option, which sets each row's background color to white; or the More Colors option, which creates a custom color. You'll use one of the theme colors.

2. In the Theme Colors section, click the color box for **Dark Blue, Text 2, Lighter 80%** (second row, fourth color box). The alternate row color is applied to the query datasheet. See Figure 3-23.

Figure 3-23 Datasheet formatted with alternate row color

Every other row in the datasheet uses the selected theme color. Oren likes how the datasheet looks with this color scheme, so he asks you to save the query.

3. Save and close the HollandCustomers query.

After viewing the query results, Oren decides that he would like to see the same fields, but only for those records with a ContractAmt field value equal to or greater than $25,000. He is interested to know which Belmont Landscapes customers in all cities and towns have signed the largest contracts, so that he can follow up with these customers personally. To create the query that will produce the results Oren wants, you need to use a comparison operator to match a range of values—in this case, any ContractAmt value greater than or equal to $25,000.

Using a Comparison Operator to Match a Range of Values

After you create and save a query, you can double-click the query name in the Navigation Pane to run the query again. You can then click the View button to change its design. You can also use an existing query as the basis for creating another query. Because the design of the query you need to create next is similar to the HollandCustomers query, you will copy, paste, and rename this query to create the new query. Using this approach keeps the HollandCustomers query intact.

To create the new query by copying the HollandCustomers query:

▶ **1.** Open the Navigation Pane. Note that the HollandCustomers query is listed in the Queries section.

   You need to use the shortcut menu to copy the HollandCustomers query and paste it in the Navigation Pane; then you'll give the copied query a different name.

▶ **2.** In the Queries section on the Navigation Pane, right-click **HollandCustomers** to select it and display the shortcut menu.

▶ **3.** Click **Copy** on the shortcut menu.

▶ **4.** Right-click the empty area near the bottom of the Navigation Pane, and then click **Paste** on the shortcut menu. The Paste As dialog box opens with the text "Copy Of HollandCustomers" in the Query Name box. Because Oren wants the new query to show the contracts with the largest amounts, you'll name the new query "LargeContractAmounts."

▶ **5.** Type **LargeContractAmounts** in the Query Name box, and then press the **Enter** key. The new query appears in the Queries section of the Navigation Pane.

▶ **6.** Double-click the **LargeContractAmounts** query to open, or run, the query. Notice that all the design changes you made to the original HollandCustomers query— decreasing the font size, resizing all the columns, and applying the alternate row color—were saved with the query.

▶ **7.** Close the Navigation Pane.

Next, you need to open the query in Design view and modify its design to produce the results Oren wants—to display only those records with ContractAmt field values that are greater than or equal to $25,000.

To modify the design of the new query:

▶ **1.** In the Views group on the Home tab, click the **View** button to display the query in Design view.

▶ **2.** Click the **ContractAmt Criteria** box, and then type **>=25000** and press the **Tab** key. See Figure 3-24.

| Figure 3-24 | Criteria entered for the ContractAmt field |

Field:	ContractNum	ContractAmt	SigningDate	ContractType	Company	First	Last	Phone
Table:	Contract	Contract	Contract	Contract	Customer	Customer	Customer	Customer
Sort:								
Show:	✓	✓	✓	✓	✓	✓	✓	✓
Criteria:		>=25000						
or:								

new condition entered

Form View

Trouble? If you receive an error message saying that you entered an expression containing invalid syntax, you might have typed a comma in the amount "25000". Commas are not allowed in selection criteria for Currency fields. Click the OK button to close the dialog box, delete the comma from the ContractAmt Criteria box, and then press the Tab key.

The condition specifies that a record will be selected only if its ContractAmt field value is $25,000 or greater. Before you run the query, you need to delete the condition for the City field. Recall that the City field is part of the query, but its values are not displayed in the query results. When you modified the query to remove the City field values from the query results, Access moved the field to the end of the design grid. So, you need to locate the City field, delete its condition, specify that the City field values should be included in the query results, and then move the field back to its original position following the Address field.

▶ **3.** Press the **Tab** key eight times until the condition for the City field is highlighted, and then press the **Delete** key. The condition for the City field is removed.

▶ **4.** Click the **Show** check box for the City field to insert a check mark so that the field values will be displayed in the query results.

▶ **5.** Use the ↓ pointer to select the City field, drag the selected field to the left of the Email field, and then click in an empty box to deselect the City field. See Figure 3-25.

| Figure 3-25 | Design grid after moving the City field |

Field:	Company	First	Last	Phone	Address	City	Email	
Table:	Customer	Customer	Customer	Customer	Customer	Customer	Customer	
Sort:								
Show:	✓	✓	✓	✓	✓	✓	✓	
Criteria:								
or:								

City field moved back to its original location

condition removed from City Criteria box

Show check box is selected

Form View

▶ **6.** In the Results group on the Design tab, click the **Run** button. Access runs the query and displays the selected fields for only those records with a ContractAmt field value of greater than or equal to $25,000. A total of 23 records is selected. See Figure 3-26.

| Figure 3-26 | Running the modified query |

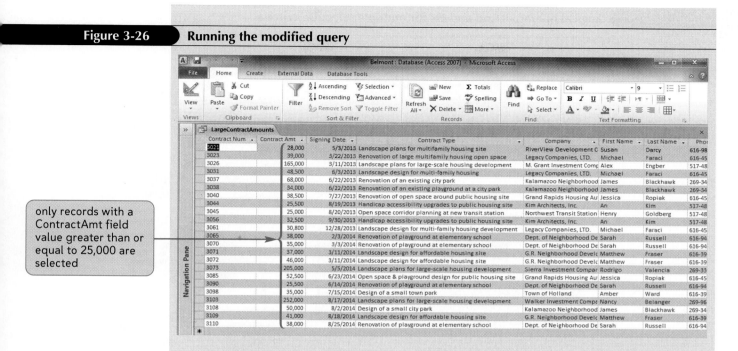

only records with a ContractAmt field value greater than or equal to 25,000 are selected

The City field values are also included in the query datasheet; you need to scroll the datasheet to the right to view them.

7. Resize the datasheet columns to their best fit, as necessary, and then save and close the LargeContractAmounts query.

Oren recently hired Steve Barry as a new consultant at Belmont Landscapes. Steve will focus primarily on customers located in Lansing. To help Steve prioritize his site visits in Lansing, Oren asks you to provide him with a list of all customers in Lansing who have signed contracts with values of greater than $25,000. To produce this list, you need to create a query containing two conditions—one for the city and another for the contract amount.

Defining Multiple Selection Criteria for Queries

Multiple conditions require you to use **logical operators** to combine two or more conditions. When you want a record selected only if two or more conditions are met, you need to use the **And logical operator**. In this case, Oren wants to see only those records with a City field value of Lansing *and* a ContractAmt field value greater than $25,000. If you place conditions in separate fields in the *same* Criteria row of the design grid, all conditions in that row must be met in order for a record to be included in the query results. However, if you place conditions in *different* Criteria rows, a record will be selected if at least one of the conditions is met. If none of the conditions are met, Access does not select the record. When you place conditions in different Criteria rows, you are using the **Or logical operator**. Figure 3-27 illustrates the difference between the And and Or logical operators.

Figure 3-27   Logical operators And and Or for multiple selection criteria

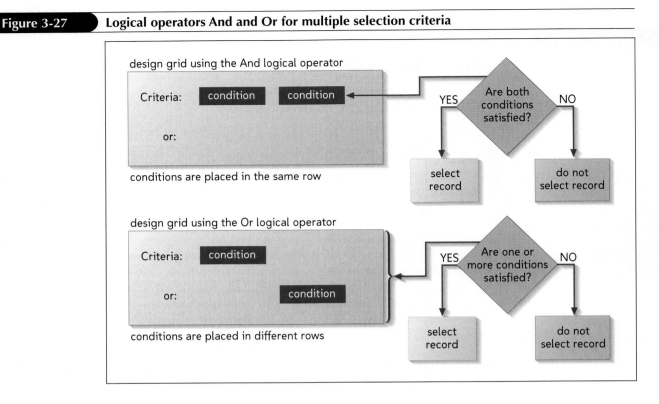

The And Logical Operator

To create the query for Oren, you need to use the And logical operator to show only the records for customers located in Lansing *and* with a contract amount greater than $25,000. You'll create a new query based on both the Customer and Contract tables to produce the necessary results. In the query design, both conditions you specify will appear in the same Criteria row; therefore, the query will select records only if both conditions are met.

To create a new query using the And logical operator:

1. Click the **Create** tab on the Ribbon.

2. In the Queries group, click the **Query Design** button.

3. Add the **Customer** and **Contract** tables to the Query window, and then close the Show Table dialog box. Resize the Customer field list to display all the field names.

4. Add the following fields from the Customer field list to the design grid in the order shown: **Company**, **First**, **Last**, **Phone**, and **City**.

5. Add the **ContractAmt** and **SigningDate** fields from the Contract table to the design grid.

   Now you need to enter the two conditions for the query.

6. Click the **City Criteria** box, and then type **Lansing**.

7. Press the **Tab** key to move to the **ContractAmt Criteria** box, type **>25000**, and then press the **Tab** key. See Figure 3-28.

Figure 3-28   **Query to find customers in Lansing with large contracts**

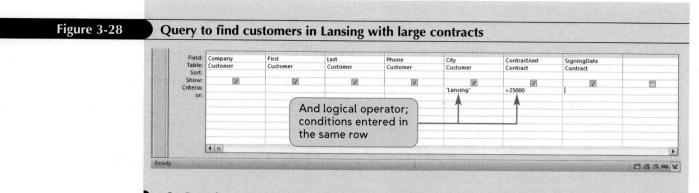

And logical operator; conditions entered in the same row

> **8.** Run the query. Access displays only those records that meet both conditions: a City field value of Lansing and a ContractAmt field value greater than $25,000. Three records are selected for two different customers. See Figure 3-29.

Figure 3-29   **Results of query using the And logical operator**

Company	First Name	Last Name	Phone	City	Contract Amt	Signing Date
M. Grant Investment Company	Alex	Engber	517-482-1400	Lansing	165,000	3/11/2013
Kim Architects, Inc.	An	Kim	517-482-9932	Lansing	25,500	8/19/2013
Kim Architects, Inc.	An	Kim	517-482-9932	Lansing	32,500	9/30/2013

> **9.** Click the **Save** button on the Quick Access Toolbar, and then save the query as **KeyLansingCustomers**.

> **10.** Close the query. When Steve begins working at Belmont Landscapes, he can run this query to see which customers in Lansing he should contact first.

Next, Oren and Taylor meet to discuss strategies for increasing business for Belmont Landscapes. They are interested in knowing which customers signed contracts for small amounts—less than $10,000—or which contracts were signed in the first two months of 2014 because business seemed unusually slow during those months. They want to use this information for two reasons: (1) to target specific customers who signed smaller contracts with Belmont Landscapes, to determine if these customers might have additional landscaping needs; and (2) to analyze the number and type of contracts signed during these slow months so they can develop strategies for increasing contract signings in the future. To help with their planning, Oren and Taylor have asked you to produce a list of all contracts with amounts less than $10,000 or that were signed between 1/1/2014 and 3/1/2014. To create this query, you need to use the Or logical operator.

The Or Logical Operator

To create the query that Oren and Taylor requested, your query must select a record when either one of two conditions is satisfied or when both conditions are satisfied. That is, a record is selected if the ContractAmt field value is less than $10,000 *or* if the SigningDate field value is between 1/1/2014 and 3/1/2014 *or* if both conditions are met. You will enter the condition for the ContractAmt field in the Criteria row and the condition for the SigningDate field in the "or" criteria row, thereby using the Or logical operator.

To display the information Oren and Taylor want to view, you'll create a new query containing the First, Last, Company, and City fields from the Customer table; and the ContractAmt, SigningDate, and ContractType fields from the Contract table. Then you'll specify the conditions using the Or logical operator.

To create a new query using the Or logical operator:

▶ 1. Click the **Create** tab on the Ribbon, and then click the **Query Design** button in the Queries group.

▶ 2. Add the **Customer** and **Contract** tables to the Query window, close the Show Table dialog box, and then resize the Customer field list.

▶ 3. Add the following fields from the Customer table to the design grid in the order shown: **First**, **Last**, **Company**, and **City**.

▶ 4. Add the following fields from the Contract table to the design grid in the order shown: **ContractAmt**, **SigningDate**, and **ContractType**.

Now you need to specify the first condition, <10000, in the ContractAmt field.

▶ 5. Click the **ContractAmt Criteria** box, and then type **<10000** and press the **Tab** key.

Because you want records selected if either of the conditions for the ContractAmt or SigningDate fields is satisfied, you must enter the condition for the SigningDate field in the "or" row of the design grid. To specify the date period for the query, you'll use the Between operator.

▶ 6. Press the ↓ key, type **Between 1/1/2014 And 3/1/2014** in the "or" box for SigningDate, and then press the **Tab** key.

To view the entire condition for the SigningDate field, you'll resize this field's column in the design grid.

▶ 7. Place the pointer on the vertical line to the right of the SigningDate field selector until the pointer changes to a ✛ shape, and then double-click to increase the column width and display the entire condition in the SigningDate field. Note that Access automatically places number signs around the date values in the condition to distinguish them from the operators. See Figure 3-30.

Figure 3-30   **Query window with the Or logical operator**

Oren wants the list displayed in descending order by SigningDate to better analyze the data.

▶ 8. Click the right side of the **SigningDate Sort** box, and then click **Descending**.

▶ 9. Run the query. Access displays only those records that meet either condition: a ContractAmt field value less than $10,000 or a SigningDate field value between 1/1/2014 and 3/1/2014. Access also selects records that meet both conditions. A total of 29 records is selected. The records in the query datasheet appear in descending order based on the values in the SigningDate field. See Figure 3-31.

Figure 3-31   **Results of query using the Or logical operator**

records with ContractAmt field values of less than 10,000

records with SigningDate field values between 1/1/2014 and 3/1/2014

records that meet both criteria

29 records selected

First Name	Last Name	Company	City	Contract Amt	Signing Date	Contract
Cathy	DeSantis		Rockford	5,000	8/24/2014	Residential landscape plan
Jan	Van Dousen	Three Tulips Café	Holland	8,500	8/2/2014	Landscape design for renova
Connor	Riley		Saint Joseph	6,500	7/28/2014	Front walk and drive design,
John	Weiss		South Haven	5,000	7/26/2014	Front walk and drive design,
Christina	Garrett	Blossom Day Care Center	Saint Joseph	6,500	7/25/2014	Schematic landscape design
Edward	Phillips		South Haven	5,000	7/25/2014	Residential landscape plan
Jerome	Smith		East Grand Rapids	5,000	6/1/2014	Residential landscape plan
Lisa	Hall	Cherrywood Senior Center	Saugatuck	6,500	5/17/2014	Schematic landscape design
Amber	Ward	Town of Holland	Holland	5,000	4/8/2014	Peer plan review for town
Devin	Finnerty	Finn's on the Waterfront	Holland	15,750	2/24/2014	Landscape design for restaur
Claire	Boucher		Saint Joseph	4,500	2/7/2014	Front walk and drive design,
Sarah	Russell	Dept. of Neighborhood Development	East Grand Rapids	38,000	2/3/2014	Renovation of playground at
John	Weiss		South Haven	1,750	1/20/2014	Landscape plan for front yard
Hwan	Tang		Holland	20,000	1/11/2014	Site layout and landscape de
Owen	Hawes		Holland	4,000	11/30/2013	Front walk and drive design,
Devin	Finnerty	Finn's on the Waterfront	Holland	7,500	9/23/2013	Landscape design for restaur
Claire	Boucher		Saint Joseph	375	9/15/2013	Consultation for front yard, r
Olivia	Pappas		South Haven	300	9/2/2013	Consultation for back yard, r
John	Weiss		South Haven	1,000	8/27/2013	Schematic plan for back yard
Owen	Hawes		Holland	2,250	7/8/2013	Residential landscape plan f
Amol	Mehta		Holland	6,500	6/22/2013	Residential landscape plan
Michael	Ingram		Kalamazoo	5,250	6/11/2013	Landscape plan for residenti
Sam	Kervin	Weston Community Parks Foundation	Grand Rapids	8,500	5/28/2013	Neighborhood park, nonprof
Melissa	Caputo		Saint Joseph	1,250	4/7/2013	Schematic plan for back yard
Anthony	Rodriguez	Grand Rapids Engineering Dept.	Grand Rapids	2,250	3/1/2013	Peer plan review for town

Record: 1 of 29

10. Save the query as **SmallContractsOrWinterSignings** and then close it.

INSIGHT

Understanding the Results of Using And vs. Or

When you use the And logical operator to define multiple selection criteria in a query, you *narrow* the results produced by the query because a record must meet more than one condition to be included in the results. When you use the Or logical operator, you *broaden* the results produced by the query because a record must meet only one of the conditions to be included in the results. This is an important distinction to keep in mind when you include multiple selection criteria in queries, so that the queries you create will produce the results you want.

Next, Oren turns his attention to some financial aspects of his business. He wants to use the Belmont database to perform calculations. He is considering imposing a 3% late fee on unpaid invoices and wants to know exactly what the late fee charges would be, should he decide to institute such a policy in the future. To produce the information for Oren, you need to create a calculated field.

Creating a Calculated Field

In addition to using queries to retrieve, sort, and filter data in a database, you can use a query to perform calculations. To perform a calculation, you define an **expression** containing a combination of database fields, constants, and operators. For numeric expressions, the data types of the database fields must be Number, Currency, or Date/Time; the constants are numbers such as .03 (for the 3% late fee); and the operators can be arithmetic operators (+ − * /) or other specialized operators. In complex expressions, you can enclose calculations in parentheses to indicate which one should be performed first. In expressions without parentheses, Access performs calculations using the following order of precedence: multiplication and division before addition and subtraction. When operators have equal precedence, Access calculates them in order from left to right.

To perform a calculation in a query, you add a calculated field to the query. A **calculated field** is a field that displays the results of an expression. A calculated field that you create with an expression appears in a query datasheet or in a form or report; however, it does not exist in a database. When you run a query that contains a calculated field, Access evaluates the expression defined by the calculated field and displays the resulting value in the query datasheet, form, or report.

To enter an expression for a calculated field, you can type it directly in a Field box in the design grid. Alternately, you can open the Zoom box or Expression Builder and use either one to enter the expression. The **Zoom box** is a dialog box that you can use to enter text, expressions, or other values. To use the Zoom box, however, you must know all the parts of the expression you want to create. **Expression Builder** is an Access tool that makes it easy for you to create an expression; it contains a box for entering the expression, an option for displaying and choosing common operators, and one or more lists of expression elements, such as table and field names. Unlike a Field box, which is too narrow to show an entire expression at one time, the Zoom box and Expression Builder are large enough to display longer expressions. In most cases, Expression Builder provides the easiest way to enter expressions because you don't have to know all the parts of the expression; you can choose the necessary elements from the Expression Builder dialog box.

REFERENCE

Using Expression Builder

- Open the query in Design view.
- In the design grid, click the Field box in which you want to create an expression.
- In the Query Setup group on the Design tab, click the Builder button.
- Use the expression elements and common operators to build the expression, or type the expression directly in the expression box.
- Click the OK button.

To produce the information Oren wants, you need to create a new query based on the Invoice table and, in the query, create a calculated field that will multiply each InvoiceAmt field value by .03 to calculate the proposed 3% late fee.

To create the new query and the calculated field:

1. Click the **Create** tab on the Ribbon, and then click the **Query Design** button in the Queries group.

   Oren wants to see data from both the Contract and Invoice tables, so you need to add these two tables to the Query window.

2. Add the **Contract** and **Invoice** tables to the Query window, and then close the Show Table dialog box. The field lists appear in the Query window, and the one-to-many relationship between the Contract (primary) and Invoice (related) tables is displayed.

3. Add the following fields to the design grid in the following order: **ContractNum** and **ContractAmt** from the Contract table; and **InvoiceItem**, **InvoicePaid**, and **InvoiceAmt** from the Invoice table.

Oren is interested in viewing data only for unpaid invoices because a late fee would apply only to them, so you need to enter the necessary condition for the InvoicePaid field. Recall that InvoicePaid is a Yes/No field. The condition you need to enter is the word "No" in the Criteria box for this field, so that Access will retrieve the records for unpaid invoices only.

▶ **4.** In the **InvoicePaid Criteria** box, type **No**. As soon as you type the letter "N," a menu appears with options for entering various functions for the criteria. You don't need to enter a function, so you can close this menu.

▶ **5.** Press the **Esc** key to close the menu.

> You must close the menu or you'll enter a function, which will cause an error.

▶ **6.** Press the **Tab** key. The query name you'll use will indicate that the data is for unpaid invoices, so you don't need to include the InvoicePaid values in the query results.

▶ **7.** Click the **InvoicePaid Show** check box to remove the check mark.

▶ **8.** Save the query with the name **UnpaidInvoicesWithLateFees**.

Now you can use Expression Builder to create the calculated field for the InvoiceAmt field.

To create the calculated field:

▶ **1.** Click the blank Field box to the right of the InvoiceAmt field. This field will contain the expression.

▶ **2.** In the Query Setup group on the Design tab, click the **Builder** button. The Expression Builder dialog box opens.

> **TIP**
> You must first save and name a query in order for its fields to be listed in the Expression Categories section.

The insertion point is positioned in the large box at the top of the dialog box, ready for you to enter the expression. The Expression Categories section of the dialog box lists the fields from the query so you can include them in the expression. The Expression Elements section contains options for including other elements in the expression, including functions, constants, and operators. If the expression you're entering is a simple one, you can type it in the box; if it's more complex, you can use the options in the Expression Elements section to help you build the expression.

The expression for the calculated field will multiply the InvoiceAmt field values by the numeric constant .03 (which represents a 3% late fee).

▶ **3.** Double-click **InvoiceAmt** in the Expression Categories section. The field name is added to the expression box, within brackets and with a space following it.

Next you need to enter the multiplication operator, which is the asterisk (*), followed by the constant.

▶ **4.** Type * (an asterisk) and then type **.03**. You have finished entering the expression. See Figure 3-32.

Figure 3-32 Completed expression for the calculated field

TIP

If you're not sure which operator to use, you can click Operators to display a list of available operators in the center section of the dialog box.

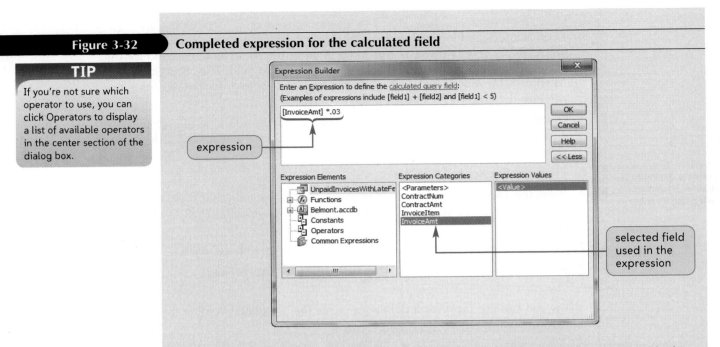

5. Click the **OK** button. Access closes the Expression Builder dialog box and adds the expression to the design grid in the Field box for the calculated field.

   When you create a calculated field, Access uses the default column name "Expr1" for the field. You need to specify a more meaningful column name so it will appear in the query results. You'll enter the name "Late Fee," which better describes the field's contents.

6. Click to the left of the text "Expr1:" at the beginning of the expression, and then press the **Delete** key five times to delete the text **Expr1**. *Do not delete the colon*; it is needed to separate the calculated field name from the expression.

7. Type **Late Fee**.

8. Run the query. Access displays the query datasheet, which contains the specified fields and the calculated field with the name "Late Fee." See Figure 3-33.

Figure 3-33 **Datasheet displaying the calculated field**

UnpaidInvoicesWithLateFees

Contract Num	Contract Amt	Invoice Item	Invoice Amt	Late Fee
3021	28,000	Construction Documents	$12,000.00	360
3021	28,000	Construction Observation	$8,500.00	255
3023	39,000	Construction Observation	$10,000.00	300
3026	165,000	Permitting	$10,000.00	300
3026	165,000	Construction Documents	$70,000.00	2100
3026	165,000	Construction Admin. & Observation	$50,000.00	1500
3031	48,500	Layout Plans	$16,000.00	480
3031	48,500	Construction Observation	$9,000.00	270
3037	68,000	Construction Documents	$30,000.00	900
3037	68,000	Construction Admin. & Observation	$15,000.00	450
3038	34,000	Construction Admin. & Observation	$8,000.00	240
3040	38,500	Construction Documents	$18,000.00	540
3040	38,500	Construction Admin. & Observation	$12,000.00	360
3043	19,000	Construction Observation	$3,000.00	90
3044	25,500	Construction Admin. & Observation	$10,000.00	300
3045	25,000	Schematic Plans	$18,000.00	540
3045	25,000	Community Meetings	$7,000.00	210
3048	7,500	Construction Observation	$1,500.00	45
3051	18,000	Construction Observation	$3,500.00	105
3056	32,500	Construction Documents	$20,000.00	600
3056	32,500	Construction Admin. & Observation	$12,500.00	375
3057	15,500	Construction Observation	$3,500.00	105
3061	30,800	Permitting	$3,000.00	90
3061	30,800	Construction Documents	$15,000.00	450
3061	30,800	Construction Observation	$6,800.00	204

specified name for the calculated field

calculated field values

Record: 1 of 100   No Filter   Search

Ready

> **Trouble?** If a dialog box opens noting that the expression contains invalid syntax, you might not have included the required colon in the expression. Click the OK button to close the dialog box, resize the column in the design grid that contains the calculated field to its best fit, change your expression to Late Fee: [Invoice Amt]*0.03 and then repeat Step 8.

The Late Fee field values are currently displayed without dollar signs and decimal places. Oren wants these values to be displayed in the same format as the InvoiceAmt field values, in case he decides to produce a report for customers showing both the invoice amounts and any imposed late fees.

Formatting a Calculated Field

You can specify a particular format for a calculated field, just as you can for any field, by modifying its properties. Next, you'll change the format of the Late Fee calculated field so that all values appear in the Currency format.

To format the calculated field:

1. Switch to Design view.

2. Right-click the **Late Fee** calculated field in the design grid to open the shortcut menu, and then click **Properties**. The Property Sheet for the calculated field opens on the right side of the window. See Figure 3-34.

Figure 3-34   **Property Sheet for the calculated field**

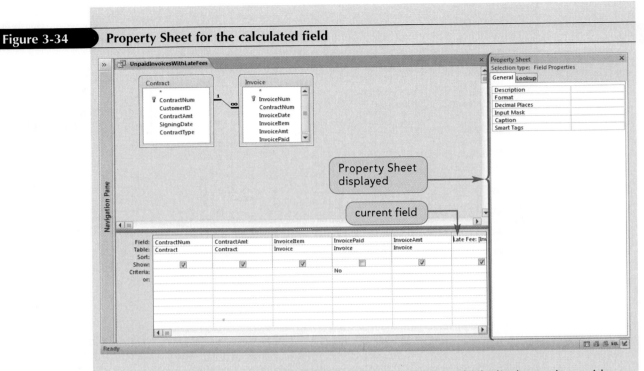

You need to change the Format property to Currency, which displays values with a dollar sign and two decimal places.

▶ **3.** Click the right side of the **Format** box in the Property Sheet to display the list of formats, and then click **Currency**.

▶ **4.** Close the Property Sheet for the calculated field, and then run the query. The amounts in the Late Fee calculated field are now displayed with dollar signs and two decimal places.

▶ **5.** Save and close the UnpaidInvoicesWithLateFees query.

PROSKILLS

Problem Solving: Creating Calculated Fields

The Calculated Field data type, a new data type in Access 2010, lets you store the result of an expression as a field in a table. However, database experts caution users against storing calculations in a table for several reasons. First, storing calculated data in a table consumes valuable space and increases the size of the database. The preferred approach is to use a calculated field in a query; with this approach, the result of the calculation is not stored in the database—it is produced only when you run the query—and it is always current. Second, the Calculated Field data type provides limited options for creating a calculation, whereas a calculated field in a query provides more functions and options for creating expressions. Third, including a field in a table using the Calculated Field data type limits your options if you need to upgrade the database at some point to a more robust DBMS, such as Oracle or SQL Server, that doesn't support this data type; you would need to redesign your database to eliminate this data type. Finally, most database experts agree that including a field in a table whose value is dependent on other fields in the table violates database design principles. To avoid such problems, it's best to create a query that includes a calculated field to perform the calculation you want, instead of creating a field in a table that uses the Calculated Field data type.

Oren wants to prepare a report on a regular basis that includes a summary of information about the contract amounts for Belmont Landscapes. He would like to know the minimum, average, and maximum contract amounts. He asks you to determine these statistics from data in the Contract table.

Using Aggregate Functions

You can calculate statistical information, such as totals and averages, on the records displayed in a table datasheet or selected by a query. To do this, you use the Access aggregate functions. **Aggregate functions** perform arithmetic operations on selected records in a database. Figure 3-35 lists the most frequently used aggregate functions.

Figure 3-35   Frequently used aggregate functions

Aggregate Function	Determines	Data Types Supported
Average	Average of the field values for the selected records	AutoNumber, Currency, Date/Time, Number
Count	Number of records selected	AutoNumber, Currency, Date/Time, Memo, Number, OLE Object, Text, Yes/No
Maximum	Highest field value for the selected records	AutoNumber, Currency, Date/Time, Number, Text
Minimum	Lowest field value for the selected records	AutoNumber, Currency, Date/Time, Number, Text
Sum	Total of the field values for the selected records	AutoNumber, Currency, Date/Time, Number

Working with Aggregate Functions Using the Total Row

If you want to quickly perform a calculation using an aggregate function in a table or query datasheet, you can use the Totals button in the Records group on the Home tab. When you click this button, a row labeled "Total" appears at the bottom of the datasheet. You can then choose one of the aggregate functions for a field in the datasheet, and the results of the calculation will be displayed in the Total row for that field.

Oren is interested to know the total amount of all contracts for the company. You can quickly display this amount using the Sum function in the Total row in the Contract table datasheet.

To display the total amount of all contracts in the Contract table:

1. Open the Navigation Pane, open the **Contract** table in Datasheet view, and then close the Navigation Pane.

2. In the Records group on the Home tab, click the **Totals** button. Access adds a row with the label "Total" to the bottom of the datasheet.

3. Scroll to the bottom of the datasheet to view the last records in the datasheet and the Total row. You want to display the sum of all the values in the Contract Amt column.

4. Click the **Contract Amt** column in the Total row. An arrow appears on the left side of the field.

5. Click the **arrow** to display the menu of aggregate functions. The functions displayed depend on the data type of the current field; in this case, the menu provides functions for a Currency field. See Figure 3-36.

| Figure 3-36 | **Using aggregate functions in the Total row** |

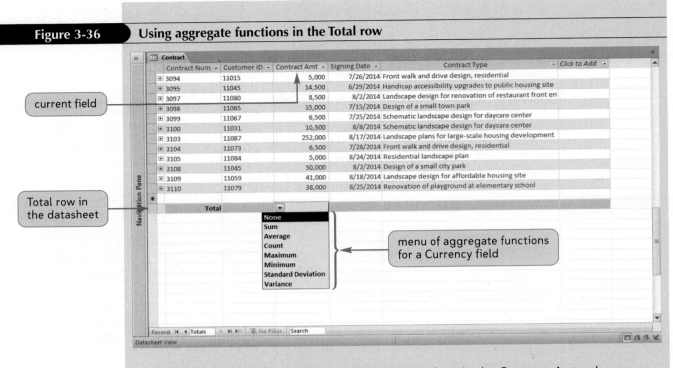

6. Click **Sum** in the menu. Access adds all the values in the Contract Amt column and displays the total 1,753,075 in the Total row for the column.

Oren doesn't want to change the Contract table to always display this total. You can remove the Total row by clicking the Totals button again; this button works as a toggle to switch between the display of the Total row and the results of any calculations in the row, and the display of the datasheet without this row.

7. In the Records group on the Home tab, click the **Totals** button. Access removes the Total row from the datasheet.

8. Close the Contract table without saving the changes.

Oren wants to know the minimum, average, and maximum contract amounts for the company. To produce this information for Oren, you need to use aggregate functions in a query.

Creating Queries with Aggregate Functions

Aggregate functions operate on the records that meet a query's selection criteria. You specify an aggregate function for a specific field, and the appropriate operation applies to that field's values for the selected records.

To display the minimum, average, and maximum of all the contract amounts in the Contract table, you will use the Minimum, Average, and Maximum aggregate functions for the ContractAmt field.

To calculate the minimum, average, and maximum of all contract amounts:

1. Create a new query in Design view, add the **Contract** table to the Query window, and then close the Show Table dialog box.

To perform the three calculations on the ContractAmt field, you need to add the field to the design grid three times.

2. Double-click **ContractAmt** in the Contract field list three times to add three copies of the field to the design grid.

   You need to select an aggregate function for each ContractAmt field. When you click the Totals button in the Show/Hide group on the Design tab, a row labeled "Total" is added to the design grid. The Total row provides a list of the aggregate functions that you can select.

3. In the Show/Hide group on the Design tab, click the **Totals** button. A new row labeled "Total" appears between the Table and Sort rows in the design grid. The default entry for each field in the Total row is the Group By operator, which you will learn about later in this tutorial. See Figure 3-37.

Figure 3-37	Total row inserted in the design grid

ContractAmt field included three times in the design grid

Total row

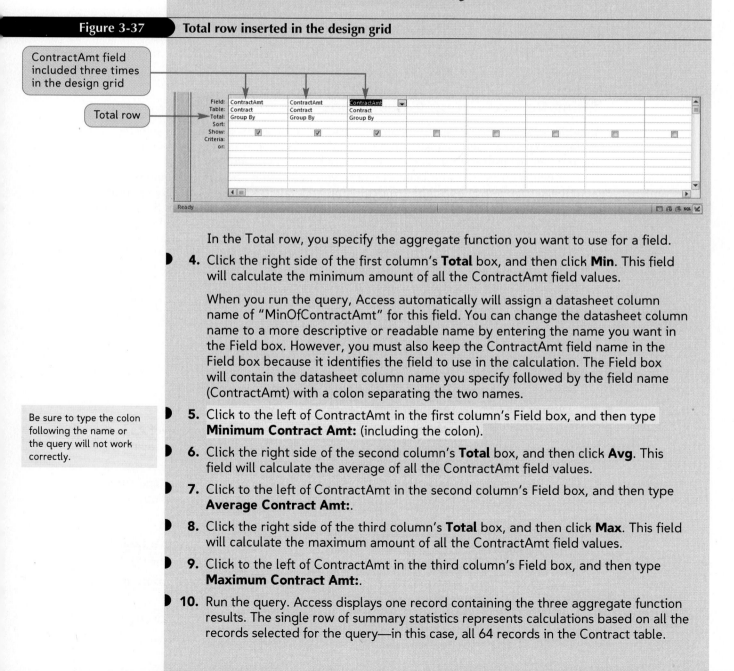

In the Total row, you specify the aggregate function you want to use for a field.

4. Click the right side of the first column's **Total** box, and then click **Min**. This field will calculate the minimum amount of all the ContractAmt field values.

   When you run the query, Access automatically will assign a datasheet column name of "MinOfContractAmt" for this field. You can change the datasheet column name to a more descriptive or readable name by entering the name you want in the Field box. However, you must also keep the ContractAmt field name in the Field box because it identifies the field to use in the calculation. The Field box will contain the datasheet column name you specify followed by the field name (ContractAmt) with a colon separating the two names.

Be sure to type the colon following the name or the query will not work correctly.

5. Click to the left of ContractAmt in the first column's Field box, and then type **Minimum Contract Amt:** (including the colon).

6. Click the right side of the second column's **Total** box, and then click **Avg**. This field will calculate the average of all the ContractAmt field values.

7. Click to the left of ContractAmt in the second column's Field box, and then type **Average Contract Amt:**.

8. Click the right side of the third column's **Total** box, and then click **Max**. This field will calculate the maximum amount of all the ContractAmt field values.

9. Click to the left of ContractAmt in the third column's Field box, and then type **Maximum Contract Amt:**.

10. Run the query. Access displays one record containing the three aggregate function results. The single row of summary statistics represents calculations based on all the records selected for the query—in this case, all 64 records in the Contract table.

▶ **11.** Resize all columns to their best fit so that the column names are fully displayed, and then click the field value in the first column. See Figure 3-38.

Figure 3-38 ▶ **Result of the query using aggregate functions**

▶ **12.** Save the query as **ContractAmtStatistics**.

Oren also wants his report to include the same contract amount statistics (minimum, average, and maximum) grouped by city.

Using Record Group Calculations

In addition to calculating statistical information on all or selected records in selected tables, you can calculate statistics for groups of records. For example, you can determine the number of customers in each city or the average contract amount by city.

To create a query for Oren's latest request, you can modify the current query by adding the City field and assigning the Group By operator to it. The **Group By operator** divides the selected records into groups based on the values in the specified field. Those records with the same value for the field are grouped together, and the datasheet displays one record for each group. Aggregate functions, which appear in the other columns of the design grid, provide statistical information for each group.

You need to modify the current query to add the Group By operator to the City field from the Customer table. The Group By operator will display the statistical information grouped by city for all the records in the query datasheet. To create the new query, you will save the ContractAmtStatistics query with a new name, keeping the original query intact, and then modify the new query.

To create a new query with the Group By operator:

▶ **1.** Display the ContractAmtStatistics query in Design view.

▶ **2.** Click the **File** tab to display Backstage view, and then click **Save Object As** in the navigation bar. The Save As dialog box opens, indicating that you are saving a copy of the ContractAmtStatistics query as a new query.

▶ **3.** Type **ContractAmtStatisticsByCity** to replace the highlighted name, and then press the **Enter** key. The new query is saved with the name you specified.

▶ **4.** Click the **Design** tab to return to the Query window in Design view.

You need to add the City field to the query. This field is in the Customer table. To include another table in an existing query, you open the Show Table dialog box.

▶ **5.** In the Query Setup group on the Design tab, click the **Show Table** button to open the Show Table dialog box.

▶ **6.** Add the **Customer** table to the Query window, close the Show Table dialog box, and then resize the Customer field list.

7. Drag the **City** field from the Customer field list to the first column in the design grid. When you release the mouse button, the City field appears in the design grid's first column, and the existing fields shift to the right. Group By, the default option in the Total row, appears for the City field.

8. Run the query. Access displays 12 records—one for each City group. Each record contains the City field value for the group and the three aggregate function values. The summary statistics represent calculations based on the 64 records in the Contract table. See Figure 3-39.

| Figure 3-39 | Aggregate functions grouped by City |

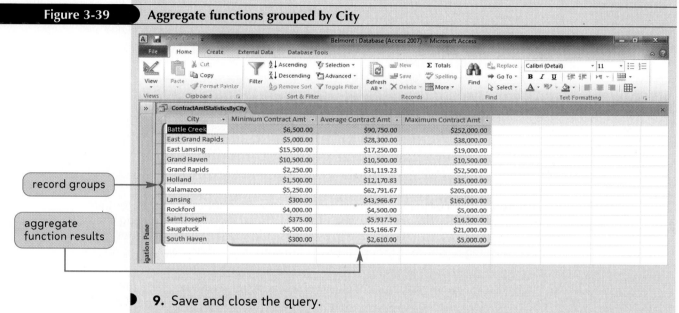

record groups

aggregate function results

9. Save and close the query.

10. Open the Navigation Pane.

You have created and saved many queries in the Belmont database. The Navigation Pane provides options for opening and managing the queries you've created, as well as the other objects in the database, such as tables, forms, and reports.

Working with the Navigation Pane

As noted in Tutorial 1, the Navigation Pane is the main area for working with the objects in a database. As you continue to create objects in your database, you might want to display and work with them in different ways. The Navigation Pane provides options for grouping database objects in various ways to suit your needs. For example, you might want to view only the queries created for a certain table or all the query objects in the database.

The Navigation Pane divides database objects into categories, and each category contains groups. The groups contain one or more objects. The default category is **Object Type**, which arranges objects by type—tables, queries, forms, and reports. The default group is **All Access Objects**, which displays all objects in the database. You can also choose to display only one type of object, such as tables.

The default group name, All Access Objects, appears at the top of the Navigation Pane. Currently, each object type—Tables, Queries, Forms, and Reports—is displayed in a bar, and the objects related to each type are listed below the bar. To group objects differently, you can select another category by using the Navigation Pane menu. You'll try this next.

TIP

You can hide the display of a group's objects by clicking the bar for the group; click the bar again to expand the group and display its objects.

To group objects differently in the Navigation Pane:

▶ **1.** At the top of the Navigation Pane, click the **All Access Objects** bar. A menu is displayed for choosing different categories and groups. See Figure 3-40.

Figure 3-40	Navigation Pane menu

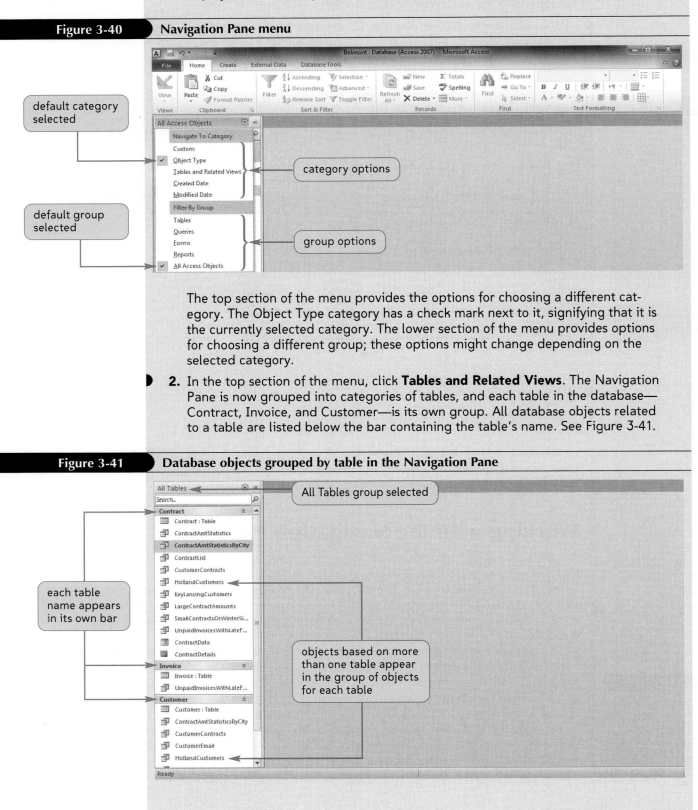

default category selected

default group selected

category options

group options

The top section of the menu provides the options for choosing a different category. The Object Type category has a check mark next to it, signifying that it is the currently selected category. The lower section of the menu provides options for choosing a different group; these options might change depending on the selected category.

▶ **2.** In the top section of the menu, click **Tables and Related Views**. The Navigation Pane is now grouped into categories of tables, and each table in the database—Contract, Invoice, and Customer—is its own group. All database objects related to a table are listed below the bar containing the table's name. See Figure 3-41.

Figure 3-41	Database objects grouped by table in the Navigation Pane

All Tables group selected

each table name appears in its own bar

objects based on more than one table appear in the group of objects for each table

Some objects appear more than once. When an object is based on more than one table, that object appears in the group for each table. For example, the HollandCustomers query is based on both the Contract and Customer tables, so it is listed in the group for both tables.

You can also choose to display the objects for only one table to better focus on that table.

▶ 3. Click the **All Tables** bar to display the Navigation Pane menu, and then click **Customer**. The Navigation Pane now shows only the objects related to the Customer table—the table itself plus the seven queries you created that include fields from the Customer table.

▶ 4. Click the **Customer** bar at the top of the Navigation Pane, and then click **Object Type** to return to the default display of the Navigation Pane.

▶ 5. Compact and repair the Belmont database, and then close the database.

Trouble? If a dialog box opens and warns that this action will cause Microsoft Access to empty the Clipboard, click the Yes button to continue.

The default All Access Objects category is a predefined category. You can also create custom categories to group objects in the way that best suits how you want to manage your database objects. As you continue to build a database and the list of objects grows, creating a custom category can help you to work more efficiently with the objects in the database.

The queries you've created and saved will help Oren, Taylor, Sarah, and others to monitor and analyze the business activity of Belmont Landscapes and its customers. Now any staff member can run the queries at any time, modify them as needed, or use them as the basis for designing new queries to meet additional information requirements.

Session 3.2 Quick Check

REVIEW

1. A(n) _____ is a criterion, or rule, that determines which records are selected for a query datasheet.
2. In the design grid, where do you place the conditions for two different fields when you use the And logical operator? The Or logical operator?
3. To perform a calculation in a query, you define a(n) _____ containing a combination of database fields, constants, and operators.
4. Which Access tool do you use to create an expression for a calculated field in a query?
5. What is an aggregate function?
6. The _____ operator divides selected records into groups based on the values in a field.
7. What is the default category for the display of objects in the Navigation Pane?

Practice the skills you learned in the tutorial using the same case scenario.

PRACTICE

Review Assignments

Data File needed for the Review Assignments: Supplier.accdb (*cont. from Tutorial 2*)

Oren asks you to update some information in the Supplier database and also to retrieve specific information from the database. Complete the following:

1. Open the **Supplier** database located in the Access1\Review folder, and then click the Enable Content button next to the Security Warning, if necessary.

2. Open the **Company** table, and then change the following field values for the record with the CompanyID MID312: Address to **2250 E Riverview St**, Phone to **269-979-0700**, Contact First Name to **Aimee**, and Contact Last Name to **Gigandet**. Close the table.

3. Open the **Product** table, find the record with Product ID 5318, and then delete the record. Close the table.

4. Create a query based on the Company table. Include the following fields in the query, in the order shown: Company, ContactFirst, ContactLast, Phone, and InitialContact. Sort the query in ascending order based on the Company field values. Save the query as **ContactList**, and then run the query.

5. Use the ContactList query datasheet to update the Company table by changing the Phone field value for Genesis Garden Center to **616-456-1783**.

6. Change the alternate row color in the ContactList query datasheet to the Theme Color named Tan, Background 2, Darker 10% (second row, third column), and then save and close the query.

7. Use Design view to create a query based on the Company and Product tables. Select the Company and City fields from the Company table, and the ProductType, Price, Unit, and Discount fields from the Product table. Sort the query results in descending order based on price. Select only those records with a City field value of Holland, but do not display the City field values in the query results. Save the query as **HollandCompanies**, run the query, and then close it.

8. Use Design view to create a query that lists all products that cost more than $5,000 and are not eligible for a discount. Display the following fields from the Product table in the query results: ProductID, ProductType, Price, Unit, and Weight. (*Hint*: The Discount field is a Yes/No field that should not appear in the query results.) Save the query as **HighPricesNoDiscount**, run the query, and then close it.

9. Use Design view to create a query that lists companies located in Grand Rapids or products that cost less than $1,000. Include the Company, City, ContactFirst, and ContactLast fields from the Company table; and the ProductType, Price, and Discount fields from the Product table. Save the query as **GrandRapidsOrLowPrices**, run the query, and then close it.

10. Use Design view to create a query that lists only those products that are eligible for a discount, along with a 5% discount amount based on the current price. Include the following fields from the Product table in the query: ProductID, ProductType, and Price. (*Hint*: The Discount field is a Yes/No field that should not appear in the query results.) Save the query as **PricesWithDiscountAmounts**. Display the discount in a calculated field named **Discount Amt** that determines a 5% discount based on the Price field values. Display the results in descending order by Price. Save and run the query.

11. Modify the format of the Discount Amt field in the PricesWithDiscountAmounts query so that it uses the Standard format and two decimal places. Run the query, resize all columns in the datasheet to best fit, and then save and close the query.

12. Create a query that calculates the lowest, highest, and average prices for all products using the field names **Lowest Price**, **Highest Price**, and **Average Price**, respectively. Run the query, resize all columns in the datasheet to best fit, save the query as **PriceStatistics**, and then close it.

13. In the Navigation Pane, copy the PriceStatistics query, and then rename the copied query as **PriceStatisticsByCompany**.

14. Modify the PriceStatisticsByCompany query so that the records are grouped by the Company field in the Company table. The Company field should appear first in the query datasheet. Save and run the query, and then close it.

15. Compact and repair the Supplier database, and then close it.

APPLY

Case Problem 1
If you have a SAM 2010 user profile, your instructor may have assigned an autogradable version of this assignment. If so, log into the SAM 2010 Web site at www.cengage.com/sam2010 to download the instructions and start files.

Data File needed for this Case Problem: Pinehill.accdb (cont. from Tutorial 2)

Pine Hill Music School   After reviewing the Pinehill database, Yuka Koyama wants to modify some records and then view specific information about the students, teachers, and contracts for her music school. She asks you to update and then query the Pinehill database to perform these tasks. Complete the following:

1. Open the **Pinehill** database located in the Access1\Case1 folder, and then click the Enable Content button next to the Security Warning, if necessary.

2. In the **Teacher** table, change the following information for the record with TeacherID 55-5310: Degree is **BM** and Hire Date is **3/12/2012**. Close the table.

3. In the **Student** table, find the record with the StudentID HAV7535, and then delete the related record in the subdatasheet for this student. Delete the record for StudentID HAV7535, and then close the Student table.

4. Create a query based on the Student table that includes the LastName, FirstName, and MobilePhone fields, in that order. Save the query as **StudentPhoneList**, and then run the query.

5. In the results of the StudentPhoneList query, change the mobile phone number for Andrea Barreau to **503-579-2277**. Close the query.

6. Use Design view to create a query based on the Teacher and Contract tables. Display the LastName field from the Teacher table, and the StudentID, EndDate, LessonType, LessonLength, and LessonCost fields, in that order, from the Contract table. Sort in ascending order first on the teacher's last name, and then in ascending order by the StudentID. Save the query as **LessonsByTeacher**, and then run it.

7. Display Backstage view, and then save the LessonsByTeacher query as **CurrentLessons**.

8. Modify the CurrentLessons query to display all contracts that end on or after 7/1/2013. Save your changes, and then run the query.

9. Display Backstage view, and then save the CurrentLessons query as **CurrentGuitarLessons**.

10. Modify the CurrentGuitarLessons query to display only those records for guitar lesson contracts that end on or after 7/1/2013. Do not include the LessonType field values in the query results. Run and save the query.

11. In the CurrentGuitarLessons query datasheet, calculate the total monthly amount for current guitar lessons.

12. Change the alternate row color in the CurrentGuitarLessons query datasheet to the Theme Color named Purple, Accent 4, Lighter 60% (third row, eight column), and then change the font size to 12. Resize all columns in the datasheet to fit the data, and then save and close the query.

13. Compact and repair the Pinehill database, and then close it.

Follow the steps and use the figures as guides to create queries for a fitness center.

CREATE

Case Problem 2

Data File needed for this Case Problem: Fitness.accdb (*cont. from Tutorial 2*)

Parkhurst Health & Fitness Center   Martha Parkhurst needs to change a few records in the Fitness database and analyze the records for members enrolled in different programs at the fitness center. To help her perform these tasks, you'll update the Fitness database and create queries to answer her questions. Complete the following:

1. Open the **Fitness** database located in the Access1\Case2 folder, and then click the Enable Content button next to the Security Warning, if necessary.

2. In the **Member** table, find the record for MemberID 1158, and then change the Street value to **89 Mockingbird Lane** and the Phone to **804-751-1847**. Close the table.

3. In the **Program** table, find the record for ProgramID 205. In the subdatasheet, delete the related record from the Member table. Then delete the record for ProgramID 205 in the Program table. Close the table.

4. Use Design view to create a query that lists members who are required to have physical examinations. In the query results, display the First, Last, and DateJoined fields from the Member table, and the MonthlyFee field from the Program table. Sort the records in descending order by the date joined. Select records only for members required to take a physical. (*Hint:* The PhysicalRequired field is a Yes/No field that should not appear in the query results.) Save the query as **PhysicalsNeeded**, and then run the query.

5. Use the PhysicalsNeeded query datasheet to update the Member table by changing the Date Joined value for Ed Curran to **10/18/2013**.

6. Use the PhysicalsNeeded query datasheet to display the total Monthly Fee for the selected members. Save and close the query.

7. Use Design view to create a query that lists the MemberID, First, Last, DateJoined, ProgramType, and MonthlyFee fields for members who joined the fitness center between June 1 and June 30, 2013. Save the query as **JuneMembers**, run the query, and then close it.

8. Create and save the query to produce the results shown in Figure 3-42. Close the query when you are finished.

Figure 3-42   RichmondOnHold query results

show only records for customers from Richmond whose memberships are on hold

sort by Last Name

apply the Orange, Accent 6, Lighter 80% alternate row Theme Color

Member ID	First Name	Last Name	Phone	Date Joined
1156	Kurt	Eisler	804-236-8961	4/17/2013
1142	Kye	Nguyen	804-236-0325	2/20/2013
1120	Carmen	Sanchez	804-674-5991	10/18/2013
1166	Abigail	Turner	804-674-6807	9/1/2013

EXPLORE

9. Create and save the query to produce the results shown in Figure 3-43. Close the query when you are finished.

Figure 3-43   **SelectedCities query results**

primary sort field

show only customers from Bon Air or Chester

secondary sort field

Total row shows the sum of the Monthly Fee values

City	First Name	Last Name	Monthly Fee	Phone	Membership Status
Bon Air	Student First	Student Last	50.00	804-323-6824	Active
Bon Air	Marlene	Halpin	50.00	804-323-0346	On Hold
Bon Air	Michelle	Kim	50.00	804-323-0291	Active
Chester	Kelly	Smith	50.00	804-751-0466	Active
Chester	Liz	Sorrento	50.00	804-751-1270	Active
Chester	Barry	Feinberg	45.00	804-751-1119	Active
Chester	Pedro	Fuente	40.00	804-751-1847	Active
Chester	Tina	Sun	40.00	804-751-9111	Active
Chester	Mary	Grant	30.00	804-751-8772	Active
Total			405.00		

◆EXPLORE   10. Create and save the query to produce results that display statistics for the MonthlyFee field, as shown in Figure 3-44. Close the query when you are finished.

Figure 3-44   **FeeStatistics query results**

format values as Standard with two decimal places

Maximum Fee	Minimum Fee	Average Fee
60.00	30.00	41.82

11. In the Navigation Pane, copy the FeeStatistics query and rename the copied query **FeeStatisticsByCity**.

12. Modify the FeeStatisticsByCity query to display the same statistics grouped by City, with City appearing as the first field. (*Hint:* Add the Member table to the query.) Run the query, and then save and close it.

13. Compact and repair the Fitness database, and then close it.

Explore some new skills to create queries for a recycling agency.

CHALLENGE

Case Problem 3

Data File needed for this Case Problem: Rossi.accdb (*cont. from Tutorial 2*)

Rossi Recycling Group   Tom Rossi needs to modify some records in the Rossi database, and then he wants to find specific information about the donors, agencies, and donations to his not-for-profit agency. Tom asks you to help him update the database and create queries. Complete the following:

1. Open the **Rossi** database located in the Access1\Case3 folder, and then click the Enable Content button next to the Security Warning, if necessary.

2. In the **Donor** table, delete the record with DonorID 36065. (*Hint:* Delete the related record first.) Close the table.

3. Create a query based on the Agency table that includes the Agency, FirstName, LastName, and City fields, in that order. Save the query as **AgenciesByCity**, and then run it.

4. Modify the AgenciesByCity query design so that it sorts records in ascending order first by City and then by Agency. Save and run the query.

5. In the AgenciesByCity query datasheet, change the contact for the Community Development agency to **Beth Dayton**. Close the query.

6. Use Design view to create a query that displays the DonorID, FirstName, and LastName fields from the Donor table, and the Description and DonationValue fields from the Donation table for all donations over $50. Sort the query in ascending order by donation value. Save the query as **LargeDonations**, and then run the query.

7. Display Backstage view, and then save the LargeDonations query as **LargeCashDonations**.

EXPLORE 8. Modify the LargeCashDonations query to display only those records with donations valuing more than $50 in cash. Do not include the Description field values in the query results. Use the query datasheet to calculate the average cash donation. Save and close the query.

9. Use Design view to create a query that displays the AgencyID (from the Agency table), and the DonationID, DonationDate, and Description fields from the Donation table. Save the query as **SeniorDonations**, and then run the query.

10. Filter the results of the SeniorDonations query datasheet to display records for all donations to the SeniorCare Program (AgencyID K82).

EXPLORE 11. Format the datasheet of the SeniorDonations query so that it does not display grid-lines, uses an alternate row Standard Color of Maroon 2, and displays a font size of 12. (*Hint*: Use the Gridlines button in the Text Formatting group on the Home tab to select the appropriate gridlines option.) Resize the columns to display the complete field names and values. Save your changes.

12. Display Backstage view, and then save the SeniorDonations query as **ComputerOrYouthDonations**.

13. Modify the ComputerOrYouthDonations query to display donations of "Computer equipment" or those to the After School Youth agency (AgencyID Y68). Sort the records in ascending order first by Description and then by AgencyID. Run, save, and then close the query.

EXPLORE 14. Use Design view to create a query (based on all three tables in the database) that displays the DonorID (Donor table), Agency, Description, and DonationValue fields for all donations that require a pickup. (*Hint:* The Pickup field is a Yes/No field that should not appear in the query results.) Save the query as **DonationsAfterPickupCharge**. Create a calculated field named **Net Donation** that displays the results of subtracting $8.75 from the DonationValue field values. Display the results in ascending order by donation value. Run the query, and then modify it to format the calculated field as Currency. Run the query again and resize the columns in the datasheet to their best fit. Save and close the query.

EXPLORE 15. Use the **Donation** table to display the sum, average, and count of the DonationValue field for all donations. Then complete the following:

   a. Specify column names of **Total Donations**, **Average Donation**, and **Number of Donations**.

   b. Save the query as **DonationStatistics**, and then run it.

   c. Modify the field properties so that the values in the Total Donations and Average Donation columns display two decimal places and the Standard format. Run the query and resize the columns in the datasheet to their best fit. Save and close the query.

   d. In the Navigation Pane, create a copy of the DonationStatistics query named **DonationStatisticsByAgency**.

   e. Modify the DonationStatisticsByAgency query to display the sum, average, and count of the DonationValue field for all donations grouped by Agency, with Agency appearing as the first field. (*Hint*: Add the Agency table to the query.) Sort the records in descending order by Total Donations. Save, run, and then close the query.

16. Compact and repair the Rossi database, and then close it.

Explore some new skills to create queries for a luxury rental company.

CHALLENGE

Case Problem 4

Data File needed for this Case Problem: GEM.accdb (*cont. from Tutorial 2*)

GEM Ultimate Vacations   Griffin and Emma MacElroy want to modify some records, and then analyze data about their clients and the luxury properties they rent. You'll help them update and query the GEM database. Complete the following:

1. Open the **GEM** database located in the Access1\Case4 folder, and then click the Enable Content button next to the Security Warning, if necessary.

2. In the **Guest** table, delete the record with a GuestID of 224, and then close the table.

3. Create a query based on the Property table that includes the PropertyName, Location, Country, NightlyRate, and PropertyType fields, in that order. Sort in ascending order based on the NightlyRate field values. Save the query as **PropertiesByRate**, and then run the query.

⊕**EXPLORE** 4. In the results of the PropertiesByRate query, change the nightly rate for the Hartfield Country Manor property to $2,500, and then use the datasheet to display the number of properties (using the Property Type column) and the average nightly rate. Save and close the query.

5. Create a query that displays the GuestLast, City, State/Prov, ReservationID, StartDate, and EndDate fields. Save the query as **GuestTripDates**, and then run the query. Change the alternate row color in the query datasheet to the Standard Color Purple 2. In Datasheet view, use an AutoFilter to sort the query results from oldest to newest Start Date. Resize the datasheet columns to their best fit, and then save and close the query.

6. Create a query that displays the GuestLast, City, ReservationID, People, StartDate, and EndDate fields for all guests from Illinois (IL). Do not include the State/Prov field in the query results. Sort the query in ascending order by City. Save the query as **IllinoisGuests** and then run it. Resize datasheet columns to their best fit, as necessary, and then save and close the query.

⊕**EXPLORE** 7. Create a query that displays the GuestLast, City, State/Prov, ReservationID, StartDate, and PropertyID fields for all guests who are not from Illinois or who are renting a property starting in the month of July 2013. (*Hint:* You must specifically type the quotation marks around the state abbreviation "IL" in the criteria.) Sort the query in descending order by StartDate. Save the query as **OutOfStateOrJuly**, and then run the query. Resize datasheet columns to their best fit, as necessary, and then save the query.

8. Display Backstage view, and then save the OutOfStateOrJuly query as **OutOfStateAndJuly**.

9. Modify the OutOfStateAndJuly query to select all guests who are not from Illinois and who are renting a property beginning in the month of July 2013. Sort the query in ascending order by StartDate. Run the query, and then save and close it.

10. Create a query that displays the ReservationID, StartDate, EndDate, PropertyID, PropertyName, People, and Rate fields for all reservations. Save the query as **RentalCost**. Add a field to the query named **Cost Per Person** that displays the results of dividing the Rate field values by the People field values. Display the results in descending order by Cost Per Person. Run the query. Modify the query by setting the Format property for the Cost Per Person field to Currency. Run the query, resize datasheet columns to their best fit, as necessary, and then save your changes.

11. Display Backstage view, and then save the RentalCost query as **TopRentalCost**.

⊕**EXPLORE** 12. Modify the TopRentalCost query in Design view to display only the top five values for the Cost Per Person field. (*Hint:* Use the Return (Top Values) box in the Query Setup group on the Design tab.) Save, run, and then close the query.

13. Use the Reservation table to determine the minimum, average, and maximum rental rate values for all reservations. Then complete the following:

   a. Specify column names of **Lowest Rate**, **Average Rate**, and **Highest Rate**.

   b. Save the query as **RateStatistics**, and then run the query.

   c. In Design view, specify the Standard format and two decimal places for each column.

   d. Run the query, resize all the datasheet columns to their best fit, save your changes, and then close the query.

   e. Create a copy of the RateStatistics query named **RateStatisticsByCountry**.

   f. Revise the RateStatisticsByCountry query to display the rate statistics grouped by Country of the property, with Country appearing as the first field. Save your changes and then run and close the query.

14. Compact and repair the GEM database, and then close it.

SAM: Skills Assessment Manager

ASSESS

For current SAM information, including versions and content details, visit SAM Central (http://samcentral.course.com). If you have a SAM user profile, you may have access to hands-on instruction, practice, and assessment of the skills covered in this tutorial. Since various versions of SAM are supported throughout the life of this text, check with your instructor for the correct instructions and URL/Web site for accessing assignments.

ENDING DATA FILES

Access1 →	Tutorial	Review	Case1
	Belmont.accdb	Supplier.accdb	Pinehill.accdb
	Case2	Case3	Case4
	Fitness.accdb	Rossi.accdb	GEM.accdb

Creating Forms and Reports

Using Forms and Reports to Display Customer and Contract Data

Case | *Belmont Landscapes*

Oren Belmont wants to continue enhancing the Belmont database to make it easier for his staff to enter, locate, and maintain data. In particular, he wants the database to include a form based on the Customer table to make it easier for employees to enter and change data about the firm's customers. He also wants the database to include a form that shows data from both the Customer and Contract tables at the same time. This form will show the contract information for each customer along with the corresponding customer data, providing a complete picture of Belmont Landscapes customers and their contracts.

In addition, Taylor Sico would like the database to include a formatted report of customer and contract data so that employees will have printed output when completing market analyses and planning strategies for selling services to customers. She wants the information to be formatted in a professional manner, to make the report appealing and easy to use.

STARTING DATA FILES

Access1 →	Tutorial	Review	Case1
	Belmont.accdb *(cont.)*	Supplier.accdb *(cont.)*	Piano.bmp
	Landscape.bmp	Tools.bmp	Pinehill.accdb *(cont.)*

Case2	Case3	Case4
Fitness.accdb *(cont.)*	Recycle.bmp	GEM.accdb *(cont.)*
Weights.bmp	Rossi.accdb *(cont.)*	Villa.bmp

SESSION 4.1 VISUAL OVERVIEW

The form object's name is displayed on the tab for the form.

The form title appears at the top of the form. By default, the form object name is used as the form title, but you can edit the title to display the text you want, as done here—a space was added between the two words for readability.

With this form layout, the Columnar layout, the field captions appear in a column on the left side of the form. If captions have not been specified for the fields, the field names would appear here instead.

The navigation buttons allow you to display the first, last, next, or previous record in the form; enter a specific record number and move to that record; and create a new record.

You can add graphic elements, such as a picture, to a form to improve its appearance or add visual appeal.

The Columnar form layout displays the corresponding field values in boxes to the right of the field captions (or field names).

Belmont : Database (Access 2007)

File | Home | Create | External Data | Database Tools

View — Views

Paste — Clipboard

Cut
Copy
Format Painter

Filter — Sort & Filter

Ascending
Descending
Remove Sort

Selection
Advanced
Toggle Filter

Refresh All — Records

New
Save
Delete

Navigation Pane

CustomerData

Customer Data

Customer ID	11001
Company	
First Name	Student First
Last Name	Student Last
Address	49 Blackstone Dr
City	Rockford
State	MI
Zip	49341
Email	student2@milocal123.com
Phone	616-866-3901

Record: 1 of 40 | No Filter | Search

Primary key

FORM DISPLAYED IN FORM VIEW

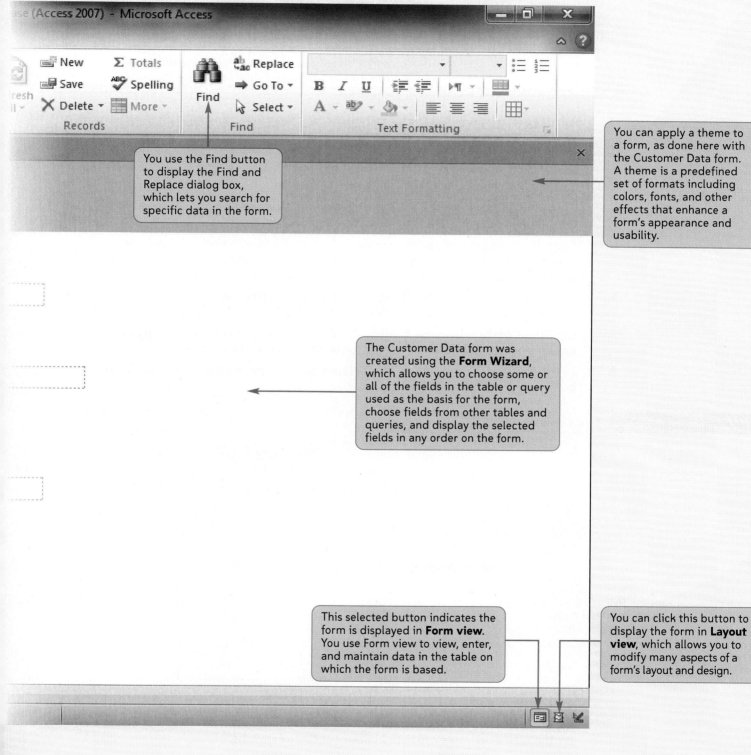

se (Access 2007) - Microsoft Access

New   Σ Totals   Replace
Save   ABC Spelling   Go To ▾   **B** *I* <u>U</u>
Delete ▾   More ▾   Find   Select ▾   A ▾
Records   Find   Text Formatting

You use the Find button to display the Find and Replace dialog box, which lets you search for specific data in the form.

You can apply a theme to a form, as done here with the Customer Data form. A theme is a predefined set of formats including colors, fonts, and other effects that enhance a form's appearance and usability.

The Customer Data form was created using the **Form Wizard**, which allows you to choose some or all of the fields in the table or query used as the basis for the form, choose fields from other tables and queries, and display the selected fields in any order on the form.

This selected button indicates the form is displayed in **Form view**. You use Form view to view, enter, and maintain data in the table on which the form is based.

You can click this button to display the form in **Layout view**, which allows you to modify many aspects of a form's layout and design.

Creating a Form Using the Form Wizard

As you learned in Tutorial 1, a form is an object you use to enter, edit, and view records in a database. You can design your own forms or have Access create them for you automatically. In Tutorial 1, you used the Form tool to create the ContractData form in the Belmont database. Recall that the Form tool creates a form automatically, using all the fields in the selected table or query.

Oren asks you to create a new form that his staff can use to view and maintain data in the Customer table. To create the form for the Customer table, you'll use the Form Wizard, which guides you through the process.

To open the Belmont database and start the Form Wizard:

▶ **1.** Start Access and open the **Belmont** database located in the Access1\Tutorial folder.

   Trouble? If the Security Warning is displayed below the Ribbon, click the Enable Content button next to the Security Warning.

▶ **2.** Open the Navigation Pane, if necessary. To create a form based on a table or query, you can select the table or query in the Navigation Pane first, or you can select it using the Form Wizard.

▶ **3.** In the Tables section of the Navigation Pane, click **Customer** to select the Customer table as the basis for the new form.

▶ **4.** Click the **Create** tab on the Ribbon. The Forms group on the Create tab provides options for creating various types of forms and designing your own forms.

▶ **5.** In the Forms group, click the **Form Wizard** button. The first Form Wizard dialog box opens. See Figure 4-1.

Figure 4-1   ▶   **First Form Wizard dialog box**

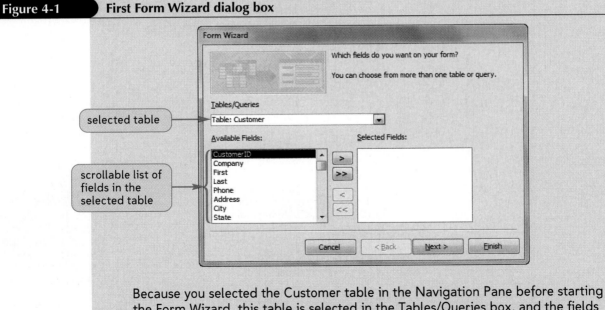

Because you selected the Customer table in the Navigation Pane before starting the Form Wizard, this table is selected in the Tables/Queries box, and the fields for the Customer table are listed in the Available Fields box.

Oren wants the form to display all the fields in the Customer table, but in a different order. He would like the Phone field to appear at the bottom of the form so that it stands out, making it easier for someone who needs to call customers to use the form and quickly identify the phone number for a customer.

To create the form using the Form Wizard:

1. Click the [>>] button to move all the fields to the Selected Fields box. Next, you need to remove the Phone field, and then add it back as the last selected field so that it will appear at the bottom of the form.

2. In the Selected Fields box, click the **Phone** field, and then click the [<] button to move the field back to the Available Fields box.

   To add the Phone field to the end of the form, you need to highlight the last field in the list, and then move the Phone field back to the Selected Fields box.

3. In the Selected Fields box, click the **Email** field.

4. With the Phone field selected in the Available Fields box, click the [>] button to move the Phone field to the end of the Selected Fields box.

5. Click the **Next** button to display the second Form Wizard dialog box, in which you select a layout for the form. See Figure 4-2.

| Figure 4-2 | Choosing a layout for the form |

The layout choices are Columnar, Tabular, Datasheet, and Justified. A sample of the selected layout appears on the left side of the dialog box.

6. Click each of the option buttons and review the corresponding sample layout.

   The Tabular and Datasheet layouts display the fields from multiple records at one time, whereas the Columnar and Justified layouts display the fields from one record at a time. Oren thinks the Columnar layout is the appropriate arrangement for displaying and updating data in the table, so that anyone using the form can focus on just one customer record at a time.

7. Click the **Columnar** option button (if necessary), and then click the **Next** button.

   Access displays the third and final Form Wizard dialog box and shows the Customer table's name as the default form name. "Customer" is also the default title that will appear on the tab for the form.

You'll use "CustomerData" as the form name and, because you don't need to change the form's design at this point, you'll display the form.

8. Click the insertion point to the right of Customer in the text box, type **Data**, and then click the **Finish** button.

9. Close the Navigation Pane to display more of the Form window. The completed form is displayed in Form view. See Figure 4-3.

Figure 4-3 **CustomerData form in Form view**

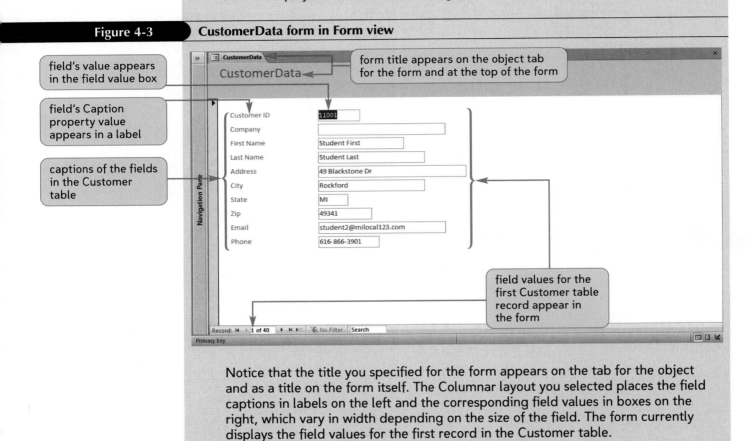

field's value appears in the field value box

field's Caption property value appears in a label

captions of the fields in the Customer table

form title appears on the object tab for the form and at the top of the form

field values for the first Customer table record appear in the form

Notice that the title you specified for the form appears on the tab for the object and as a title on the form itself. The Columnar layout you selected places the field captions in labels on the left and the corresponding field values in boxes on the right, which vary in width depending on the size of the field. The form currently displays the field values for the first record in the Customer table.

After viewing the form, Oren decides that he doesn't like its appearance. The font used in the labels on the left is somewhat light in color and small, making them a bit difficult to read. Also, he thinks inserting a graphic on the form would add visual interest, and modifying other form elements—such as the color of certain text, the type of line used for the field value boxes, and so on—would improve the look of the form. You can make all of these changes working with the form in Layout view.

Modifying a Form's Design in Layout View

TIP

Some form design changes require you to switch to Design view, which gives you a more detailed view of the form's structure.

After you create a form, you might need to modify its design in Layout view to improve its appearance or to make the form easier to use. In Layout view, you see the form as it appears in Form view, but you can still modify the form's design; in Form view, you cannot make any design changes. Because you can see the form and its data while you are modifying the form, Layout view makes it easy for you to see the results of any design changes you make. You can continue to make changes, undo modifications, and rework the design in Layout view to achieve the look you want for the form.

The first modification you'll make to the CustomerData form is to change its appearance by applying a theme.

Applying a Theme to a Form

By default, a form you create is formatted with the Office theme, which determines the color and font used on the form. Access, like other Microsoft Office programs, provides many built-in themes, including the Office theme, making it easy for you to create objects with a unified look. You can also create a customized theme if none of the built-in themes suit your needs. To change a form's appearance, you can easily apply a new theme to it.

REFERENCE

Applying a Theme to a Form

- Display the form in Layout view.
- In the Themes group on the Design tab, click the Themes button.
- In the displayed gallery, click the theme you want to apply to all objects; or, right-click the theme to display the shortcut menu, and then choose to apply the theme to the current object only or to all matching objects.

Oren would like to see if the CustomerData form's appearance can be improved with a different theme. To apply a theme, you first need to switch to Layout view.

To apply a theme to the CustomerData form:

1. In the Views group on the Home tab, click the **View** button. The form is displayed in Layout view. See Figure 4-4.

Figure 4-4   **Form displayed in Layout view**

Themes button

Design tab displays options for changing the form's appearance

orange outline indicates the selected object

Customer ID	11001
Company	
First Name	Student First
Last Name	Student Last
Address	49 Blackstone Dr
City	Rockford
State	MI
Zip	49341
Email	student2@milocal123.com
Phone	616-866-3901

Trouble? If the Field List or Property Sheet opens on the right side of your window, close it before continuing.

You can use Layout view to modify an existing form. In Layout view, an orange outline identifies the currently selected object on the form; in this case, the field value for the CustomerID field, 11001, is selected. You need to apply a theme to the CustomerData form.

2. In the Themes group on the Design tab, click the **Themes** button. A gallery opens showing the available themes for the form. See Figure 4-5.

Figure 4-5	Themes gallery displayed

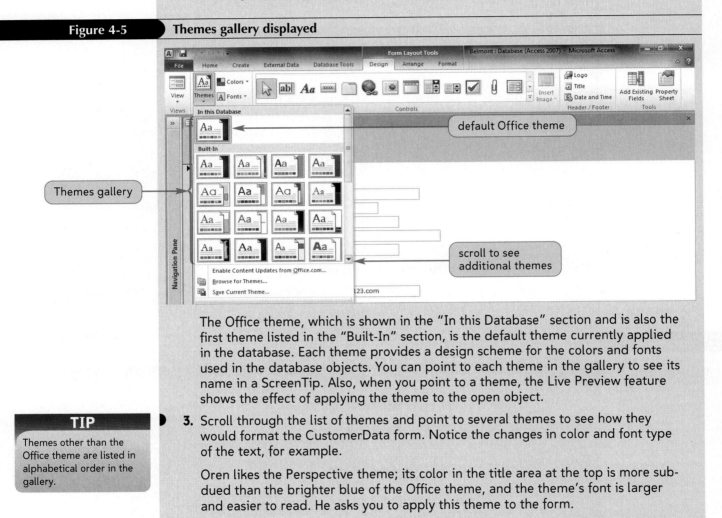

The Office theme, which is shown in the "In this Database" section and is also the first theme listed in the "Built-In" section, is the default theme currently applied in the database. Each theme provides a design scheme for the colors and fonts used in the database objects. You can point to each theme in the gallery to see its name in a ScreenTip. Also, when you point to a theme, the Live Preview feature shows the effect of applying the theme to the open object.

TIP

Themes other than the Office theme are listed in alphabetical order in the gallery.

3. Scroll through the list of themes and point to several themes to see how they would format the CustomerData form. Notice the changes in color and font type of the text, for example.

Oren likes the Perspective theme; its color in the title area at the top is more subdued than the brighter blue of the Office theme, and the theme's font is larger and easier to read. He asks you to apply this theme to the form.

4. Scroll the Themes gallery to the bottom, and then right-click the **Perspective** theme (third row from the bottom, third theme from the left). A shortcut menu opens with options for applying the theme. See Figure 4-6.

Figure 4-6	Shortcut menu for applying the theme

Perspective theme

shortcut menu displayed when you right-click a theme

The menu provides options for applying the theme to all matching objects—for example, all the forms in the database—or to the current object only. You can also choose to make the theme the default theme in the database, which means any new objects you create will be formatted with the selected theme. Because Oren is not sure if all forms in the Belmont database will look better with the Perspective theme, he asks you to apply it only to the CustomerData form.

5. On the shortcut menu, click **Apply Theme to This Object Only**.

Choose this option to avoid applying the theme to other forms in the database.

The gallery closes, and the Perspective theme formats the form's colors and fonts.

Working with Themes

Themes provide a quick and easy way for you to format the objects in a database with a consistent look, which is a good design principle to follow. In general, all objects of a type in a database—for example, all forms—should have a consistent design. However, keep in mind that when you select a theme in the Themes gallery and choose the option to apply the theme to all matching objects or to make the theme the default for the database, Access applies it to *all* the existing forms and reports in the database as well as to new forms and reports you create. Although this ensures a consistent design, this approach can cause problems. For example, if you have already created a form or report and its design is suitable, applying a theme that includes a larger font size could cause the text in labels and field value boxes to be cut off or to extend into other objects on the form or report. The colors applied by the theme could also interfere with elements on existing forms and reports. To handle these unintended results, you would have to spend time checking the existing forms and reports and fixing any problems introduced by applying the theme. A better approach is to select the option "Apply Theme to This Object Only," available on the shortcut menu for a theme in the Themes gallery, for each existing form and report. If the newly applied theme causes problems for any individual form or report, you can then reapply the original theme to return the object to its original design.

Next, Oren asks you to add a picture to the form for visual interest. The picture, which is included on various stationery items for Belmont Landscapes—business cards, flyers, and so on—is a small graphic of a piece of landscaping equipment. You'll add this picture to the form.

Adding a Picture to a Form

A picture is one of many controls you can add and modify on a form. A **control** is an item on a form, report, or other database object that you can manipulate to modify the object's appearance. The controls you can add and modify in Layout view for a form are available in the Controls group and the Header/Footer group on the Design tab. The picture you need to add is contained in a file named Landscape.bmp, which is located in the Access1\Tutorial folder provided with your Data Files.

To add the picture to the form:

1. Make sure the form is still displayed in Layout view.

2. In the Header/Footer group on the Design tab, click the **Logo** button. The Insert Picture dialog box opens.

3. Navigate to the **Access1\Tutorial** folder provided with your Data Files, click the **Landscape** file, and then click the **OK** button. The picture appears as a selected object on top of the form's title. See Figure 4-7.

| Figure 4-7 | Form with picture added |

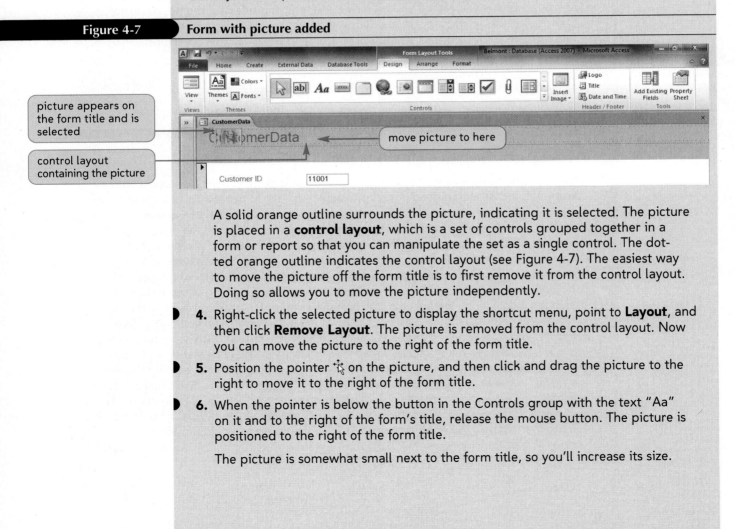

picture appears on the form title and is selected

control layout containing the picture

move picture to here

A solid orange outline surrounds the picture, indicating it is selected. The picture is placed in a **control layout**, which is a set of controls grouped together in a form or report so that you can manipulate the set as a single control. The dotted orange outline indicates the control layout (see Figure 4-7). The easiest way to move the picture off the form title is to first remove it from the control layout. Doing so allows you to move the picture independently.

4. Right-click the selected picture to display the shortcut menu, point to **Layout**, and then click **Remove Layout**. The picture is removed from the control layout. Now you can move the picture to the right of the form title.

5. Position the pointer on the picture, and then click and drag the picture to the right to move it to the right of the form title.

6. When the pointer is below the button in the Controls group with the text "Aa" on it and to the right of the form's title, release the mouse button. The picture is positioned to the right of the form title.

The picture is somewhat small next to the form title, so you'll increase its size.

7. With the picture still selected, place the pointer ↕ on the bottom edge of the orange outline below the picture, and then click and drag down to increase the height of the picture (see Figure 4-8).

8. Click in a blank area on the main form (to the right of the field values) to deselect the picture. See Figure 4-8.

Figure 4-8   **Form with theme applied and picture repositioned**

CustomerData

CustomerData

> picture moved to the right of the form title and resized

Perspective theme colors and fonts applied to the form elements

Navigation Pane

Customer ID	11001
Company	
First Name	Student First
Last Name	Student Last
Address	49 Blackstone Dr
City	Rockford
State	MI
Zip	49341
Email	student2@milocal123.com
Phone	616-866-3901

Record: ◄ ◄ 1 of 40 ► ►► ►* No Filter Search

Layout View

Trouble? Don't be concerned if your picture is not in the exact location or is not the same exact size as the one shown in Figure 4-8. Just make sure the picture is not blocking any part of the form title; that it appears to the right of the form title and above the main part of the form; and that it is not any larger than the shaded title area.

The addition of the picture to the form provides more color and visual interest. Next, Oren asks you to change the color of the form title to brown so that it will coordinate better with the picture next to the title.

Changing the Color of the Form Title

The Font group on the Format tab provides many options you can use to change the appearance of text on a form. For example, you can bold, italicize, and underline text; change the font, font color, and font size; and change the alignment of text. Before you change the color of the "CustomerData" title on the form to brown, you'll change the title to two words so it is easier to read.

TIP

Changing the form's title does not affect the form object name; it is still CustomerData, as shown on the object tab.

To change the form title's text and color:

1. Click the **CustomerData** form title. An orange box surrounds the title, indicating it is selected.

2. Click between the letters "r" and "D" to position the insertion point, and then press the **spacebar**. The title on the form is now "Customer Data."

3. Click in the main form area again to deselect the title, and then click **Customer Data** to reselect the title. The orange outline appears around the words of the title.

4. Click the **Format** tab on the Ribbon.

5. In the Font group on the Format tab, click the **Font Color button arrow** $\boxed{\text{A}}$ ▾ to display the gallery of available colors. The gallery provides theme colors and standard colors, as well as an option for creating a custom color.

6. In the Theme Colors palette, point to the seventh color box in the fifth row of boxes. The ScreenTip indicates this is the Brown, Accent 3, Darker 25% color.

7. Click the **Brown, Accent 3, Darker 25%** color box.

8. Click in a blank area of the main form to deselect the title text. The brown color is applied to the form title text, tying it to the picture on the form. See Figure 4-9.

Figure 4-9	**Form title with new color applied**

form title in a darker brown font and edited with a space between words

You have made a couple of changes to the form, and should save it now.

9. Click the **Save** button 🖫 on the Quick Access Toolbar to save the modified form.

Oren suggests a different type of line for the field value boxes. He thinks the solid line currently used on the form somewhat overshadows the field values within the boxes, and that a more subtle type of line might look better and make the field values easier to read.

Changing the Type of Line on a Form

A line on a form, such as the box around each field value, is another type of control that you can modify in Layout view. The Control Formatting group on the Format tab provides options for changing the thickness, type, and color of any line on a form. Next, you'll change the type of line for the field values boxes on the CustomerData form.

To change the type of line for the field value boxes:

1. Click the field value **11001** for the CustomerID field. An orange outline appears around the field value box to indicate it is selected.

2. In the Control Formatting group on the Format tab, click the **Shape Outline** button. A gallery opens with options for applying color. At the bottom of the gallery are options for modifying the line thickness and line type.

3. Point to **Line Type** to display a submenu with various line formats, point to the **Dots** option (the fourth line type in the submenu) to display its ScreenTip, and then click the **Dots** line type.

4. Click in a blank area of the main form to deselect the box. The Customer ID field value box changes to a dotted line.

Oren thinks the dotted line type is much better and makes the field value easier to see. He asks you to change the line type for the rest of the field value boxes on the form. To do so, you can select the remaining field value boxes and apply the new line type to all of them at the same time.

5. Click the **Company** field value box (the box is currently empty), press and hold the **Shift** key, click each remaining field value box below the Company field value box, and then release the **Shift** key. All the field value boxes except the first one should be selected; each box is outlined in orange to indicate it is selected. See Figure 4-10.

Figure 4-10	Form with multiple field value boxes selected

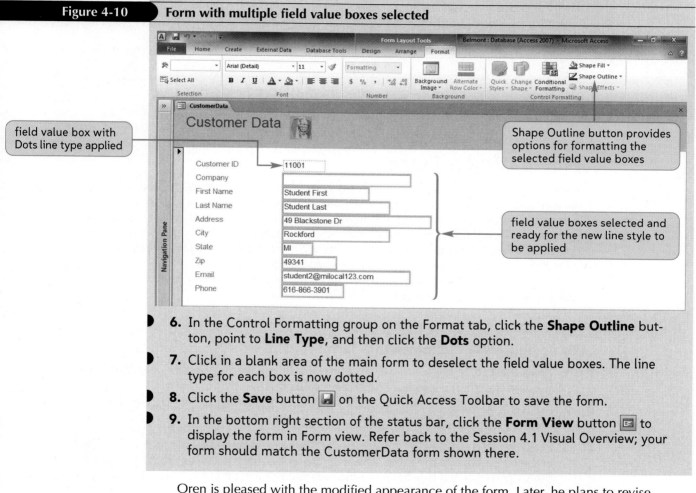

field value box with Dots line type applied

Shape Outline button provides options for formatting the selected field value boxes

field value boxes selected and ready for the new line style to be applied

6. In the Control Formatting group on the Format tab, click the **Shape Outline** button, point to **Line Type**, and then click the **Dots** option.

7. Click in a blank area of the main form to deselect the field value boxes. The line type for each box is now dotted.

8. Click the **Save** button 🖫 on the Quick Access Toolbar to save the form.

9. In the bottom right section of the status bar, click the **Form View** button 🖽 to display the form in Form view. Refer back to the Session 4.1 Visual Overview; your form should match the CustomerData form shown there.

Oren is pleased with the modified appearance of the form. Later, he plans to revise the existing ContractData form and make the same changes to it, so that it matches the appearance of the CustomerData form.

Written Communication: Understanding the Importance of Form Design

Similar to any document, a form must convey written information clearly and effectively. When you create a form, it's important to consider how the form will be used, so that its design will accommodate the needs of people using the form to view, enter, and maintain data. For example, if a form in a database mimics a paper form that users will enter data from, the form in the database should have the same fields in the same order as those on the paper form. This will enable users to easily tab from one field to the next in the database form to enter the necessary information from the paper form. Also, it's important to include a meaningful title on the form to identify its purpose, and to enhance the appearance of the form. A form that is visually appealing makes working with the database more user-friendly and can improve the readability of the form, thereby helping to prevent errors in data entry. Also, be sure to use a consistent design for the forms in your database whenever possible. Users will expect to see similar elements—titles, pictures, fonts, and so on—in each form contained in a database. A mix of form styles and elements among the forms in a database could lead to problems when working with the forms. Finally, make sure the text on your form does not contain any spelling or grammatical errors. By producing a well-designed and well-written form, you can ensure that users will be able to work with the form in a productive and efficient manner.

Navigating a Form

Oren wants to use the CustomerData form to view some data in the Customer table. As you saw earlier, you use Layout view to modify the appearance of a form. To view, navigate, and change data using a form, you need to display the form in Form view. As you learned in Tutorial 1, you navigate a form in the same way that you navigate a table datasheet. Also, the navigation mode and editing mode keystroke techniques you used with datasheets in Tutorial 3 are the same when navigating a form.

The CustomerData form is already displayed in Form view, so you can use it to navigate through the fields and records of the Customer table.

To navigate the CustomerData form:

1. Press the **Tab** key twice to move to the First Name field value box, and then press the **End** key to move to the Phone field value box.

2. Press the **Home** key to move back to the Customer ID field value box. The first record in the Customer table still appears in the form.

3. Press the **Ctrl+End** keys to move to the Phone field value box for record 40, which is the last record in the table. The record number for the current record appears in the Current Record box between the navigation buttons at the bottom of the form.

4. Click the **Previous record** navigation button ◀ to move to the Phone field value box in record 39.

5. Press the ↑ key twice to move to the Zip field value box in record 39.

6. Click the insertion point between the numbers "7" and "5" in the Address field value to switch to editing mode, press the **Home** key to move the insertion point to the beginning of the field value, and then press the **End** key to move the insertion point to the end of the field value.

> **7.** Click the **First record** navigation button |◄| to move to the Address field value box in the first record. The entire field value is highlighted because you switched from editing mode to navigation mode.

> **8.** Click the **Next record** navigation button |▶| to move to the Address field value box in record 2, the next record.

Next, Oren asks you to display the record for the Three Tulips Café, a Belmont Landscapes customer. The paper form containing the original contact information for this customer was damaged. Oren recently contacted the owner of the café and obtained all the customer information again. Now Oren wants to use the form to view the data for this customer to make sure it is correct.

Finding Data Using a Form

As you learned in Tutorial 3, the Find command lets you search for data in a datasheet so you can display only those records you want to view. You can also use the Find command to search for data in a form. You choose a field to serve as the basis for the search by making that field the current field, and then you enter the value you want Access to match in the Find and Replace dialog box.

REFERENCE

Finding Data in a Form or Datasheet

- Open the form or datasheet, and then select the field you want to search.
- In the Find group on the Home tab, click the Find button to open the Find and Replace dialog box.
- In the Find What box, type the field value you want to find.
- Complete the remaining options, as necessary, to specify the type of search to conduct.
- Click the Find Next button to begin the search.
- Click the Find Next button to continue searching for the next match.
- Click the Cancel button to stop the search operation.

You need to find the record for the Three Tulips Café. Oren doesn't recall the CustomerID value for this customer, so you'll search for the record using the Company field.

To find the record using the CustomerData form:

> **1.** Click in the **Company** field value box (which is empty for the current record) to establish Company as the current field. This is the field you need to search.

> Instead of searching for the entire company name, Three Tulips Café, you can search for a record that contains part of the name anywhere in the Company field value. Performing a partial search such as this is often easier than matching the entire field value and is useful when you don't know or can't remember the entire field value.

> **2.** In the Find group on the Home tab, click the **Find** button. The Find and Replace dialog box opens. The Look In box shows that the current field (in this case, Company) will be searched. You'll search for records that contain the word "tulips" in the company name.

3. In the Find What box, type **tulips**. Note that you do not have to enter the word as "Tulips" with a capital letter "T" because the Match Case option is not selected in the Find and Replace dialog box. Access will find any record containing the word "tulips" with any combination of uppercase and lowercase letters.

4. Click the **Match** arrow to display the list of matching options, and then click **Any Part of Field**. Access will find any record that contains the word "tulips" in any part of the Company field. See Figure 4-11.

| Figure 4-11 | Completed Find and Replace dialog box |

search value entered

current field

specifies that Access will search for the value in any part of the current field

5. Click the **Find Next** button. The CustomerData form now displays record 35, which is the record for the Three Tulips Café (CustomerID 11080). The word "Tulips" is selected in the Company field value box because you searched for this word. Oren reviews the information for the record and determines it is correct.

The search value you enter can be an exact value or it can include wildcard characters. A **wildcard character** is a placeholder you use when you know only part of a value or when you want to start or end with a specific character or match a certain pattern. Figure 4-12 shows the wildcard characters you can use when finding data.

| Figure 4-12 | Wildcard characters |

Wildcard Character	Purpose	Example
*	Match any number of characters. It can be used as the first and/or last character in the character string.	th* finds the, that, this, therefore, and so on
?	Match any single alphabetic character.	a?t finds act, aft, ant, apt, and art
[]	Match any single character within the brackets.	a[fr]t finds aft and art but not act, ant, and apt
!	Match any character not within brackets.	a[!fr]t finds act, ant, and apt but not aft and art
-	Match any one of a range of characters. The range must be in ascending order (a to z, not z to a).	a[d-p]t finds aft, ant, and apt but not act and art
#	Match any single numeric character.	#72 finds 072, 172, 272, 372, and so on

Next, Oren wants to view the customer records for any customers with phone numbers beginning with the area code 517. He is curious to know how many customers are in cities serviced by that area code, and what the cities are. You could search for any field containing the digits 517 in any part of the field, but this search would also find records with the digits 517 in any part of the phone number. To find only those records with the 517 area code, you'll use the * wildcard character.

To find the records using the * wildcard character:

▶ **1.** Make sure the Find and Replace dialog box is still open.

▶ **2.** Click anywhere in the CustomerData form to make it active, and then press the **Tab** key eight times to move to the Phone field value box. This is the field you want to search.

▶ **3.** Click the title bar of the Find and Replace dialog box to make it active, and then drag the Find and Replace dialog box to the right so you can see the Phone field on the form. The Look In box setting is still Current field, which is now the Phone field; this is the field that will be searched.

▶ **4.** Double-click **tulips** in the Find What box to select the entire value, and then type **517***.

▶ **5.** Click the **Match** arrow, and then click **Whole Field**. Because you're using a wildcard character in the search value, you want Access to search the whole field.

   With the settings you've entered, Access will find records in which any field value in the Phone field begins with the digits 517.

▶ **6.** Click the **Find Next** button. Access displays record 36, which is the first record found for a customer with the area code 517. This customer is located in East Lansing. Notice that the search process started from the point of the previously displayed record in the form, which was record 35.

▶ **7.** Click the **Find Next** button. Access displays record 8, which is the next record found for a customer with the area code 517. This customer is located in Lansing. Notice that the search process cycles back through the beginning of the records in the underlying table.

▶ **8.** Click the **Find Next** button. Access displays record 12, the third record found; this customer is also located in Lansing.

▶ **9.** Click the **Find Next** button. Access displays record 25 for another customer located in Lansing, with the area code 517.

▶ **10.** Click the **Find Next** button. Access displays record 33 for another customer located in Lansing.

▶ **11.** Click the **Find Next** button. Access displays a dialog box informing you that the search is finished.

▶ **12.** Click the **OK** button to close the dialog box. Oren notes that all customers with an area code of 517 are located in either Lansing or East Lansing.

▶ **13.** Click the **Cancel** button to close the Find and Replace dialog box.

Oren has identified some customer updates he wants you to make. You'll use the CustomerData form to update the data in the Customer table.

Maintaining Table Data Using a Form

Maintaining data using a form is often easier than using a datasheet because you can focus on all the changes for a single record at one time. In Form view, you can edit the field values for a record, delete a record from the underlying table, or add a new record to the table. You already know how to navigate a form and find specific records. Now you'll use the CustomerData form to make the changes Oren wants to the Customer table.

First, you'll update the record for the Cherrywood Senior Center. The center has a new contact person, so you need to update the first name, last name, phone number, and email address for this customer. Oren happens to know that the Cherrywood Senior Center is record 22 in the Customer table. If you know the number of the record you want to view, you can enter the number in the Current Record box to move to that record.

To change the record using the CustomerData form:

1. Click in the Current Record box at the bottom of the form, select **33**, type **22**, and then press the **Enter** key. Record 22 (Cherrywood Senior Center) is now current.

   You need to update this record with the information for the new contact person at the center, Dan Lewis.

2. In the First Name field value box, double-click **Lisa** to select the entry, and then type **Dan**.

3. Press the **Tab** key to move to and select the value in the Last Name field value box, and then type **Lewis**.

4. Click the insertion point before the first character in the Email field value box, press the **Delete** key seven times to delete the characters before the @ symbol, and then type **dlewis4**. The Email field value is now dlewis4@csc77.com.

5. Click the insertion point at the end of the value in the Phone field value box, press the **Backspace** key three times, and then type **890**. The Phone field value is now 269-857-1890. The updates to the record are complete. See Figure 4-13.

> **TIP**
>
> Note that the pencil symbol appears in the upper-left corner of the form, indicating that the form is in editing mode.

Figure 4-13   **Customer record after changing field values**

pencil symbol indicates editing mode

Customer Data

Customer ID	11058
Company	Cherrywood Senior Center
First Name	Dan
Last Name	Lewis
Address	77 Forest Hill Rd
City	Saugatuck
State	MI
Zip	49453
Email	dlewis4@csc77.com
Phone	269-857-1890

field values changed

record 22 is the current record

Record: 14 ◄ 22 of 40 ► ►I ►＊ No Filter   Search

Form View

Next, Oren asks you to add a record for a new customer. The customer has not yet returned a signed contract, but Oren expects to receive the contract soon and wants to be sure the Customer table is updated first with the new customer record. You'll use the CustomerData form to add the new record.

To add the new record using the CustomerData form:

▶ **1.** In the Records group on the Home tab, click the **New** button. Record 41, the next available new record, becomes the current record. All field value boxes are empty, and the insertion point is positioned in the Customer ID field value box.

▶ **2.** Refer to Figure 4-14 and enter the value shown for each field. Press the **Tab** key to move from field to field.

Figure 4-14	Completed form for the new record

Trouble? Compare your screen with Figure 4-14. If any field value is incorrect, correct it now, using the methods described earlier for editing field values.

▶ **3.** After entering the Phone field value, press the **Tab** key. Record 42, the next available new record, becomes the current record, and the record for CustomerID 11090 is saved in the Customer table.

Oren would like a printed copy of the record for the new customer only. He wants to give the printout to a staff member as a reminder to look for the new contract for this customer when it comes in.

Previewing and Printing Selected Form Records

Access prints as many form records as can fit on a printed page. If only part of a form record fits on the bottom of a page, the remainder of the record prints on the next page. Access allows you to print all pages or a range of pages. In addition, you can print the currently selected form record.

Before printing record 41, the record for Lily's Boutique, you'll preview the form record to see how it will look when printed.

To preview the form and print the data for record 41:

▶ **1.** Click the **Previous record** navigation button ◀ to redisplay record 41.

▶ **2.** Click the **File** tab to display Backstage view, click the **Print** tab in the navigation bar, and then click **Print Preview**. The Print Preview window opens, showing the form records for the Customer table. Notice that each record appears in its own form, and that shading is used to distinguish one record from another. See Figure 4-15.

Figure 4-15   **Form records displayed in Print Preview**

Print Preview tab contains options for viewing and printing the form and records

form records

click to close Print Preview and return to Form view

shading distinguishes one record from another

To print selected records, you need to close Print Preview and then use the Print dialog box.

▶ **3.** In the Close Preview group on the Print Preview tab, click the **Close Print Preview** button. You return to Form view with the record for Lily's Boutique still displayed.

▶ **4.** Click the **File** tab to display Backstage view again, click the **Print** tab in the navigation bar, and then click **Print**. The Print dialog box opens.

▶ **5.** Click the **Selected Record(s)** option button to print the current form record (record 41).

Trouble? Check with your instructor to be sure you should print the form; then continue to the next step. If you should not print the form, click the Cancel button, and then skip to Step 7.

▶ **6.** Click the **OK** button to close the dialog box and print the selected record.

▶ **7.** Close the CustomerData form.

▶ **8.** If you are not continuing to Session 4.2, click the **File** tab, and then click **Close Database** in the navigation bar to close the Belmont database.

The CustomerData form will enable Oren and his staff to enter and maintain data easily in the Customer table. In the next session, you'll create another form for working with data in both the Customer and Contract tables at the same time. You'll also create a report showing data from both tables.

Session 4.1 Quick Check

REVIEW

1. Describe the difference between creating a form using the Form tool and creating a form using the Form Wizard.
2. What is a theme and how do you apply one to an existing form?
3. A(n) _____ is an item on a form, report, or other database object that you can manipulate to modify the object's appearance.
4. Which table record is displayed in a form when you press the Ctrl+End keys while you are in navigation mode?
5. Which wildcard character matches any single alphabetic character?
6. To print only the current record displayed in a form, you need to select the _____ option button in the Print dialog box.

SESSION 4.2 VISUAL OVERVIEW

The report title appears at the top of the report. By default, the report object name is used as the report title, but you can edit the title to display the text you want, as done here, with spaces added between words for readability.

Fields from the primary Customer table appear first in the report.

Fields from the related Contract table appear below the fields from the primary table.

For a **grouped report**, the data from a record in the primary table (the Customer table in this report) appears as a group, followed on subsequent lines of the report by the joined records from the related table (the Contract table in this report).

By default, the Report Wizard includes the current date at the bottom of each page in the report.

The Navigation buttons allow you to display the first, last, next, or previous page in the report, or to enter a specific page number and move to that page.

The report object's name is displayed on the tab for the report.

REPORT IN PRINT PREVIEW

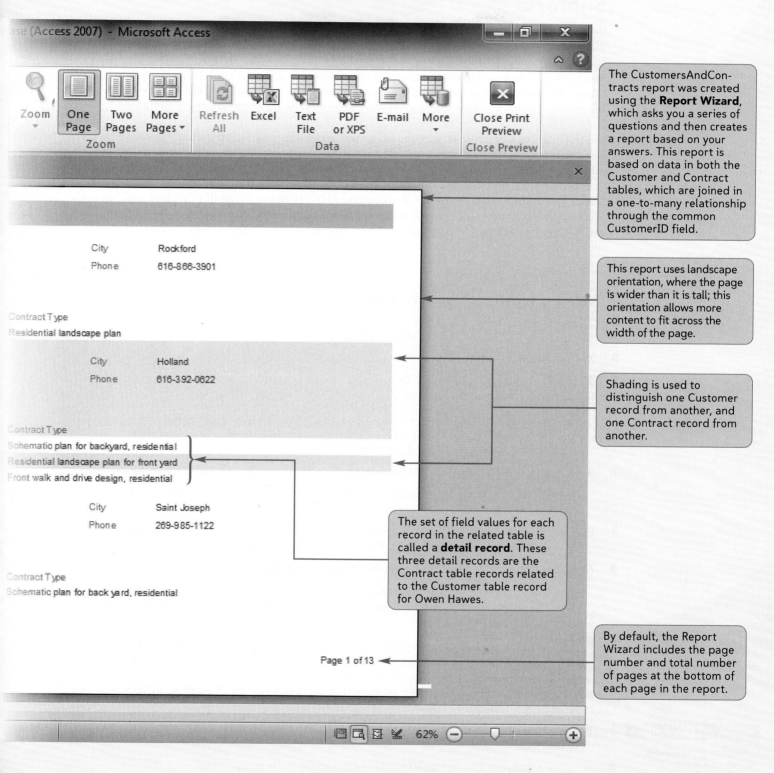

The CustomersAndContracts report was created using the **Report Wizard**, which asks you a series of questions and then creates a report based on your answers. This report is based on data in both the Customer and Contract tables, which are joined in a one-to-many relationship through the common CustomerID field.

This report uses landscape orientation, where the page is wider than it is tall; this orientation allows more content to fit across the width of the page.

Shading is used to distinguish one Customer record from another, and one Contract record from another.

The set of field values for each record in the related table is called a **detail record**. These three detail records are the Contract table records related to the Customer table record for Owen Hawes.

By default, the Report Wizard includes the page number and total number of pages at the bottom of each page in the report.

Creating a Form with a Main Form and a Subform

Before developing a report for the Belmont database, Oren would like you to create a form so that he can view the data for each customer and the customer's contracts at the same time. The type of form you need to create will include a main form and a subform. To create a form based on two tables, you must first define a relationship between the two tables. In Tutorial 2, you defined a one-to-many relationship between the Customer (primary) and Contract (related) tables, so you can now create a form based on both tables.

When you create a form containing data from two tables that have a one-to-many relationship, you actually create a **main form** for data from the primary table and a **subform** for data from the related table. Access uses the defined relationship between the tables to join them automatically through the common field that exists in both tables.

Oren and his staff will use the form when contacting customers about their contracts. The main form will contain the customer ID, company name (if any), first and last names, phone number, and email address for each customer. The subform will contain the information about the contracts for each customer. You'll use the Form Wizard to create the form.

To create the form using the Form Wizard:

1. If you took a break after the previous session, make sure that the Belmont database is open and the Navigation Pane is closed.

2. Click the **Create** tab on the Ribbon.

3. In the Forms group on the Create tab, click the **Form Wizard** button. The first Form Wizard dialog box opens.

   When creating a form based on two tables, you first choose the primary table and select the fields you want to include in the main form; then you choose the related table and select fields from it for the subform.

4. If necessary, click the **Tables/Queries** arrow, and then click **Table: Customer**.

   Oren wants the form to include only the CustomerID, Company, First, Last, Phone, and Email fields from the Customer table.

5. Click **CustomerID** in the Available Fields box (if necessary), and then click the `>` button to move the field to the Selected Fields box.

6. Repeat Step 5 for the **Company**, **First**, **Last**, **Phone**, and **Email** fields.

   The CustomerID field will appear in the main form, so you do not have to include it in the subform. Otherwise, Oren wants the subform to include all the fields from the Contract table.

7. Click the **Tables/Queries** arrow, scroll the list up, and then click **Table: Contract**. The fields from the Contract table appear in the Available Fields box. The quickest way to add the fields you want to include is to move all the fields to the Selected Fields box, and then remove the only field you don't want to include (CustomerID).

8. Click the `>>` button to move all the fields in the Contract table to the Selected Fields box.

9. Click **Contract.CustomerID** in the Selected Fields box, and then click the `<` button to move the field back to the Available Fields box.

10. Click the **Next** button. The next Form Wizard dialog box opens. See Figure 4-16.

TIP

The table name (Contract) is included in the CustomerID field name to distinguish it from the same field (CustomerID) in the Customer table.

Figure 4-16 Choosing a format for the main form and subform

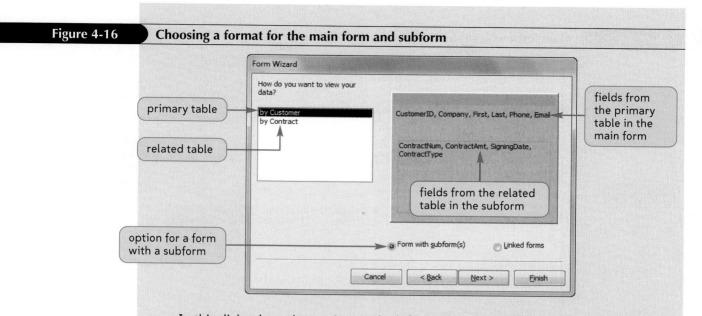

In this dialog box, the section on the left shows the order in which you will view the selected data: first by data from the primary Customer table, and then by data from the related Contract table. The form will be displayed as shown on the right side of the dialog box, with the fields from the Customer table at the top in the main form, and the fields from the Contract table at the bottom in the subform. The selected "Form with subform(s)" option button specifies a main form with a subform. The Linked forms option creates a form structure in which only the main form fields are displayed. A button with the subform's name on it appears on the main form; you can click this button to display the associated subform records.

The default options shown in Figure 4-16 are correct for creating a form with Customer data in the main form and Contract data in the subform.

To finish creating the form:

1. Click the **Next** button. The next Form Wizard dialog box opens, in which you choose the subform layout.

   The Tabular layout displays subform fields as a table, whereas the Datasheet layout displays subform fields as a table datasheet. The layout choice is a matter of personal preference. You'll use the Datasheet layout.

2. Click the **Datasheet** option button to select it (if necessary), and then click the **Next** button. The next Form Wizard dialog box opens, in which you choose titles for the main form and the subform.

   You'll use the title "CustomerContracts" for the main form and the title "ContractSubform" for the subform. These titles will also be the names for the form objects.

3. In the Form box, click the insertion point to the right of the last letter, and then type **Contracts**. The main form name is now CustomerContracts.

4. In the Subform box, delete the space between the two words so that the subform name appears as **ContractSubform**.

5. Click the **Finish** button. The completed form opens in Form view. See Figure 4-17.

Figure 4-17 **Main form with subform in Form view**

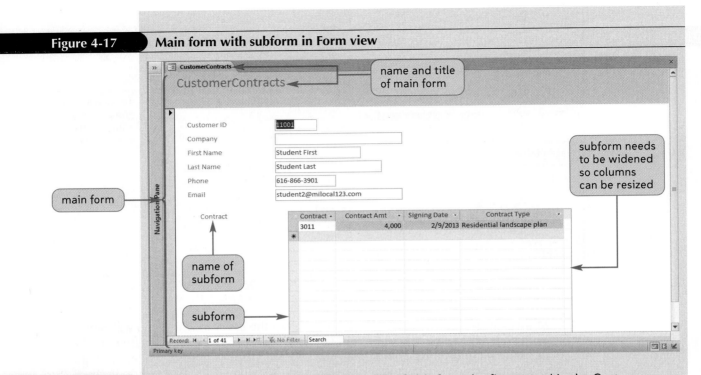

In the main form, Access displays the fields from the first record in the Customer table in a columnar format. The records in the main form appear in primary key order by CustomerID. CustomerID 11001 has one related record in the Contract table; this record, for ContractNum 3011, is shown in the subform, which uses the datasheet format. The main form name, "CustomerContracts," appears on the object tab and as the form title. The name of the subform appears to the left of the subform. Note that only the word "Contract" and not the complete name "ContractSubform" appears on the form. Access displays only the table name for the subform itself, but displays the complete name of the object, "ContractSubform," when you view and work with objects in the Navigation Pane. The subform designation is necessary in a list of database objects, so that you can distinguish the Contract subform from other objects, such as the Contract table; but the subform designation is not needed in the CustomerContracts form. Only the table name is required to identify the table containing the records in the subform.

You need to make some changes to the form. First, you'll edit the form title to add a space between the words so that it appears as "Customer Contracts." Then, you'll resize the subform. Oren is concerned that the subform is not wide enough to allow for all the columns to be resized and fully display their field values, especially the Contract Type column. To make these changes, you need to switch to Layout view.

To modify the CustomerContracts form in Layout view:

1. In the Views group on the Home tab, click the **View** button to switch to Layout view.

2. Click **CustomerContracts** in the blue area at the top of the form. The form title is selected.

3. Click between the letters "r" and "C" to place the insertion point, and then press the **spacebar**. The title on the form is now "Customer Contracts."

4. Click in a blank area of the form to the right of the field value boxes to deselect the title. Next, you'll increase the width of the subform.

5. Click the subform. An orange outline surrounds the subform, indicating it is selected.

6. Position the pointer on the right edge of the selected subform until the pointer changes to a ↔ shape, and then click and drag to the right approximately two inches (see Figure 4-18).

7. Use the ↔ pointer to resize each column in the subform datasheet to its best fit. Your form should now look like the one shown in Figure 4-18.

Figure 4-18	Modified form in Layout view

form title edited to include a space between words

subform navigation buttons appear at the bottom of the subform; you need to scroll the main form to see them

main form navigation buttons

subform columns resized to best fit

subform widened

8. Click the **Save** button 🖫 on the Quick Access Toolbar to save both the main form and the subform.

9. In the Views group on the Design tab, click the **View** button to display the CustomerContracts form in Form view.

Trouble? If the fields in the main form are partially out of view, use the vertical scroll bar to scroll to the top of the form and display the fields.

The form includes two sets of navigation buttons. You use the set of navigation buttons at the bottom of the Form window to select records from the primary table in the main form (see Figure 4-18). The second set of navigation buttons is currently not visible; you need to scroll down the main form to see these buttons, which appear at the bottom of the subform. You use the subform navigation buttons to select records from the related table in the subform.

You'll use the navigation buttons to view different records.

To navigate to different main form and subform records:

▶ 1. In the main form, click the **Last record** navigation button �. Record 41 in the Customer table (for Lily's Boutique) becomes the current record in the main form. The subform shows that this customer currently has no contracts; recall that you just entered this record using the CustomerData form. Oren can use the subform to enter the information for this customer's contract when he receives it, and that information will be updated in the Contract table.

▶ 2. In the main form, click the **Previous record** navigation button ◀. Record 40 in the Customer table (for Weston Community Parks Foundation) becomes the current record in the main form. The subform shows that this customer has two contracts.

▶ 3. In the main form, select **40** in the Current Record box, type **34**, and then press the **Enter** key. Record 34 in the Customer table (for Dept. of Neighborhood Development) becomes the current record in the main form. The subform shows that this customer has four contracts.

▶ 4. Double-click the pointer ↔ at the right edge of the Contract Type column in the subform, so that the complete values for this field are visible.

▶ 5. Use the vertical scroll bar for the main form to scroll down and view the bottom of the subform, if necessary. Note the navigation buttons.

▶ 6. In the subform, click the **Last record** navigation button �. Record 4 in the Contract table becomes the current record in the subform.

▶ 7. Save and close the CustomerContracts form.

TIP

As you move through the form/subform, notice that some field values in the subform are not completely visible. You can resize any subform field to its best fit to fully display the field values.

You've finished your work for Oren on the forms in the Belmont database. Next, Taylor Sico asks you to create a report that she can use to prepare a new advertising campaign.

Creating a Report Using the Report Wizard

As you learned in Tutorial 1, a report is a formatted printout of the contents of one or more tables or queries in a database. In Access, you can create your own reports or use the Report Wizard to create them for you. Whether you use the Report Wizard or design your own report, you can change the report's design after you create it.

INSIGHT

Creating a Report Based on a Query

You can create a report based on one or more tables or queries. When you use a query as the basis for a report, you can use criteria and other query features to retrieve only the information you want to display in the report. Experienced Access users often create a query just so they can create a report based on that query. When thinking about the type of report you want to create, consider creating a query first and basing the report on the query, to produce the exact results you want to see in the report.

Taylor wants you to create a report that includes data from both the Customer and Contract tables, as shown in the Session 4.2 Visual Overview. Like the CustomerContracts form you just created, which includes a main form and a subform, the report will be based on both tables, which are joined in a one-to-many relationship through the common CustomerID field. You'll use the Report Wizard to create the report for Taylor.

To start the Report Wizard and select the fields to include in the report:

1. Click the **Create** tab on the Ribbon.

2. In the Reports group on the Create tab, click the **Report Wizard** button. The first Report Wizard dialog box opens.

   As was the case when you created the form with a subform, initially you can choose only one table or query to be the data source for the report. Then you can include data from other tables or queries. You will select the primary Customer table first.

3. If necessary, click the **Tables/Queries** arrow, and then click **Table: Customer**.

   You select fields in the order you want them to appear on the report. Taylor wants the CustomerID, Company, First, Last, City, and Phone fields from the Customer table to appear on the report, in that order.

4. Click **CustomerID** in the Available Fields box (if necessary), and then click the ⟨ > ⟩ button. The field moves to the Selected Fields box.

5. Repeat Step 4 to add the **Company**, **First**, **Last**, **City**, and **Phone** fields to the report.

6. Click the **Tables/Queries** arrow, scroll the list up, and then click **Table: Contract**. The fields from the Contract table appear in the Available Fields box.

   The CustomerID field will appear on the report with the customer data, so you do not need to include it in the detail records for each contract. Otherwise, Taylor wants all the fields from the Contract table to be included in the report.

7. Click the ⟨ >> ⟩ button to move all the fields from the Available Fields box to the Selected Fields box.

8. Click **Contract.CustomerID** in the Selected Fields box, click the ⟨ < ⟩ button to move the field back to the Available Fields box, and then click the **Next** button. The second Report Wizard dialog box opens. See Figure 4-19.

Figure 4-19	Choosing a grouped or ungrouped report

TIP

You can display tips for creating reports and examples of reports by clicking the "Show me more information" button.

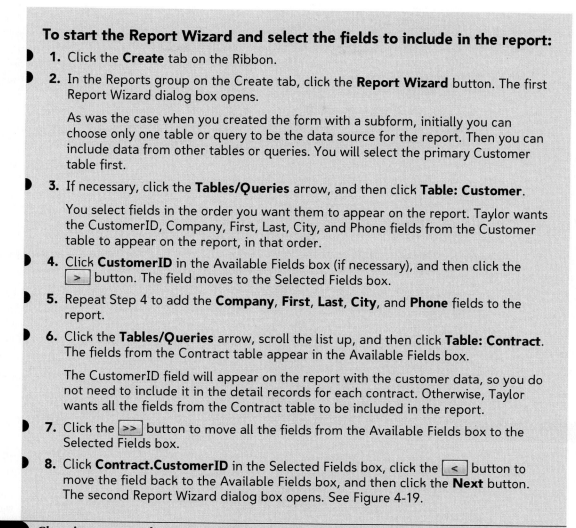

You can choose to arrange the selected data grouped by table, which is the default, or ungrouped. You're creating a grouped report; the data from a record in the Customer table will appear in a group, followed by the related records for each customer from the Contract table. An example of an ungrouped report would be a report of records from the Customer and Contract tables in order by ContractNum. Each contract and its associated customer data would appear together on one or more lines of the report; the data would not be grouped by table.

The default options shown on your screen are correct for the report Taylor wants, so you can continue responding to the Report Wizard questions.

To finish creating the report using the Report Wizard:

▶ **1.** Click the **Next** button. The next Report Wizard dialog box opens, in which you choose additional grouping levels.

Two grouping levels are shown: one for a customer's data, and the other for a customer's contracts. Grouping levels are useful for reports with multiple levels, such as those containing monthly, quarterly, and annual totals, or for those containing city and country groups. Taylor's report requires no further grouping levels, so you can accept the default options.

▶ **2.** Click the **Next** button. The next Report Wizard dialog box opens, in which you choose the sort order for the detail records. See Figure 4-20.

Figure 4-20	Choosing the sort order for detail records

The records from the Contract table for a customer represent the detail records for Taylor's report. She wants these records to appear in increasing, or ascending, order by the value in the SigningDate field, so that the contracts will be shown in chronological order. The Ascending option is already selected by default. To change to descending order, you click this same button, which acts as a toggle between the two sort orders. Also, you can sort on multiple fields, as you can with queries.

▶ **3.** Click the **arrow** on the first box, click **SigningDate**, and then click the **Next** button. The next Report Wizard dialog box opens, in which you choose a layout and page orientation for the report. See Figure 4-21.

Figure 4-21   **Choosing the report layout**

sample of the selected layout

orientation options

layout options

4. Click each layout option and examine each sample that appears.

   You'll use the Outline layout for Taylor's report. Also, because some of the fields in both the Customer and Contract tables contain lengthy field values, you'll change the page orientation to landscape. This will provide more space across the page to display longer field values.

5. In the Layout section, click the **Outline** option button.

6. In the Orientation section, click the **Landscape** option button, and then click the **Next** button. The final Report Wizard dialog box opens, in which you choose a report title, which also serves as the name for the report object in the database.

   Taylor wants the report title "Customers and Contracts" at the top of the report. Because the name you enter in this dialog box is also the name of the report object, you'll enter the report name as one word and edit the title on the report later.

7. In the box for the title, enter **CustomersAndContracts** and then click the **Finish** button. The Report Wizard creates the report based on your answers, saves it as an object in the Belmont database, and opens the report in Print Preview.

   To view the entire page, you need to change the Zoom setting.

8. In the Zoom group on the Print Preview tab, click the **Zoom button arrow**, and then click **Fit to Window**. The first page of the report is displayed in Print Preview.

   When a report is displayed in Print Preview, you can use the pointer to toggle between a full-page display and a close-up display of the report.

9. Click the pointer 🔍 at the center of the report. The display changes to show a close-up view of the report. See Figure 4-22.

Figure 4-22	Close-up view of the report

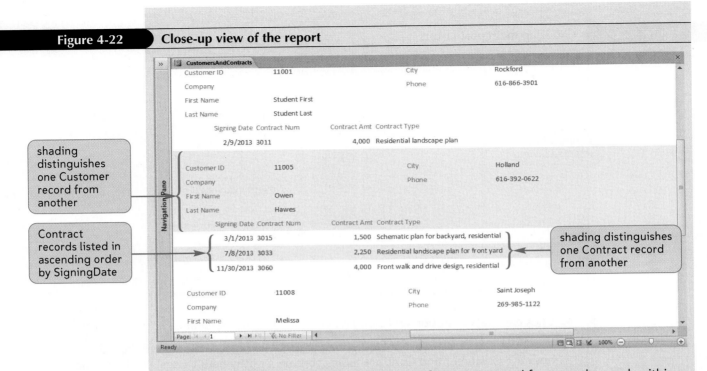

shading distinguishes one Customer record from another

Contract records listed in ascending order by SigningDate

shading distinguishes one Contract record from another

Shading is used both to distinguish one Customer record from another and, within a group of each customer's Contract records, one Contract record from another.

Trouble? Depending on your computer settings, the shading and colors used in your report might look different. This difference should not cause any problems.

The detail records for the Contract table fields appear in ascending order based on the values in the SigningDate field. Because the SigningDate field is used as the basis for sorting records, it appears as the first field in this section, even though you selected the fields in the order in which they appear in the Contract table.

10. Use the vertical scroll bar to scroll to the bottom of the first page, checking the text in the report as you scroll. Notice the current date and page number at the bottom of the first page of the report; the Report Wizard included these elements as part of the report's design.

11. Use the horizontal scroll bar to scroll to the right and view the page number in the footer.

Trouble? Depending on your computer's settings, the text of the page number might not be completely within the page border. If so, you'll see blank pages every other page as you complete Steps 12 and 13. You'll fix this problem shortly.

12. Click the pointer 🔍 on the report to zoom back out, and then click the **Next Page** navigation button ▶ to move to page 2 of the report.

13. Continue to move through the pages of the report, and then click the **First Page** navigation button ◀ to return to the first page.

Earlier, when meeting with Oren, Taylor viewed and worked with the CustomerData form. She likes how the form looks with the Perspective theme applied, and would like her report formatted with the same theme. You need to switch to Layout view to make this change.

Modifying a Report's Design in Layout View

Similar to Layout view for forms, Layout view for reports enables you to make modifications to the report's design. Many of the same options—such as those for applying a theme and changing the color of text—are provided in Layout view for reports.

Applying a Theme to a Report

The same themes available for forms are also available for reports. You can choose to apply a theme to the current report object only, or to all reports in the database. In this case, you'll apply the Perspective theme only to the CustomersAndContracts report because Taylor isn't certain if it is the appropriate theme for other reports in the Belmont database.

To apply the Perspective theme to the report:

1. On the status bar, click the **Layout View** button ⊞. The report is displayed in Layout view.

2. In the Themes group on the Design tab, click the **Themes** button. The "In this Database" section at the top of the gallery shows both the default Office theme and the Perspective theme. The Perspective theme is included here because you applied it earlier to the CustomerData form.

3. At the top of the gallery, right-click the **Perspective** theme to display the shortcut menu, and then click **Apply Theme to This Object Only**. The gallery closes and the theme is applied to the report.

   The larger font used by the Perspective theme has caused both the report title text and the Contract Num field label to be cut off on the right. First, you'll fix the problem with the report title and edit the title text as well.

4. Click the **CustomersAndContracts** title at the top of the report to select it.

5. Place the pointer on the right edge of the orange outline surrounding the title, and then click and drag the ↔ pointer to the right until the title is fully displayed.

6. Click between the letters "s" and "A" in the title, press the **spacebar**, change the capital letter "A" to **a**, place the insertion point between the letters "d" and "C," and then press the **spacebar**. The title is now "Customers and Contracts."

7. Click to the right of the report title in the shaded area.

   Taylor is concerned that the larger font size of the theme might have caused other text in the report to be cut off—especially some of the Company names, which are lengthy. You need to check the report for such problems.

8. Scroll the report until you see the record for CustomerID 11045, Kalamazoo Neighborhood Development. Notice that the right part of the company name is not visible. The same is true later in the report for the record for CustomerID 11059, G.R. Neighborhood Development Corp.

To fix this problem, you need to resize the City and Phone field labels to make them smaller, allowing more room for the Company field value box, which you can then resize. You also need to resize the Contract Num field label so it is fully displayed.

Resizing a Field on a Report in Layout View

Working in Layout view, you can resize and reposition fields to improve the appearance of the report or to address the problem of some field values not being completely displayed. In the CustomersAndContracts report, you need to make space for the longer

Company field values by resizing the City and Phone field labels first, and then resizing the Company field value box. To make sure all the Company field values will fit, you should make any adjustments based on the longest company name—Kalamazoo Neighborhood Development. Then you'll resize the Contract Num field label so it is fully displayed; and finally, you'll check the page number in the footer to make sure it fits completely on the page.

To resize the field labels and field value box:

▶ **1.** Make sure the Report window is still displaying the record for CustomerID 11045, Kalamazoo Neighborhood Development. To select and resize multiple fields, you use the Shift key.

▶ **2.** Click the **City** field label for CustomerID 11045, press and hold the **Shift** key, and then click the **Phone** field label for the same record. Both field labels are selected and can be resized. See Figure 4-23.

Figure 4-23	Field labels selected and ready to be resized

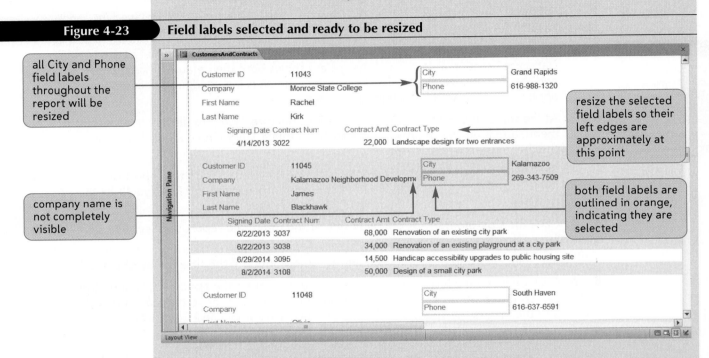

all City and Phone field labels throughout the report will be resized

company name is not completely visible

resize the selected field labels so their left edges are approximately at this point

both field labels are outlined in orange, indicating they are selected

You'll resize the field labels on their left edges, making them smaller and moving the labels closer to their corresponding field values.

▶ **3.** Position the pointer ↔ on the left edge of either selected field label, and then click and drag to the right. As you drag, black outlines indicate the size of the labels.

▶ **4.** Release the mouse button when the left edge of the field labels is approximately aligned with the beginning of the word "for" in the Contract Type field value box above (see Figure 4-23). The City and Phone field labels are now smaller, moving them closer to their values and making more space available for the Company field value box. Note that *all* City and Phone field labels for the entire report have been resized, not just those for the current record.

Next you'll resize the Company field value box so that the longest value (Kalamazoo Neighborhood Development) is fully displayed. This will ensure that all other company names will be completely visible in the report as well.

▶ **5.** Click the Company field value **Kalamazoo Neighborhood Development** for Customer ID 11045. An orange outline appears around the field value box, indicating it is selected.

6. Position the pointer on the right side of the field value box until the pointer changes to a ↔ shape.

7. Click and drag the pointer to the right until the complete company name is visible, and then release the mouse button.

8. Click the **Contract Num** field label below the record for Customer ID 11045 to select the label, and then use the ↔ pointer to resize its right side until the field label is fully displayed. See Figure 4-24.

| Figure 4-24 | Report after resizing field labels and field value boxes |

all City and Phone field labels resized and closer to their field values

Company field value is now fully displayed

Contract Num field label is now fully displayed

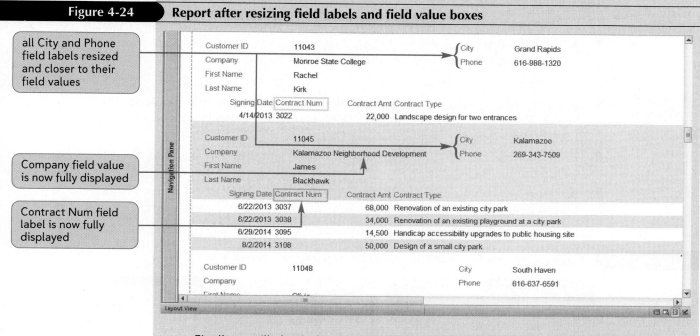

Finally, you'll check the page number in the footer to make sure the text is completely on the page.

9. Scroll the report to the bottom and to the right and view the page number text.

Trouble? If the text "Page 1 of 1" is not fully within the page border, click the text to select it, position the pointer on its right edge until the pointer changes to ↔, and then click and drag to the left until the page number text is roughly right-aligned with the text in the report.

Next, Taylor asks you to enhance the report's appearance by inserting the same picture on the CustomersAndContracts report as you included on the CustomerData form, and to change the color of the report title to the same brown color used on the form.

Changing the Title Font Color and Inserting a Picture in a Report

You can change the color of text on a report to enhance its appearance. You can also add a picture to a report for visual interest or to identify a particular section of the report. Because Taylor plans to print the report using a color printer, she asks you to change the report title color to brown and to include the Landscape picture to the right of the report title.

To change the color of the report title and insert the picture:

▶ **1.** Scroll to the top of the report, and then click the title **Customers and Contracts** to select it.

▶ **2.** Click the **Format** tab on the Ribbon. The options for modifying the format of a report are the same as those available for forms.

▶ **3.** In the Font group on the Format tab, click the **Font Color button arrow** A ▾, and then click the **Brown, Accent 3, Darker 25%** color box (fifth row, seventh box in the Theme Colors palette). The color is applied to the report title.

Now you'll insert the picture to the right of the report title text.

▶ **4.** Click the **Design** tab on the Ribbon. Again, the options provided on this tab for reports are the same as those you worked with for forms.

▶ **5.** In the Header/Footer group on the Design tab, click the **Logo** button.

▶ **6.** Navigate to the **Access1\Tutorial** folder, and then double-click the **Landscape** file. The picture is inserted in the top-left corner of the report, partially covering the report title.

▶ **7.** Position the pointer ⬚ on the selected picture, and then click and drag it to the right of the report title.

▶ **8.** Release the mouse button when the pointer is to the right of the report title text and below the button in the Controls group with "Aa" on it, and then click in a blank area of the shaded bar to deselect the picture. See Figure 4-25.

Figure 4-25	Report after changing the title font color and inserting the picture

font color of the title is now brown

picture added and moved to the right of the title

Trouble? Don't be concerned if the pointer in your report is not in the exact same location as the one shown in the figure. Just make sure it is to the right of the title text and within the shaded area.

Taylor is pleased with the report's appearance and shows it to Oren. He also approves of the report's contents and design, but has one final suggestion to enhance the report. He'd like to draw attention to the contract amounts that are greater than $25,000 by formatting them with a bold, red font. Because Oren doesn't want all the contract amounts to appear in this font, you need to use conditional formatting.

Using Conditional Formatting in a Report

Conditional formatting in a report (or form) is special formatting applied to certain field values depending on one or more conditions—similar to criteria you establish for queries. If a field value meets the condition or conditions you specify, the formatting is applied to the value.

Oren would like the CustomersAndContracts report to show any contract amount that is greater than $25,000 in a bold, dark red font. This formatting will help to highlight the more significant contracts for Belmont Landscapes.

To apply conditional formatting to the ContractAmt field in the report:

1. Make sure the report is still displayed in Layout view, and then click the **Format** tab on the Ribbon.

2. Click the first ContractAmt field value, **4,000**, for ContractNum 3011. An orange outline appears around the field value box, and a lighter orange outline appears around each ContractAmt field value box throughout the entire report. The conditional formatting you specify will affect all the values for the field.

3. In the Control Formatting group on the Format tab, click the **Conditional Formatting** button. The Conditional Formatting Rules Manager dialog box opens. Because you selected a ContractAmt field value box, this field is displayed in the "Show formatting rules for" box. Currently, there are no conditional formatting rules set for the selected field. You need to create a new rule.

4. Click the **New Rule** button. The New Formatting Rule dialog box opens. See Figure 4-26.

Figure 4-26   New Formatting Rule dialog box

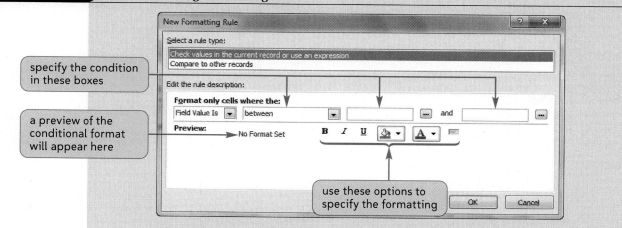

The default setting for "Select a rule type" specifies that Access will check field values and determine if they meet the condition. This is the setting you want. You need to enter the condition in the "Edit the rule description" section of the dialog box. The setting "Field Value Is" means that the conditional format you specify will be applied only when the value for the selected field, ContractAmt, meets the condition.

5. Click the **arrow** for the box containing the word "between," and then click **greater than**. Oren wants only those contract amounts greater than $25,000 to be formatted.

6. Press the **Tab** key to move to the next box, and then type **25000**.

7. In the Preview section, click the **Font color button arrow** A ▾ , and then click the **Dark Red** color box (first color box in the last row of Standard Colors).

8. In the Preview section, click the **Bold** button B . The specifications for the conditional formatting are complete. See Figure 4-27.

Figure 4-27	Conditional formatting set for the ContractAmt field

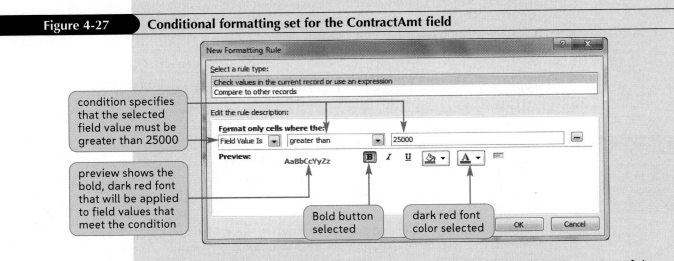

condition specifies that the selected field value must be greater than 25000

preview shows the bold, dark red font that will be applied to field values that meet the condition

Bold button selected

dark red font color selected

9. Click the **OK** button. The new rule you specified appears in the Rule section of the dialog box as Value > 25000; the Format section on the right shows the conditional formatting (dark red, bold font) that will be applied based on this rule.

10. Click the **OK** button. The conditional format is applied to the ContractAmt field values. To get a better view of the report and the formatting, you'll switch to Print Preview.

11. On the status bar, click the **Print Preview** button 🔍 .

12. Move to page 9 of the report. Notice that the conditional formatting is applied only to ContractAmt field values greater than $25,000. See Figure 4-28.

Figure 4-28	Viewing the finished report in Print Preview

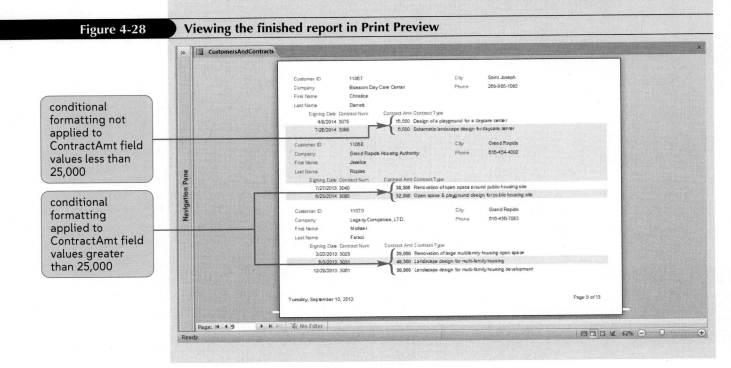

conditional formatting not applied to ContractAmt field values less than 25,000

conditional formatting applied to ContractAmt field values greater than 25,000

PROSKILLS

Problem Solving: Understanding the Importance of Previewing Reports

When you create a report, it is a good idea to display the report in Print Preview occasionally as you develop the report. Doing so will give you a chance to find any formatting problems or other issues so that you can make any necessary corrections before printing the report. It is particularly important to preview a report after you've made changes to its design to ensure that the changes you made have not created new problems with the report's format. Before printing any report, you should preview it so you can determine where the pages will break and make any necessary adjustments. Following this problem-solving approach will not only ensure that the final printed report looks exactly the way you want it to, but will also save you time and help to avoid wasting paper.

The report is now complete. You'll print just the first page of the report so that Oren and Taylor can view the final results and share the report design with other staff members before printing the entire report. (*Note:* Ask your instructor if you should complete the following printing steps.)

To print page 1 of the report:

1. In the Print group on the Print Preview tab, click the **Print** button. The Print dialog box opens.

2. In the Print Range section, click the **Pages** option button. The insertion point now appears in the From box so that you can specify the range of pages to print.

3. Type **1** in the From box, press the **Tab** key to move to the To box, and then type **1**. These settings specify that only page 1 of the report will be printed.

4. Click the **OK** button. The Print dialog box closes, and the first page of the report is printed.

5. Save and close the CustomersAndContracts report.

You've created many different objects in the Belmont database. Before you close it, you'll open the Navigation Pane to view all the objects in the database.

To view the Belmont database objects in the Navigation Pane:

1. Open the Navigation Pane and scroll down, if necessary, to display the bottom of the pane. The CustomersAndContracts report is selected because it is the object you just closed.

   The Navigation Pane displays the objects grouped by type: tables, queries, forms, and reports. Notice the CustomerContracts form. This is the form you created containing a main form based on the Customer table and a subform based on the Contract table. The ContractSubform object is also listed; you can open it separately from the main form. See Figure 4-29.

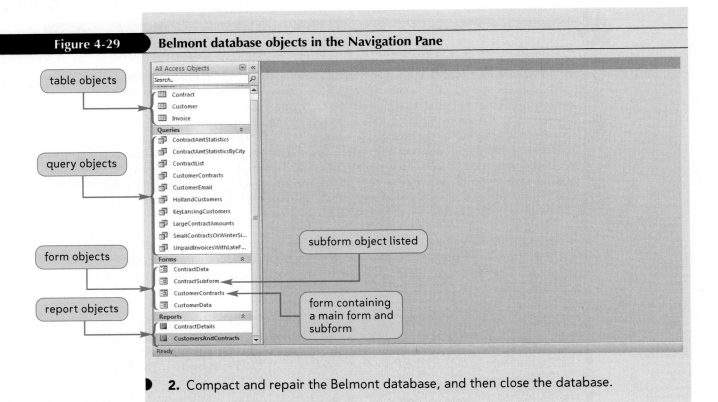

Figure 4-29   **Belmont database objects in the Navigation Pane**

table objects

query objects

form objects

report objects

subform object listed

form containing a main form and subform

2. Compact and repair the Belmont database, and then close the database.

Oren is satisfied that the forms you created—the CustomerData form and the CustomerContracts form—will make it easier to enter, view, and update data in the Belmont database. The CustomersAndContracts report presents important information about Belmont Landscapes customers in an attractive and professional format, which will help Taylor and other staff members in their marketing efforts.

Session 4.2 Quick Check

REVIEW

1. In a form that contains a main form and a subform, what data is displayed in the main form and what data is displayed in the subform?
2. Describe how you use the navigation buttons to move through a form containing a main form and a subform.
3. When you create a report based on two tables that are joined in a one-to-many relationship, the field values for the records from the related table are called the _____ records.
4. True or False: To resize a field on a report, you first need to display the report in Design view.
5. When working in Layout view for a report, which key do you press and hold down so that you can click to select multiple fields?
6. _____ in a report (or form) is special formatting applied to certain field values depending on one or more conditions.

Practice the skills you learned in the tutorial using the same case scenario.

PRACTICE

Review Assignments

Data Files needed for the Review Assignments: Supplier.accdb (*cont. from Tutorial 3*) **and Tools.bmp**

Oren asks you to enhance the Supplier database with forms and reports. Complete the following steps:

1. Open the **Supplier** database located in the Access1\Review folder provided with your Data Files.

2. Use the Form Wizard to create a form based on the Product table. Select all fields for the form and the Columnar layout; specify the title **ProductData** for the form.

3. Apply the Foundry theme to the ProductData form *only*.

4. Insert the Tools picture, which is located in the Access1\Review folder provided with your Data Files, in the ProductData form. Remove the picture from the control layout, and then move the picture to the right of the form title.

5. Edit the form title so that it appears as "Product Data" (two words), and change the font color of the form title to the Tan, Accent 5, Darker 25% theme color.

6. Change the line type for the field value boxes—except the Discount Offered check box—to Dots.

7. Resize the text box for the Weight in Lbs field value so it is the same width as the Size text box above it.

8. Use the ProductData form to update the Product table as follows:

   a. Use the Find command to search for "wall" anywhere in the ProductType field and then display the record for a retaining wall (ProductID 5227). Change the Price in this record to **11.50** and the Discount Offered to **yes**.

   b. Add a new record with the following field values, leaving the Color, Material, and Weight in Lbs fields blank:

   Product ID: **5630**
   Company ID: **GEN359**
   Product Type: **Annual**
   Price: **2.90**
   Unit: **Each**
   Color: [do not enter a value]
   Material: [do not enter a value]
   Size: **1 quart**
   Weight in Lbs: [do not enter a value]
   Discount Offered: **yes**

   c. Save and close the form.

9. Use the Form Wizard to create a form containing a main form and a subform. Select all fields except Product from the Company table for the main form, and select ProductID, ProductType, Price, Unit, and Color—in that order—from the Product table for the subform. Use the Datasheet layout. Specify the title **CompaniesAndProducts** for the main form and **ProductSubform** for the subform.

10. Change the form title text to **Companies and Products**.

11. Resize the subform to the right, increasing its width by approximately two inches, and then resize all columns in the subform to their best fit, working left to right. Navigate through each record in the main form to make sure all the field values in the subform are completely displayed, resizing subform columns as necessary. Save and close the CompaniesAndProducts form.

12. Use the Report Wizard to create a report based on the primary Company table and the related Product table. Select the CompanyID, Company, ContactFirst, ContactLast, City, and Phone fields—in that order—from the Company table, and the ProductID, ProductType, Price, and Unit fields from the Product table. Do not specify any additional grouping levels, and sort the detail records in ascending order by ProductID. Choose the Outline layout and Portrait orientation. Specify the title **ProductsByCompany** for the report.

13. Change the report title text to **Products by Company**.

14. Apply the Foundry theme to the ProductsByCompany report *only*.

15. Resize the following controls in the report in Layout view, and then scroll through the report to make sure all field values are fully displayed:

   a. Resize the report title so that the text of the title, Products by Company, is fully displayed.

   b. Resize the City and Phone field labels to reduce their size from the left by roughly one half and move them closer to their field value boxes.

   c. Resize the Product ID field label on its left side, increasing its width so the label is fully displayed.

16. Change the color of the report title text to the Tan, Accent 5, Darker 25% theme color.

17. Insert the Tools picture, which is located in the Access1\Review folder provided with your Data Files, in the report. Move the picture to the right of the report title.

18. Apply conditional formatting so that the City field values equal to Lansing appear as dark red and bold.

19. Preview each page of the report, verifying that all the fields fit on the page. If necessary, return to Layout view and make changes so the report prints within the margins of the page and so that all field names and values are completely displayed.

20. Save the report, print its first page (only if asked by your instructor to do so), and then close the report.

21. Compact and repair the Supplier database, and then close it.

Case Problem 1

If you have a SAM 2010 user profile, your instructor may have assigned an autogradable version of this assignment. If so, log into the SAM 2010 Web site at www.cengage.com/sam2010 to download the instructions and start files.

APPLY

Data Files needed for this Case Problem: Pinehill.accdb (*cont. from Tutorial 3*) and **Piano.bmp**

Pine Hill Music School   Yuka Koyama wants to use the Pinehill database to track and view information about the classes her music school offers. She asks you to create the necessary forms and a report to help her manage this data. Complete the following:

1. Open the **Pinehill** database located in the Access1\Case1 folder provided with your Data Files.

2. Use the Form Wizard to create a form based on the Student table. Select all the fields for the form and the Columnar layout. Specify the title **StudentData** for the form.

3. Apply the Clarity theme to the StudentData form *only*.

4. Edit the form title so that it appears as "Student Data" (two words), and change the font color of the form title to the Blue-Gray, Accent 4, Lighter 40% theme color.

5. Use the Find command to display the record for Jeff Tealey, and then change the Address field value for this record to **304 Forest Ave**.

6. Use the StudentData form to add a new record to the Student table with the following field values:

   Student ID: **NEL7584**

   First Name: **Kayla**

   Last Name: **Nelson**

Address: **15540 Belleview Dr**
City: **Portland**
State: **OR**
Zip: **97229**
Home Phone: **541-563-3156**
Mobile Phone: **541-563-8882**
Birth Date: **10/13/2003**
Gender: **F**

7. Save and close the StudentData form.

8. Use the Form Wizard to create a form containing a main form and a subform. Select all the fields from the Teacher table for the main form, and select the ContractID, StudentID, and LessonType fields from the Contract table for the subform. Use the Datasheet layout. Specify the title **ContractsByTeacher** for the main form and the title **ContractSubform** for the subform.

9. Change the form title text for the main form to **Contracts by Teacher**.

10. Change the line type for the field value boxes—except the Takes Beginners check box—to Dots.

11. Resize all columns in the subform to their best fit, and then move through all the records in the main form and check to make sure that all subform field values are fully displayed, resizing the columns as necessary.

12. Save and close the ContractsByTeacher form.

13. Use the Report Wizard to create a report based on the primary Student table and the related Contract table. Select the StudentID, FirstName, LastName, and HomePhone fields from the Student table, and select all fields from the Contract table except StudentID, StartDate, and EndDate. Do not select any additional grouping levels, and sort the detail records in ascending order by ContractID. Choose the Outline layout and Landscape orientation. Specify the title **StudentContracts** for the report.

14. Apply the Clarity theme to the StudentContracts report *only*.

15. Resize the report title so that the text is fully displayed; edit the report title so that it appears as "Student Contracts" (two words); and change the font color of the title to the Blue-Gray, Accent 4, Lighter 40% theme color.

16. Resize the following controls in the report in Layout view, and then scroll through the report to make sure all field values are fully displayed:

    a. Resize the Contract ID field label on its left side, increasing its width so the label is fully displayed.

    b. Resize the Lesson Length field label on its left side, increasing its width so the label is fully displayed.

    c. Scroll to the bottom of the report and check to make sure the page number is completely within the page border. If necessary, resize the control on its right side, reducing its width so that the page number text is roughly right-aligned with the text in the report.

17. Insert the Piano picture, which is located in the Access1\Case1 folder provided with your Data Files, in the report. Move the picture to the right of the report title.

18. Apply conditional formatting so that any LessonCost field value greater than 200 appears as bold and with the Maroon 5 color applied.

19. Preview the entire report to confirm that it is formatted correctly. If necessary, return to Layout view and make changes so that all field labels and field values are completely displayed. (*Hint:* You might need to resize the Teacher ID field label so it is fully displayed; if so, resize the Contract ID field label to the left more, to make room for resizing the Teacher ID field label.) When you are finished, save the report, print its first page (only if asked by your instructor to do so), and then close the report.

20. Compact and repair the Pinehill database, and then close it.

Challenge yourself by creating and working with a form and report for a fitness center.

CHALLENGE

Case Problem 2

Data Files needed for this Case Problem: Fitness.accdb (*cont. from Tutorial 3*) and Weights.bmp

Parkhurst Health & Fitness Center Martha Parkhurst is using the Fitness database to track and analyze the business activity of the fitness center members and their programs. To make her work easier, you'll create a form and report in the Fitness database. Complete the following steps:

1. Open the **Fitness** database located in the Access1\Case2 folder provided with your Data Files.

2. Use the Form Wizard to create a form containing a main form and a subform. Select all the fields from the Program table for the main form, and select the MemberID, First, Last, and Phone fields from the Member table for the subform. Use the Tabular layout. Specify the title **ProgramMembers** for the main form and the title **MemberSubform** for the subform.

3. Apply the Slipstream theme to the ProgramMembers form *only*.

4. Edit the form title so that it appears as "Program Members" (two words), and change the font color of the form title to the Green, Accent 3, Lighter 80% theme color. Deselect the form title after changing the color.

⊕ EXPLORE
5. In Layout view, use the Insert Image button in the Controls group on the Design tab to insert the Weights picture, which is located in the Access1\Case2 folder provided with your Data Files. (*Hint:* In the Insert Picture dialog box, make sure the All Files option is selected in the box next to the File name box.) Click to select the picture in the dialog box, and then click the OK button. (Do *not* double-click the picture file in the dialog box.) Notice that the pointer changes to ⁺🖻. Place this pointer below the subform name "Member" and then click to place the picture on the form. Use the ⁺🖑 pointer to move the picture below the subform name, and then use the resizing pointers—on the sides, corners, top, and/or bottom of the picture, as needed—to resize the picture and make it smaller. Continue to move and resize the picture until it is positioned roughly one-quarter inch below the subform name "Member" and is about the same width as the subform name.

6. Save the ProgramMembers form, display the form in Form view, and then navigate to the second record in the subform for the first main record (MemberID 1110). Change the Phone field value for this record to **804-553-7986**.

7. Navigate to the ninth record in the main form, and then change the value in the Last Name column in the fourth record in the subform (MemberID 1155) to **Larsen**. Close the form.

⊕ EXPLORE
8. Use the Report Wizard to create a report based on the primary Program table and the related Member table. Select all fields except PhysicalRequired from the Program table, and then select the following fields from the Member table: MemberID, First, Last, City, Phone, DateJoined, and Status. In the third Report Wizard dialog box, specify the City field as an additional grouping level. Sort the detail records by DateJoined in *descending* order. Choose the Outline layout and Landscape orientation for the report. Specify the title **ProgramsAndMembers** for the report.

9. Apply the Slipstream theme to the ProgramsAndMembers report *only*.

10. Resize the report title so that the text is fully displayed; edit the report title so that it appears as "Programs and Members"; and change the font color of the title to the Green, Accent 3, Lighter 80% theme color.

11. Resize the Membership Status field label to the right, making it wider so that the label is fully displayed.

12. Scroll to the bottom of the report and check to make sure the page number is completely within the page border. If necessary, resize the control on its right side, reducing its width so that the page number text is roughly right-aligned with the text in the report.

13. Insert the Weights picture (located in the Access1\Case2 folder) in the report. Move the picture to the right of the report title. Resize the picture so that it is approximately one-inch wide.

⊕ **EXPLORE** 14. In the Control Formatting group on the Format tab, use the Shape Fill button to apply the Green, Accent 3, Lighter 60% theme color to the picture. (*Hint:* Make sure the picture is selected first.)

⊕ **EXPLORE** 15. Apply conditional formatting so that all Status field values equal to "On Hold" are formatted with an italic font and the background color Green 3. Note that you must include quotation marks around the words "On Hold" because there is a space between them.

16. Preview the report to confirm that it is formatted correctly and all field names and values are fully displayed. Save the report, print its first page (only if asked by your instructor to do so), and then close the report.

17. Compact and repair the Fitness database, and then close it.

Explore some new skills to create forms and a report for a not-for-profit agency.

CHALLENGE

Case Problem 3

Data Files needed for this Case Problem: Rossi.accdb (*cont. from Tutorial 3*) and **Recycle.bmp**

Rossi Recycling Group Tom Rossi wants to work with and display data about the donations made to the Rossi Recycling Group. You'll help him by creating forms and a report in the Rossi database. Complete the following steps:

1. Open the **Rossi** database located in the Access1\Case3 folder provided with your Data Files.

2. Use the Form Wizard to create a form based on the Donation table. Select all the fields for the form and the Columnar layout. Specify the title **DonationInfo** for the form.

3. Apply the Verve theme to the DonationInfo form *only*.

4. Edit the form title so that it appears as "Donation Info" (two words), and change the font color of the form title to the Pink, Accent 2, Darker 25% theme color.

⊕ **EXPLORE** 5. Use the appropriate button in the Font group on the Format tab to underline the form title. Resize the title, as necessary, so that the complete title text appears on the same line.

⊕ **EXPLORE** 6. Use the appropriate button in the Font group on the Format tab to left-align the Donation Value field values. Save the form.

⊕ **EXPLORE** 7. Use the DonationInfo form to update the Donation table as follows:

   a. Use the Find command to search for records that contain "tools" anywhere in the Donation Description field. Display the record with the field value Power tools, and then change the Donation Value for this record to **565**.

   b. Add a new record with the following values:
   Donation ID: **2219**
   Donor ID: **36077**
   Agency ID: **W22**
   Donation Date: **12/21/2013**
   Donation Description: **Toys**
   Donation Value: **45**
   Pickup Required: **No**

    c. Find the record with DonationID 2150, and then delete it. (*Hint:* After displaying the record in the form, you need to select it by clicking the right-pointing triangle in the bar to the left of the field labels. Then use the appropriate button in the Records group on the Home tab to delete the record. When asked to confirm the deletion, click the Yes button.) Close the form.

8. Use the Form Wizard to create a form containing a main form and a subform. Select all the fields from the Donor table for the main form, and select the DonationID, AgencyID, DonationDate, Description, and DonationValue fields from the Donation table for the subform. Use the Datasheet layout. Specify the name **DonorsAndDonations** for the main form and the title **DonationSubform** for the subform.

9. Apply the Verve theme to the DonorsAndDonations form *only*.

10. Edit the form title so that it appears as "Donors and Donations." Resize the form title so that the text fits on one line. Change the font color of the title to the Pink, Accent 2, Darker 25% theme color.

⊕ **EXPLORE** 11. Use the appropriate button in the Font group on the Format tab to apply the theme color Pink, Accent 1, Lighter 80% as a background color for all the field value boxes in the main form. Then use the appropriate button in the Control Formatting group to change the outline of all the main form field value boxes to have a line thickness of 1 pt. (*Hint:* Select all the field value boxes before making these changes.)

12. Resize the subform to the right to make it as wide as possible, and then resize all columns in the subform to their best fit, *working right to left*. Navigate through each record in the main form to make sure all the field values in the subform are completely displayed, resizing subform columns as necessary. Save the form.

13. Use the appropriate wildcard character to find all records with a Phone field value that begins with the area code 316. Change the record with the Phone field value of 316-282-2226 (Donor ID 36062) to **316-282-2556**. Close the form.

⊕ **EXPLORE** 14. Use the Report Wizard to create a report based on the primary Agency table and the related Donation table. Select the Agency and Phone fields from the Agency table, and select all fields except AgencyID and Pickup from the Donation table. In the third Report Wizard dialog box, select DonorID as an additional grouping level. Sort the detail records in *descending* order by DonationValue. Choose the Outline layout and Portrait orientation. Specify the name **AgenciesAndDonations** for the report.

15. Apply the Verve theme to the AgenciesAndDonations report *only*.

16. Resize the report title so that the text is fully displayed; edit the report title so that it appears as "Agencies and Donations"; and change the font color of the title to the Pink, Accent 2, Darker 25% theme color.

17. Select both the Donation Description field label and its field value box, and then resize them from the left side, making them smaller and moving them further to the right. Then select both the Donation Date field label and its field value box, and then resize them on both the left and right sides to move them further to the right and fully display their values. Finally, resize the Donation ID field label so it is fully displayed. Save the report.

18. Insert the Recycle picture, which is located in the Access1\Case3 folder provided with your Data Files, in the report. Move the picture to the right of the report title.

19. Apply conditional formatting so that any DonationValue greater than or equal to 200 is formatted as bold and with the Maroon font color.

20. Preview the report to confirm that it is formatted correctly and all field labels and field values are fully displayed. Save the report, print its first page (only if asked by your instructor to do so), and then close the report.

21. Compact and repair the Rossi database, and then close it.

With the figures provided as guides, create a form and a report for a luxury rental agency.

CREATE

Case Problem 4

Data Files needed for this Case Problem: GEM.accdb (*cont. from Tutorial 3*) and Villa.bmp

GEM Ultimate Vacations   Griffin and Emma MacElroy want to use the GEM database to track and analyze data about their clients and the luxury properties they rent. You'll help them by creating a form and a report to meet this goal. Complete the following steps:

1. Open the **GEM** database located in the Access1\Case4 folder provided with your Data Files.

2. Create the form shown in Figure 4-30.

Figure 4-30   Completed GuestsAndReservations form

Flow theme applied to this form object only

Turquoise, Accent 2, Darker 25% theme color applied to the form title text (be sure to apply the Flow theme first)

Villa picture inserted and its height and width increased

subform columns resized to their best fit

subform object title is ReservationSubform

Datasheet layout specified

---

3. Using the form you just created, navigate to the second record in the subform for the third main record, and then change the People field value to **7**.

4. Use the Find command to move to the record for Kelly Skolnik, and then change the value in the End Date column for ReservationID 507 to **5/22/13**.

5. Use the appropriate wildcard character to find all records with a Phone field value that begins with the area code 630. Change the Phone field value of 630-442-4831 (Guest ID 230) to **630-442-5943**. Save and close the form.

EXPLORE

6. Use the Report Wizard to create the report shown in Figure 4-31.

   (*Hint*: To apply the background color to the field names from the Reservation table, press and hold down the Shift key and click to select the six field names, and then use the Background Color button in the Font group on the Format tab.) You might need to resize some field labels so there is white space between the field label boxes after you apply the background color.

Figure 4-31   **Completed GuestReservations report**

Turquoise, Accent 2, Darker 25% theme color applied to the report title text

Flow theme applied to this report object only

Outline layout and Landscape orientation specified

Property ID field label resized so it is fully displayed

detail records sorted by ReservationID in ascending order

Villa picture inserted and made wider

Turquoise, Accent 2, Lighter 80% theme color applied to the field name backgrounds

Phone field value resized from the left and right to pull the values into the report and fully display them

7. Scroll to the bottom of the report and check to make sure the page number is completely within the page border. If necessary, resize the control on its right side, reducing its width so that the page number text is roughly right-aligned with the text in the report.

8. Apply conditional formatting so that all People field values greater than 7 are formatted in a bold, dark red font. Save the report.

⊕ EXPLORE

9. Preview the report so you see two pages at once. (*Hint*: Use a button on the Print Preview tab.) Check the report to confirm that all field labels and field values are fully displayed; then resize any, if necessary. Print page 1 of the report (only if asked by your instructor to do so).

10. Save and close the report, compact and repair the GEM database, and then close it.

SAM: Skills Assessment Manager

For current SAM information, including versions and content details, visit SAM Central (http://samcentral.course.com). If you have a SAM user profile, you may have access to hands-on instruction, practice, and assessment of the skills covered in this tutorial. Since various versions of SAM are supported throughout the life of this text, check with your instructor for the correct instructions and URL/Web site for accessing assignments.

ASSESS

ENDING DATA FILES

Access1

Tutorial
Belmont.accdb

Review
Supplier.accdb

Case1
Pinehill.accdb

Case2
Fitness.accdb

Case3
Rossi.accdb

Case4
GEM.accdb

Teamwork

Working with a Team to Create a Database

Teamwork is the collaborative effort of individuals working together to achieve a goal. Most organizations rely on teams to complete work tasks, regardless of whether those teams are formal and ongoing or informally organized to achieve a specific goal. Some teams might even be virtual, such as teams that use telecommunications technologies and social networks to complete tasks from different corporate or geographical locations.

When an organization decides to use a database to manage information, the database is rarely planned, created, and maintained by a single individual. In most cases, a team of individuals is assigned to work on different stages of database development. For example, a team might research the needs of the organization, the best database management system to use to meet those needs, and the skills required of the team members to create, update, and maintain the database. Then another team might take over the task of actually creating the database and its objects, inputting the data, and installing the database on the organization's network. Finally, yet another team might conduct training sessions to teach users how to use the database to extract the data they require to perform their jobs.

Regardless of the type of database being created, the roles that individual team members play when working on a team are similar to what you might expect in any situation that requires a collaborative effort.

The Roles of Team Members

If a team is to be successful, individual members must see the value in their respective contributions and what the team as a whole gets out of each member's contribution. This means two important requirements must be met: task performance and social satisfaction. Task performance usually is handled by one or more members who are task specialists. Task specialists spend a lot of time and effort ensuring that the team achieves its goals. They initiate ideas, give opinions, gather information, sort details, and provide motivation to keep the team on track.

Social satisfaction is handled by individuals who strengthen the team's social bonds through encouragement, empathy, conflict resolution, compromise, and tension reduction. Have you ever been on a team where the tension was high, and someone stepped in to tell a joke or tried to soften the blow of criticism? That person held the role of managing social satisfaction.

Both the task specialist and social satisfaction specialist are important roles on teams. These are not the only roles, however. Other roles include team leaders, work coordinators, idea people, and critics. The roles of individual team members are not always mutually exclusive. For example, the task specialist might also be the team leader, and the idea person might also fill the social satisfaction role. As you begin working with your team in this exercise, watch how these roles are filled and how they change as your team completes its work. Perhaps you'll want to discuss upfront which role each member is comfortable filling to see how complementary your collective skill sets turn out to be. What if your team lacks a role? Then you'll need to figure out, as a team, how to move forward so you can complete your work successfully. The following are tips that everyone should respect as work on a team begins:

- Remember that everyone brings something of value to the team.
- Respect and support each other as you work toward the common goal.

- When criticism or questions arise, try to see things from the other person's perspective.
- If someone needs assistance, find ways to encourage or support that person so the team is not affected.
- Deal with negative or unproductive attitudes immediately so they don't damage team energy and attitude.
- Get outside help if the team becomes stuck and can't move forward.
- Provide periodic positive encouragement or rewards for contributions.

The Importance of Technology in Teamwork

Many teams now depend on technology to accomplish work tasks. For example, corporate intranets and networks, email and voice mail, texting and instant messaging, teleconferencing and software collaboration tools, social networks, and cell phones can support teamwork. Each time you work in a group, decide at the outset how the team will use different technologies to communicate and document work activities. Determine how the team will organize and combine deliverable documents or presentation materials. Use whatever technology tools make the most sense for your team, your task, and your skills.

PROSKILLS

Create a Database

Many organizations use Access to manage business data, but Access can also be a valuable tool to track personal data. For example, you might create an Access database to store information about items in a personal collection, such as CDs, DVDs, or books; items related to a hobby, such as coin or stamp collecting, travel, or family history; or items related to sports teams, theater clubs, or other organizations to which you might belong. In this exercise, you'll work with your team members to create a database that will contain information of your choice, using the Access skills and features presented in Tutorials 1 through 4. As a group, you'll choose something the team is interested in tracking, such as members and activities of a college service organization or recruiters and job opportunities at your school.

Using Templates

Access includes templates for creating databases and tables. A **database template** is a database containing predefined tables, queries, forms, and reports. A **table template** is a template containing predefined fields. Using a database or table template can save you time and effort when creating a database. For example, if the fields available in one of the table templates are similar to the data you want to store, you can use the table template to quickly create a table with the fields and field properties already created and set for you. You can then modify the table, as necessary, to suit your needs. Before you begin to create a database with your team members, review the following steps for using database and table templates.

To create a database using a database template:

1. Make sure Backstage view is displayed.
2. Click the appropriate option in the Available Templates section, or click a link in the Office.com Templates section.

3. Click the name of the template you want to use; for example, if you choose to work with a sample template, you might click the Projects Web Database template or the Tasks template.

4. Specify the name for your database and a location in which to save the database file.

5. Click the Create button (or the Download button if you are using an online template).

6. Use the resulting database objects to enter, modify, or delete data or database objects.

To create a table using a table template:

1. With your database file open, click the Create tab on the Ribbon.

2. In the Templates group, click the Application Parts button. A menu opens listing the templates provided, including table templates.

3. Click the table template you want to use.

4. Modify the resulting table as needed, by adding or deleting fields, changing field properties, and so on.

Work in a Team to Create a Database

Working with your team members, you can decide to use a database and/or table template for this exercise if the templates fit the data you want to track. Note, however, that you still need to create the additional database objects indicated in the following steps—tables, queries, forms, and reports—to complete the exercise successfully.

Note: Please be sure *not* to include any personal information of a sensitive nature in the database you create to be submitted to your instructor for this exercise. Later on, you can update the data in your database with such information for your own personal use.

1. Meet with your team to determine what data you want to track in your new Access database. Determine how many tables you need and what data will go into each table. Sketch the layout of the columns (fields) and rows (records) for each table. Also discuss the field properties for each field, so that team members can document the characteristics needed for each field as they collect data. Consider using a standard form to help each person as he or she collects the necessary data.

   Next, assign data gathering and documentation tasks to each team member and set a deadline for finishing this initial task. Consider using Excel workbooks for this task, as you can use them to import the data later when working in Access. When all the data for the fields is collected, meet again as a team to examine the data collected and determine the structure of the database you will create. Finally, assign each team member specific tasks for creating the database objects discussed in the following steps.

2. Create a new Access database to contain the data your team wants to track.

3. Create two or three tables in the database that can be joined through one-to-many relationships.

4. Using the preliminary design work done by team members, define the properties for each field in each table. Make sure to include a mix of data types for the fields (for example, do not include only Text fields in each table).

5. As a team, discuss and specify a primary key for each table.

6. Define the necessary one-to-many relationships between the tables in the database with referential integrity enforced.

7. Enter 20 to 30 records in each table. If appropriate, your team can import the data for a table from another source, such as an Excel workbook or a text file.

8. Create 5 to 10 queries based on single tables and multiple tables. Be sure that some of the queries include some or all of the following: exact match conditions, comparison operators, and logical operators.

9. For some of the queries, use various sorting and filtering techniques to display the query results in various ways. Save these queries with the sort and/or filter applied.

10. If possible, and depending on the data your team is tracking, create at least one calculated field in one of the queries.

11. If possible, and depending on the data your team is tracking, use aggregate functions to produce summary statistics based on the data in at least one of the tables.

12. Create at least one form for each table in the database. Enhance each form's appearance with pictures, themes, line colors, and so on.

13. Create at least one form with a main form and subform based on related tables in the database. Enhance the form's appearance as appropriate.

14. Create at least one report based on each table in the database. Enhance each report's appearance with pictures, themes, color, and so on.

15. Apply conditional formatting to the values in at least one of the reports.

16. Submit your team's completed database to your instructor as requested. Include printouts of any database objects, such as reports, if required. Also, provide written documentation that describes the role of each team member and his or her contributions to the team. This documentation should include descriptions of any challenges the team faced while completing this exercise and how the team members worked together to overcome those challenges.

GLOSSARY/INDEX

TASK REFERENCE

TASK	PAGE #	RECOMMENDED METHOD
Access, start	AC 7	Click ![], click All Programs, click Microsoft Office, click Microsoft Access 2010
Aggregate functions, use in a datasheet	AC 151	Open table or query in Datasheet view, in Records group on Home tab click Totals button, click Total field row, click function
Aggregate functions, use in a query	AC 153	Display the query in Design view, click Totals button in the Show/Hide group on the Query Tools Design tab
Calculated field, add to a query	AC 146	*See* Reference box: Using Expression Builder
Column, resize width in a datasheet	AC 13	Double-click ↔ on the right border of the column heading
Data, find	AC 179	*See* Reference box: Finding Data in a Form or Datasheet
Data Type gallery, add fields to a table with	AC 82	Click Fields tab, click More Fields in Add & Delete group, click field or Quick Start selection to add
Database, compact and repair	AC 39	*See* Reference box: Compacting and Repairing a Database
Database, compact on close	AC 39	Click File tab, click Options, click Current Database, click Compact on Close
Database, create a blank	AC 7	Start Access, click Blank database, type the database name, select the drive and folder, click OK, click Create
Database, open	AC 24	*See* Reference box: Opening a Database
Datasheet view for tables, switch to	AC 87	In the Views group on the Table Tools Design tab, click the View button
Design view, switch to	AC 70	In the Views group on the Home tab, click the View button
Field, add to a table	AC 69	*See* Reference box: Adding a Field Between Two Existing Fields
Field, define in a table	AC 60	*See* Reference box: Defining a Field in Design View
Field, delete from a table	AC 83	*See* Reference box: Deleting a Field from a Table Structure
Field, move to a new location in a table	AC 88	Display the table in Design view, click the field's row selector, drag the field with the pointer
Field property change, update	AC 86	Click ![], select the option for updating the field property
Filter By Selection, activate	AC 127	*See* Reference box: Using Filter By Selection
Form Wizard, activate	AC 188	Click Create tab, click Form Wizard in Forms group, choose the table or query for the form, select fields, click Next
Object, open	AC 19	Double-click the object in the Navigation Pane
Object, save	AC 17	Click ![], type the object name, click OK
Picture, insert in a form	AC 200	In Layout view, click Design tab, click Logo button in the Header/Footer group, select the picture file, click OK
Primary key, specify	AC 67	*See* Reference box: Specifying a Primary Key in Design View
Property sheet, open	AC 149	Right-click the object or control, click Properties
Query datasheet, sort	AC 125	*See* Reference box: Sorting a Query Datasheet
Query, define	AC 117	Click the Create tab, click the Query Design button in the Queries group
Query, run	AC 119	Double-click query in Navigation Pane or, in Results group on Query Tools Design tab, click Run button

TASK	PAGE #	RECOMMENDED METHOD
Query results, sort	AC 125	*See* Reference box: Sorting a Query Datasheet
Quick Start selection, add	AC 82	Click Fields tab, click More Fields in Add & Delete group, click Quick Start selection
Record, add new	AC 17	In the Records group on the Home tab, click the New button
Record, delete	AC 115	*See* Reference box: Deleting a Record
Record, move to first	AC 27	Click ⏮
Record, move to last	AC 27	Click ⏭
Record, move to next	AC 27	Click ▶
Record, move to previous	AC 27	Click ◀
Records, print selected in a form	AC 184	Click File tab, click Print in navigation bar, click Print, click Selected Record(s), click OK
Records, redisplay all after filter	AC 129	In Sort & Filter group on Home tab, click the Toggle Filter button
Report, print	AC 37	*See* Reference box: Printing a Report
Report, print specific pages of	AC 203	Click File tab, click Print in navigation bar, click Print, click Pages, enter number of pages to print in From and To boxes, click OK
Report Wizard, activate	AC 193	Click Create tab, click Report Wizard button in Reports group, choose the table or query for the report, select fields, click Next
Sort, specify ascending in datasheet	AC 123	Click a column heading arrow, click Sort A to Z
Sort, specify descending in datasheet	AC 123	Click a column heading arrow, click Sort Z to A
Table, create in Datasheet view	AC 9	*See* Reference box: Creating a Table in Datasheet View
Table, open in a database	AC 19	Double-click the table in the Navigation Pane
Table, save in a database	AC 17	*See* Reference box: Saving a Table
Theme, apply to a form	AC 171	*See* Reference box: Applying a Theme to a Form